The Truman Administration
and the
Problems of Postwar Labor

By the Same Author

The Versatiles (With Alfred E. Twomey)

The Truman Administration and the Problems of Postwar Labor, 1945-1948

by
ARTHUR F. McCLURE

Rutherford · Madison · Teaneck
Fairleigh Dickinson University Press

Associated University Presses, Inc.

Cranbury, New Jersey 08512

SBN–8386–6999–9

Printed in the United States of America

For
Judy, Allison, Kyle, Amy

And for my friends
Mr. and Mrs. Edwin B. Stevens

Preface

THIS BOOK REPRESENTS AN ATTEMPT TO PROVIDE A GENERAL
study of the involvement of President Harry S Truman
and his administration in the labor problems that marked
the post-World War II years of 1945 through 1948. Truman's main concern during these years was to harmonize
the seemingly conflicting interests of labor and management so that all could benefit through economic progress.
His insistence that labor had responsibilities as well as
rights was a stand that was not always popular during
his first term.

Yet despite many difficulties, Truman received great
support from labor in the 1948 election. After four
politically and economically troubled years, his militant
individualism somehow gained for him the respect and
votes of most of the nation's members of organized labor.

What had happened? How did he do it? It is my
hope that these and other questions may be answered
in the following pages.

I am deeply grateful to many people for ideas, suggestions, admonition, and encouragement; but the responsibility is mine for the facts, opinions, and errors as presented.

I wish to express my sincere gratitude to my doctoral
dissertation director, Dr. Donald R. McCoy of the University of Kansas, whose constructive guidance and un-

failing patience contributed immeasurably to the study in its present form.

Special thanks is extended to Dr. Philip C. Brooks, Mr. Philip Lagerquist, and the staff of the Harry S Truman Library for their gracious hospitality and helpful suggestions during my research. A special note of gratitude is due the Harry S Truman Library Institute for National and International Affairs whose grant-in-aid made possible a large portion of the research.

Several persons and organizations merit acknowledgment: Miss Jane F. Smith, Chief, Social and Economic Branch, Office of Civil Archives, National Archives; Mr. David C. Mearns, Chief, Manuscripts Division, Library of Congress; the staffs of the AFL-CIO Library, United States Department of Labor Library, and the University of Kansas Libraries; and Mrs. Stella Christopher, of the Central Missouri State College Library.

A great debt is owed to my friend and colleague, Dr. William E. Foley, Central Missouri State College, for reading the manuscript and for offering valuable suggestions for its improvement. It is not possible to acknowledge all my indebtedness to those many college students who have helped me with this book, but I wish particularly to mention Judy B. Bond, my faithful secretary.

Finally, to my wife, Judy, who went a step beyond practical help and wise counsel to extend her loving encouragement, I am deeply indebted.

Warrensburg, Missouri

A. F. McC.

Contents

List of Illustrations

Introduction

SOON AFTER HARRY S TRUMAN BECAME PRESIDENT OF THE
United States in 1945, America's problems in labor relations became as serious as in any period of its history.
The year following the end of the war with Japan showed
the worst record of labor conflicts in the history of the
United States, and during President Truman's first four
years in office labor problems posed some of the most
difficult questions for Presidential policy and planning.

Concerning domestic policy in general, Truman saw
himself not only as the man who would continue many
of Franklin Roosevelt's New Deal proposals, but in particular he saw himself as the instrument with which to
implement the late President Roosevelt's famous "Economic Bill of Rights." In Roosevelt's message to the
Congress on the State of the Union in January, 1944, he
spoke of his postwar plans to raise the standard of living
as the "Economic Bill of Rights." This was designed
to be a counterpart of the Constitution's political Bill
of Rights in order to meet the demands of a modern
industrial America at peace. Roosevelt spoke of the time
when all men had:

The right to a useful and remunerative job. . . .
The right to earn enough. . . .
The right of every farmer to . . . a decent living.
The right of every businessman . . . to trade in . . . free-
   dom from unfair competition. . . .

11

The right of every family to a decent home.

The right to adequate medical care. . . .

The right to adequate protection from . . . fears of old age, sickness, accident and unemployment.

The right to a good education.

All these rights spell security. And after the war is won, we must be prepared to move forward in the implementation of these rights. . . .[1]

Roosevelt's proposals were reasserted by Truman in a twenty-one point program sent to Congress by special message on September 6, 1945.[2] It became clear from the numbered points of the speech that Truman had staked out for his administration a sweeping legislative program in the fields of social welfare that embraced in its essential aspects the whole range of the measures that came to be known after 1948 as the "Fair Deal." This speech became one of Truman's most significant pronouncements concerning postwar domestic policy. He often repeated many of its main points in later speeches.

Among the things Truman listed as essential were full employment legislation, expanded unemployment compensation, a permanent Fair Employment Practices Committee, an increased minimum wage, comprehensive housing legislation, a National Science Foundation, grants for hospital construction, permanent farm price supports, protection and assistance for small business, and expanded public works for resource conservation and development. The similarity between these points and those of Roosevelt's "Economic Bill of Rights" was for Truman "an affirmation of fidelity to the cause and the direction of liberal Democracy, rekindling the social outlook of the New Deal."[3]

While Truman was seeking to rekindle that outlook he was also faced with the problem of reconverting the nation's economy from a wartime to a peacetime one. The end of the war brought industrial relations problems relative to reconversion that were almost as difficult as those involved in prosecuting the war. The most serious labor relations problem that faced the Truman administration was the rash of strikes that broke out in 1945. Most of the stoppages before the end of the war were small, spontaneous, and unauthorized strikes—many of them over minor issues which were either quickly settled or else turned over to government agencies for decisions or settlements to be thrashed out after work was resumed. After V.J.-Day, however, the stoppages, on the average, were bigger, longer, and more difficult to solve, because the disputes involved such fundamental issues as the wage structure and its relation to prices and profits.

With the beginning of reconversion to peacetime production came layoffs for workers in most war production industries and reductions in the number of working hours per week, which meant less take-home pay. Most employees had been working at least a forty-eight hour week, which, with overtime for the last eight hours, meant the equivalent of pay for fifty-two hours at straight-time rates. The change to a forty hour week cut their weekly earnings substantially. Such reduction naturally intensified the demand for wage-rate changes which had been more and more insistently advanced by the unions since 1943.[4] Prior to that time the unions had supported wage stabilization. They had, however, insisted on more rigorous price control and finally upon a rollback of prices, since the price index had continued to advance after the "Little Steel" formula was developed in 1942. When it was demonstrated that prices could not be held within the fifteen per cent limit that basic wage rates were permitted to advance, the unions urged more and more strongly a wage-stabilization policy that would permit general increases in basic wage rates at least equal to changes in the cost of living.

Their demands were tempered by general adherence to

the no-strike pledge on the part of union leaders and also perhaps by the fact that, with long hours, upgrading and administrative judgment in the rates paid to individuals, the consequences of the virtual freezing of basic wage rates under the "Little Steel" formula were somewhat mitigated. In addition, of course, although there was no concession with respect to general wage-rate changes, the National War Labor Board permitted some improvement in working conditions through concessions to the unions on a number of fringe issues.[5]

By the end of the war, however, there was less and less opportunity for these adjustments, while prices continued slowly but persistently to rise. With the ending of the war basic wage rates took on added importance, for organized labor was certain that industry's practice would result in paring away the gains that individuals had obtained in a wartime labor market. It was against this background, then, that the unions faced a large reduction in take-home pay as a result of the elimination of overtime work. Reduction in the length of the work week had always stimulated demands for wage-rate increases to maintain take-home pay.

In addition to all this there was the belief on the part of organized labor that profits both before and after taxes were large enough for many companies to sustain some increase of wages without necessitating a price increase. Therefore some of the larger unions announced soon after V.J.-Day that they would seek wage increases sufficient to maintain for forty hours of work the same weekly earnings their members had received during wartime; they contended that employers, with their accumulated wartime profits and bright outlook for an era of high production and good markets, could well afford to pay such increases. During the war the National War Labor Board had been given the final authority to determine disputes affecting the war effort, and the Board was required to approve substantially all wage increases before they could be put into effect. Almost immediately after the termination of the war a change in wage policy was announced, permitting employers to increase wages without an NWLB approval, provided the increases were not used as grounds for seeking price increases. It was also announced that the NWLB would go out of existence at the end of 1945. The NWLB, therefore, declined to accept any additional dispute cases unless the parties agreed beforehand that they would abide by its decision.

These developments opened the way for workers to seek wage increases without specific government approval and widened the range for free collective bargaining. Many of the strikes that developed in connection with the disputes which followed were long and stubborn. The unions were strong and in earnest about maintaining high earnings; they remembered the reductions in pay and in national income after World War I, which had led to a period of hardship and the depression of 1921.

These industrial conflicts of the reconversion period played a major part in creating a climate in which the Taft-Hartley Act of 1947 could be passed. Actions by some unions and their leaders made all unions vulnerable to attack and aroused public irritation and resentment.

In addition, labor's internal feuds had directly weakened its political power. It also lost public support as a result of jurisdictional disputes and of occasional abuses of power, such as coercion of employers to recognize unions despite the wishes of employees, unreasonable expulsions and denials of membership under closed-shop contracts, unjustifiable boycotts, and failure to bargain in good faith. Communist domination of some unions and control of other unions by racketeers had similar results.

During the 1930's organized labor, and particularly the CIO, had accepted the help of Communists in organizing workers. Because experienced union organizers were urgently needed during the rapid union expansion of the 1930's and 1940's, many Communists and sympathizers were able to secure influential positions in the new unions. Communist influence was never as great as popularly supposed, particularly among most of the large cio unions such as the steelworkers, clothing workers, and textile workers. There was, however, an appreciable Communist influence in the automobile workers, electrical workers, and the longshore workers. Communist influence in unions reached a peak during World War II because of the close military alliance between the United States and Russia. But after the war American Communists became bitterly hostile to the foreign policy of the United States. At the same time American public opinion became increasingly anti-Communist. Communists were belabored in the press, and this increased anti-Communist climate of opinion sometimes fostered the excesses of Communist-haters. Much of this public distrust was centered upon organized labor in general.

The postwar labor movement was also not as sensitive to public opinion about strikes and other union actions as it should have been, but it was adamantly against any revision of the Wagner Act, which guaranteed the right of collective bargaining to labor. Labor organizations also failed to propose solutions for problems on which the public was with some justice aroused against labor. The postwar press contributed to this with its general hostility toward labor, and the public usually assumed that the union was responsible for a strike, often without inquiring whether management was in some cases equally or even more responsible because of failure to seek a reasonable basis of settlement.

Business groups, led by the National Association of Manufacturers and the U. S. Chamber of Commerce, had for years been advocating amendment of the Wagner Act. Labor's fighting among rival organizations had prevented

it from agreeing on moderate reforms which might have
forestalled more far-reaching changes. Employers differed
in their attitudes toward both the Wagner Act and the
unions. Many of them over the years came to accept collective bargaining. The most active spokesmen for business, however, never gave up their opposition to the Wagner Act because of their feeling that the law created an
imbalance in favor of labor in its dealings with management. After the constitutionality of the Wagner Act was
established, both the NAM and the Chamber of Commerce
began a long campaign for amendment and for regulation
of unions by state and federal governments.

After the war the drive for "equalizing" and restrictive
legislation in order to balance the position of labor and
management again went into full swing. These forces
worked through local and state affiliated organizations,
through the press and radio, and by contacts with representatives of the groups whom the NAM called "the great,
unorganized, inarticulate, so-called 'middle-class'; the
younger generation . . . and the opinion makers of the
nation."[6] Full-page ads in the *New York Times* during
the spring of 1947 appealed to anti-union sentiment in the
name of the interests of individual citizens, the "right
to work," and equality. These continuous publicity attacks relied on a public reaction aroused against unions
by the postwar strike wave. The campaigns were made
not in the name of the interest of employers so much as
in the name of the interests of the public and of individual
employees. The long propaganda campaign was directed
in part at real problems on which experience clearly
showed need for new legislation.

The NAM was the leader of what was generally referred
to as the "postwar antilabor forces." The NAM's campaign
helped to heighten and cement the public's anger with
organized labor. The public became more aware of the
abuses of the labor movement. Such practices as the closed

shop, the boycott, strikes of questionable moral justification, the discrimination of unions against minority groups,
restrictions on output, and laxity in the administration
of union finances served to focus critical attention upon
the union movement. These things were actually aspects
of unionism long before the passage of the Wagner Act.
However, with the growing power of labor unions, these
abuses took on greater proportions in the public mind
after World War II. People who were basically anti-labor
in thinking made the most of union shortcomings and
could point to the general undesirability of unions and
collective bargaining.

There was also a decided anti-labor force in Congress
during the postwar years. From 1932 until 1946 the nation had sent Democratic majorities to both houses of
Congress. Supported by organized labor, the Democratic
Congresses refused to alter the Wagner Act. In the elections of 1946 the Republicans elected enough candidates
to control both branches of Congress. Although it was
this Eightieth Congress that enacted the Taft-Hartley Act,
it would be a mistake to attribute all of the suggested
restrictive measures of the postwar years to the Republicans. During the Seventy-Ninth Congress, for example,
Democratic members of the House provided approximately
one-fifth of the bills introduced to control union activities.
Most of these bills came from Southern Democrats who
were usually conservative on labor questions, but they
were significant because of the fact that it indicated that
the suggestions for the control of union activities crossed
party lines.

Organized labor reacted to the attacks upon it with a
vigorous campaign of its own. From the end of the war
until the day the Taft-Hartley Act was passed in 1947 by
Congress over Truman's veto, organized labor's position
was to oppose every suggestion of limitation upon the rights
of unions. In regard to labor controls, they took a stand

which hurt their cause deeply. They felt they had attained their rightful place in the economy with the passage of the Wagner Act and they insisted that there be no changes in it. Most influential union leaders would not concede that any modifications in the Wagner Act were needed. Many seemed to feel that even slight changes would pave the way for much more sweeping revisions.

With so much sentiment in Congress and all over the country for curbs on labor unions, it would have been wise for some of the more sober labor leaders to have worked with the more reasonable management and congressional leaders on measures that would have put an end to some of the abuses by unions, the existence of which even union leaders sometimes had to acknowledge. A willingness to discuss the need for some changes in the law regulating union–management relationships might have eventually brought a more moderate piece of legislation than the Taft-Hartley Act during the postwar years.

It is the involvement of President Truman and his administration in this atmosphere of conflict that will be the central theme of this study. No previous work has focused on President Truman's personal involvement in labor problems, with the exception of his participation in the Taft-Hartley controversy. Historians have frequently overlooked the fact that he actively participated in shaping the many other facets of postwar labor relations. Presidential policy toward labor legislation, public reaction to the seizure of struck industrial plants by executive order, and the public pronouncements concerning labor relations by President Truman are but several of the significant areas that will be investigated in the present study.

These aspects of Truman's labor policies have been in serious need of a general historical examination. One of the purposes of this investigation will be to outline Truman's labor policies, 1945–1948. Another will be to indicate how and why they developed. A third will be to show their political and economic impact. In these ways it is hoped that this study will be helpful in placing the labor program of Truman's first Presidential term in its proper historical perspective.

Notes: Introduction

1. Samuel I. Rosenman (comp.), *The Public Papers and Addresses of Franklin D. Roosevelt: 1944–1945* (New York: Harper and Brothers Company, 1950), p. 41.
2. *Public Papers of the Presidents of the United States: Harry S. Truman, 1945.* (Washington: U. S. Government Printing Office, 1961), pp. 263–309. Hereinafter cited as *Public Papers of the Presidents.*
3. Richard Neustadt, "Congress and the Fair Deal: A Legislative Balance Sheet," *Public Policy*, V (Cambridge: Harvard University Press, 1954), p. 357.
4. *New York Times*, September 16, 1945.
5. *New York Times*, February 1, 1945.
6. Harry A. Millis and Emily Clark Brown, *From the Wagner Act to Taft-Hartley* (Chicago: University of Chicago Press, 1950), p. 288.

The Truman Administration
and the
Problems of Postwar Labor

1

Labor Relations During World War II

THE LABOR PROBLEMS FACING PRESIDENT TRUMAN HAD BEEN largely inherited from the administration of Franklin D. Roosevelt. The formulation of a government labor policy and the settlement of long-standing industrial grievances had been interrupted by World War II. Both stood high, however, on President Roosevelt's agenda for postwar action. In his last budget message he had urged the importance of promoting labor–management cooperation by "working out a sound long-range labor policy."[1] After Roosevelt's sudden death in April, 1945, the job of implementing a postwar labor policy fell upon the shoulders of his successor, Harry S Truman. The new Chief Executive had to supervise the reconversion of America's economy from war to peace. The problems of reconversion were nowhere greater than in the field of industrial relations. The large degree of compulsion in wartime labor measures left both labor and management eager to get back to less controlled methods of dealing with each other. This eagerness stemmed in part from their conviction that wartime government controls had favored their industrial adversaries at their own expense. Consequently, when the war was over and many government controls were removed there was a great wave of labor trouble.[2]

There were several factors that reflected some of the rea-

23

sons for the critical strike situations that quickly developed. One factor was that it was necessary for labor and management to relearn the process of collective bargaining which had fallen into disuse during the war. For four years the government through compulsory arbitration by the NWLB had settled the more critical disputes for them. A second factor was that the great economic changes of the war period produced dislocations and psychological tensions within the labor force and the ranks of management which were released when the controls were withdrawn and resulted in a large number of work stoppages. A third and very important factor was that the rapid rise in the cost of living led labor organizations to make larger demands than they might otherwise have made, enter into contracts of short duration, and make agreements with reopening clauses on wages. These conditions made for unstable collective bargaining relationships. Many of the strikes occurred in areas basic to industrial production and led to restriction of the nation's economic readjustment. These postwar tensions did much to furnish the basis for a storm of public resentment against labor unions and their leaders.

The groundwork for much of this protest, however, had been laid during and even before the war years. In the 1930's the federal government supported laws favorable toward unions; the legislative branch enacted them, and the courts eventually proclaimed their constitutionality. What turned out to be a period of unusual government friendliness toward organized labor actually had its beginnings before the start of the New Deal era. But it was not until the decade of the 1930's was nearly over that the full import of changed government attitudes was apparent. By 1940, there had occurred a virtual revolution in labor law. The two federal statutes that dealt with collective bargaining relationships were the Norris-LaGuardia Anti-Injunction Act of 1932 and the Wagner or National Labor Relations Act of 1935.

The former act provided protection against the free issuance of court injunctions during labor disputes. The NLRA, which declared that equality of bargaining power between management and workers was a part of government policy, marked the start of a new era in the government–labor relationship. Workers for many years had had the right to organize to bargain collectively. Management, however, had had the equivalent rights of combatting labor organizations and refusing to bargain with them. The revolutionary impact of the law lay in the stripping away of these management rights and allowing the matter of union choice to rest exclusively with workers. Any management attempt to influence or coerce workers in their exercise of this choice of a union to represent them was an "unfair labor practice" and the remedies were provided to correct such practices where they occurred.[3]

As the 1940's began, labor–management relations were in an unsettled state. The attitude of many in management was that they had lost a battle rather than a war. On the union side, many leaders approached management with suspicion and hostility. But there also was suspicion among the labor leaders toward each other. The 1930's had witnessed a great upheaval in the ranks of organized labor which led to the eventual split from the AFL by the CIO in 1938. Outwardly, the argument was over the issue of whether the workers in the mass production industries should be organized on the basis of the jobs they performed or the industries in which they worked. Underlying this issue was the seething hostility that stemmed from the jealousies of rival leaders.

There were other aspects to the unsettled state of affairs in labor relations in the early 1940's. The schism in the labor movement did not respond to the several attempts to promote unity between the factions. Far too much energy was being expended in the expression of mutual hostility by prominent CIO and AFL leaders. Frequently, as in the case of jurisdictional disputes, both the employers and the public had to suffer the consequences of internal union warfare. Another complication stemmed from the new governmental attitudes toward unions. Management spokesmen challenged the "one-sidedness" of the NLRA and pressure was exerted to obtain the repeal or amendment of the law. Nor was the National Labor Relations Board, which administered the NLRA, immune from attacks by labor. The AFL claimed that the NLRB was pro-CIO while the latter organization frequently charged the reverse.

Labor and management needed time to adjust to their new relationships, to recognize the new dimensions of their respective powers, and to appreciate the social responsibilities that flowed from the possession of these powers. Time was needed for the government as well as for labor and management to appreciate the full implications of a new legal setting. The time in which these adjustments might have been made ran out, however, as the nation became involved in World War II.

It was apparent even before America's entry into the war that some method for settling labor disputes in defense industries was necessary. Strikes were widespread during the winter of 1940–1941. They resulted from the rush of unions to organize workers in the new defense plants and the rapid rise in the cost of living induced by increased industrial activity. It was clear that the failure of organized labor and management to resolve voluntarily all their differences at the bargaining table jeopardized national safety when war was in the offing. The public interest called for industrial peace.

On March 19, 1941, the National Defense Mediation Board was created by President Roosevelt to adjust labor disputes in war plants.[4] The Board was composed of representatives of the public, labor, and management. The President's executive order provided that the Board should attempt to resolve disputes by helping the parties settle controversies, by providing means for voluntary arbitration, and by investigating issues in a dispute and making recommendations for its settlement. Although labor and management were not required to accept the Board's help, Presidential seizure of struck plant facilities was provided for in instances where it was thought to be essential to national defense. There were three such plant seizures under this order.[5]

The strikes of 1941 were accompanied by public demands for tighter controls. A number of bills were introduced by Representative Howard Smith of Virginia providing for a thirty-day cooling-off period before strikes or lockouts could be called in defense industries.[6] Strikes were forbidden except when approved by a majority vote of the workers. Strikes caused by jurisdictional disputes among unions and boycotts that affected defense contracts were also outlawed. This bill was passed by the House on December 3, 1941, but was shelved during the excitement after the Japanese attack on Pearl Harbor of December 7.

Following Pearl Harbor national unity reached a height seldom achieved in America's history. The great feeling of unity was illustrated by the no-strike pledge of labor's leaders in December, 1941. Few responsible labor organizations called strikes, and national unions stood ready to discipline any local that embarked on unauthorized strikes. Considering the great size and heterogeneous nature of the labor movement, it reached a remarkably high degree of unanimity in the early months of the war.

On January 12, 1942, the President, by executive order, replaced the National Defense Mediation Board with the National War Labor Board.[7] Also composed of representatives of the public, labor, and management, the new Board was given the authority to settle all labor disputes affecting the war effort. The NWLB was sometimes called "the Supreme Court of labor disputes" and assumed the dual responsibility of resolving industrial disputes and achieving wage stabilization.[8] The NWLB exerted more force than the NDMB, since refusal to obey its decisions frequently resulted in plant seizure and government operation.

In 1942, which was the first full year of the war for the United States, strike activity sharply declined from the previous year. The patriotism of management and labor alike was apparent in the fact that man-hours lost in 1942 were only one-sixth of the time lost the preceding year. This did not signify, however, a reduction of disagreements. Friction arose over wages. On the theory that wage controls should follow the price controls implemented by the government, the NWLB was ordered by the White House to stabilize wages at a level equal to the rise in the cost of living up to that time. When 180,000 members of the Steel Workers of America threatened to strike at the Bethlehem, Youngstown, Inland, and Republic steel companies the NWLB granted the workers a fifteen per cent pay raise on the theory that it corresponded to the rise in the cost of living between January 1, 1941, and May, 1942.[9] This action became known as the "Little Steel Formula." Labor severely criticized the NWLB, arguing that it had undermined the principle of collective bargaining and prevented workers from improving their standard of living. Despite labor's criticism, the NWLB applied the Little Steel formula of 1942 in settling later wartime wage disputes.

The problem of strikes became acute in 1943, as labor unions attempted to break through the Little Steel formula. The most serious of these were the strikes of John L. Lewis's United Mine Workers, which suspended work four times in 1943 and forced the government to seize the coal mines and to grant substantial wage increases. The coal strike of May, 1943, was referred to the NWLB, but the United Mine Workers, which was demanding a $2.00 per day increase, refused to take part in the NWLB hearings. The NWLB finally negotiated an agreement for a $1.50 increase, which technically saved the Little Steel formula since the wage increase was within the formula's fifteen per cent range.[10] In actuality, the formula had been bypassed because of certain fringe benefits added to the wage increase. The press almost universally denounced as unpatriotic the labor leadership in the coal mines.

Management and the public also had to bear the brunt of jurisdictional strikes and inter-union quarrels in other industries that led to stoppages that served only to promote the selfish interests of different labor factions. Strikes and threats of strikes aroused tremendous public resentment. The public could not help being gravely concerned over the failure of union labor to provide any guarantee that essential public services, upon which the entire nation was dependent, might not be interrupted by strikes even when the demands of war made their continued operation a vital matter of national security. Joel Seidman, in his *American Labor from Defense to Reconversion,* adequately summed up the feelings of an angry public when he related the reactions of the nation to the 1943 coal stoppages.

> Because of the dependence of the nation upon coal for heat and power, because coal lay at the basis of our industrial civilization, because the comfort and welfare of the civilian population as well as the lives of the fighting forces depended so intimately upon the continued production of coal, the successive stoppages of mining aroused public opinion against the striking union and its leader to a degree that our history had seldom witnessed.[11]

Despite the opposition of organized labor, Congress, on June 25, 1943, passed the Smith-Connally or War Labor Disputes Act over the President's veto.[12] This highly controversial measure as first introduced in the Senate merely gave the President power to take over war plants affected by labor disputes. However, the House of Representatives subjected it to amendments which radically changed the nature of the original bill. The bill as finally passed also embodied provisions declaring unlawful all interference by labor with the war effort, and gave subpoena power to the National War Labor Board, providing for strike notices and strike ballots in defense industries, and forbidding political contributions by labor unions. The Act provided for its termination six months after the end of war hostilities.[13]

President Roosevelt in his veto message stated that he was in accord with the general purpose of the bill, but there were certain provisions, which he specifically pointed out, that had no place in legislation to prevent strikes in wartime and which would in fact foment slowdowns and strikes. He especially referred to sections eight and nine.

Section eight required the representative of employees of a war contractor to give notice of a labor dispute which seriously threatened to interrupt war production to the Secretary of Labor, the National War Labor Board, and the National Labor Relations Board, in order to give the employees the opportunity to express themselves by secret ballot as to whether they would permit such interruption of war production. It was made mandatory by section eight that the National Labor Relations Board on the thirtieth day after the giving of the notice had to take a secret ballot among the employees on the question of whether they would stop work.

Roosevelt stated that section eight would force a labor leader who was trying to prevent a strike in accordance with his no-strike pledge to give notice which would cause the taking of a strike ballot and might actually precipitate a strike. It was the President's opinion that the thirty days allowed before the strike vote was taken under government supervision might become a "boiling" period instead of a "cooling" period, and that the thought and energies of the workers would be diverted from war production to vote getting.

Section nine, which prohibited for the duration of the war political contributions by labor organizations was objected to by Roosevelt on the ground that it was irrelevant to a bill prohibiting strikes during the war in plants operated by the government. It was Roosevelt's contention that if there were merit in the prohibition, it should not be confined to wartime, and careful consideration should be given to the appropriateness of extending the prohibition to nonprofit organizations other than labor unions.[14] Labor leaders immediately voiced their displeasure at the passage of the Smith-Connally Act. They denounced the law as being an attempt to enslave men. The Congress of Industrial Organizations Executive Board met in an extraordinary session on July 7, 1943, and announced its approval of President Philip Murray's reiteration of the no-strike pledge given to Roosevelt after the passage of the bill. It also stated its opposition vigorously to the measure by issuing the following statement:

> The labor-baiting and Administration-hating forces in Congress enacted this vicious anti-labor measure to wreak vengeance for the acts of one individual who flouted the needs of the nation for continuous production of vital war materials, ignored the machinery established for the adjustment of all labor disputes in order to guarantee continuous production, and recklessly caused a national strike in the coal fields.[15]

There was a ready answer to these charges in Congress. Republican Senator Robert A. Taft, in an address made in July, defended Congress's action by stating that by passing the Smith-Connally Act, the House and Senate had shown that they were not "rubber-stamp" bodies. He also insisted that the measure would tend to prevent slowdowns and strikes rather than accelerate them as the President feared.[16] But despite Taft's insistence, within one month after its passage, the act had led to the filing of fifty strike notices, nine of which were later withdrawn. On July 29, Attorney General Francis Biddle, in an opinion requested by Roosevelt, said that, under the War Labor Disputes Act, representatives of any group of employees—not necessarily the majority—might give notice of a labor dispute to the Secretary of Labor, the National War Labor Board, and the National Labor Relations Board. Thirty days after such notice, if the dispute was not settled, the National Labor Relations Board had to take a secret ballot of the employees of the plant as to whether they desired to strike.[17]

On August 7, 1943, Philip Murray, President of the CIO, in a letter to Roosevelt, protested the interpretation by Attorney General Biddle of the strike provisions of the act and requested a reconsideration. Murray wrote:

> Organized labor, determined to prevent for the duration of the war any stoppage of work, is faced with the ugly opinion of the Attorney General which actually encourages stoppages of work . . . the seriousness of the situation warrants the resubmission of the entire matter to the Attorney General and that an opportunity be afforded to organized labor to present to him the problems in the situation in the hope that an interpretation may be obtained more consistent with both the intent and desire of Congress and the war needs of the country.[18]

At the meeting of the Executive Council of the American Federation of Labor, held during the early part of August, repeal of the act was demanded. However, the appeal by the CIO to the AFL that the two should join forces in seeking the defeat of the measure and defeating at the polls those members of Congress who had supported the bill was rejected.[19]

There were more strikes and more workers involved in strikes in 1944 than in 1943. It might be assumed from this that the Smith-Connally Act had little real impor-tance. However, it was quite significant in showing just how strong anti-labor attitudes ran in Congress. It showed a definite shift in the feelings of Congress, and served as an indicator for the possibility of more such legislation after the war.

Union leaders and workers denounced the legislation as a "slave" act, but experience showed that they "wore their shackles lightly."[20] Union leaders learned to take advantage of the machinery of the law to bring pres-sure against employers. Workers often voted for strikes they never really had any intention of participating in so they could strengthen their bargaining position.[21] Actions such as these, however, only served to strengthen the argu-ments of those people who wanted to restrict union activi-ties.

Although the Smith-Connally Act was the only impor-tant labor relations measure enacted by Congress during the war years, there were other signs that tremendous anti-labor feelings existed. Many labor bills were intro-duced that would have limited strikes, violence, the closed shop, and prohibition of political contributions by unions. The bill that came the closest to adoption was the Hobbs bill, which would have subjected unions to anti-racketeer-ing laws.[22] The Hobbs bill passed the House in 1943, but failed in the Senate. However, the defeat was only tem-porary, since the Hobbs Act became law when reintro-duced in essentially the same form in the Seventy-Ninth Congress in 1946.

By 1945 the legislative position of organized labor was considerably weakened. The Wagner Act still remained unchanged, but the mood of Congress showed an increas-ing impatience with some of the wartime activities of labor. It was to become clear that there were hard days ahead for the American labor movement after the war ended.

* * * * * *

Notes: Chapter 1

1. Samuel I. Rosenman (comp.), *The Public Papers and Addresses of Franklin D. Roosevelt: 1944–1945* (New York: Harper & Brothers, Company, 1950), p. 41.
2. Joseph Rayback, *A History of American Labor* (New York: The Macmillan Company, 1959), p. 389.
3. *Ibid.,* pp. 320–329.
4. Joel Seidman, *American Labor From Defense to Reconversion* (Chicago: University of Chicago Press, 1953), p. 45.
5. Robert K. Murray, "Government and Labor During World War II," *Current History,* XXXIII (September, 1959), p. 148.
6. Seidman, *op. cit.,* p. 71.
7. Murray, *op. cit.,* p. 147.
8. Seidman, *op. cit.,* p. 81.
9. Harold U. Faulkner, *American Economic History* (New York: Harper & Brothers, 1960), p. 708.
10. Seidman, *op. cit.,* p. 140.
11. *Ibid.,* p. 133.
12. Rayback, *op. cit.,* p. 382.
13. "The Smith-Connally Act," *Lawyers Guild Review,* III (July–August, 1943), p. 46.
14. *New York Times,* June 26, 1943.
15. *Ibid.,* July 8, 1943.
16. *Ibid.,* July 11, 1943.
17. "The Smith-Connally Act," *Temple University Law Quarterly,* XVIII (April, 1944), p. 277.
18. *New York Times,* August 8, 1943.
19. "The Smith-Connally Act," *Temple University Law Quarterly, op. cit.,* p. 276.
20. Seidman, *op. cit.,* p. 189.
21. *Ibid.,* pp. 189–190.
22. *Ibid.,* p. 191.

2

Truman's Pre-Presidential Labor Record

AS PRESIDENT OF THE UNITED STATES HARRY S TRUMAN FACED some of the most serious labor problems in our history. Yet historians who have examined his role in this atmosphere of conflict have largely ignored the importance of Truman's earlier years in shaping his attitudes concerning labor. By overstressing his later political pronouncements regarding the Taft-Hartley Act, they have obscured many of Truman's true feelings toward governmental participation in labor relations. Truman's "pro-labor" image has been enhanced by this overemphasis and a historical imbalance has resulted. In reality, Truman's actions throughout his public career presented a much different impression. During his tenure in the United States Senate he forcefully demonstrated his conviction that organized labor had to act responsibly in its economic actions while considering the welfare of the community as a whole.

In his *Memoirs* Harry Truman looked back at the postwar labor problems that he had faced. He admitted that the labor unrest that had developed during the first days of his administration "presented one of the most difficult and persistent of all the domestic problems" he dealt with as President. But he also candidly said that "Labor unrest is inevitable in a free economy; it is part of the struggle for adjustment to shifting economic conditions."[1]

An examination of Truman's often overlooked pre-Presidential attitudes toward labor provides a better understanding of the policies that Truman and his administration later applied to postwar labor problems. By examining some of the speeches, statements, and letters Truman made as a Senator, a fairly clear idea of his attitudes regarding organized labor can be formulated.

President Truman's record as a Senator indicated that he was generally sympathetic to labor. In the Senate he supported such things as the Wagner Act, the prohibition of the use of strikebreakers and spies in labor disputes, the Fair Labor Standards Act, and the exemption of unions from filing financial reports.

Even before his election to the Senate he had accepted a dollar-a-year appointment from Federal Emergency Relief Administrator Harry Hopkins in October, 1933, as Reemployment Director of Missouri.[2] As economic unrest swept the country, 1934 was a year of rioting and strikes among labor groups in Missouri. Truman looked upon his job as one of "redistributing wealth that was amassed in the robust years."[3] In a speech at the University of Missouri in January, 1934, he said that "if it is necessary to cut each working day to two hours to give everybody a job, then let's cut it to two hours and give the same wage we used to earn for a ten-hour day."[4]

After he was elected to the Senate in 1934, Truman compiled an almost perfect New Deal voting record. But despite his sympathetic feeling toward organized labor and its problems, he was disposed to insist on labor's obligations to the public welfare as well as to the protection of its rights. This insistence sometimes meant that he ran counter to the Roosevelt administration—such as on the issue of sit-down strikes. In 1937 he voted for a resolution condemning the sit-down strikes of that year in automobile plants as an unfair labor practice. Such issues made him feel that "business must be fair to labor, but labor will have to take a realistic view of the situation."[5] Truman was also concerned that:

> The great gains which labor has made must not be imperiled. But labor, like business must recognize and fulfill its obligation to society. The alternative is government regulations. The decision rests with labor.[6]

No branch of American industry felt the depression more than transportation, particularly the railroad system. As a Senator, Truman was especially concerned about railroad wages. Many railroad companies had proposed wage cuts for their employees as a means of relief for their financial problems. But Truman, in a May, 1938, Senate speech said:

> A reduction in wages is not what the railroads need. Railroad wages are not too high. Railroad employees do not now receive enough wages. . . . What the railroads need to do is reduce rates and increase traffic. They have gone at the problem in the opposite way. They want to do the thing backwards by raising rates and decreasing wages. The railroads will never prosper until they change their views on that question.[7]

Truman's stand in support of railway labor later paid him rich political dividends when he ran for a second Senate term in 1940.

In that campaign Truman received the support of Missouri labor organizations that had the combined membership of approximately 150,000. The railroad labor organizations represented a major part of this support. A. F. Whitney, President of the Brotherhood of Railway Trainmen, and Alvanley Johnston, President of the Brotherhood of Locomotive Engineers, supplied Truman with campaign workers.[8] Along the rail lines of Missouri "Committees for Truman" were formed at railroad stations.[9]

The weekly newspaper *Labor,* which was published by the railroad labor organizations in Washington, D.C., issued a special Truman edition in July, 1940. The headline said that "Harry Truman's Magnificent Record Entitles Him to Another Term."[10] With its publication of 500,000 copies this issue of *Labor* helped to offset an otherwise generally hostile press.

Many of the accolades in the paper came from influential New Deal Senators with whom Truman had served since 1934. Among those endorsers were Senators James Byrnes of South Carolina, Alben Barkley of Kentucky, Robert Wagner of New York, and Lewis Schwellenbach of Washington who later became Truman's Secretary of Labor.

William Green, President of the AFL, endorsed Truman by sending a letter to Frank Murphy, Secretary of the Missouri State Federation of Labor. The letter read in part:

> Dear Sir and Brother: I am writing this letter to direct your attention to the very favorable record Senator Harry S. Truman has made on measures of interest to labor during his term of service in the United States Senate . . . you are requested to notify all affiliates to your State Federation of Labor as to Senator Truman's favorable record with the request that they and their friends support him in the coming election.
>
> Fraternally,
>
> *William Green*
>
> President, American Federation of Labor[11]

A special meeting of the Executive Board of the Missouri State Federation of Labor held in Kansas City, July 8, 1940, officially endorsed Truman for reelection.[12]

After his reelection in 1940, Truman returned to the Senate where in 1941 a number of bills were presented in Congress that would have limited labor union activities.

An examination of some of the Truman Senatorial letters proved to be quite valuable in determining some of Truman's basic ideas concerning organized labor. When a union official wrote to him after Pearl Harbor telling him to vote against all of the bills directed against the "rights of labor," Truman replied that it was up to labor itself to remedy the evils in its own organization which had brought about the violent anti-labor feelings in Congress. He went on to say that labor had deserted its friends in Congress and "left them out on a limb," and that they would have to remedy the situation in order that "those who are their friends will have some ground to stand on."[13]

In another letter he revealed his feeling that unions should support the war effort wholeheartedly and forget their selfish interests. He added that "it seems to me that it is about time for industry and labor to stop throwing bombs at one another and throw them at the enemy."[14]

On another occasion he wrote to a constituent expressing concern about the labor strife that existed in 1941:

> I am anxious to see labor get back in the good graces of Congress and the people, and if you have ever had a good friend to labor, I have tried to be that. But the policy [of strikes] that has been followed has been along lines to create ill feeling, and I hope they will get busy and correct that situation before it is too late. The country ought to come first with everybody, and I think labor is just as patriotic as I am.[15]

Such statements revealed that although Truman was sympathetic toward labor, he was unwilling to accept many of its complaints. He particularly denounced labor's use of the jurisdictional strike. These strikes were caused by rival unions seeking to become the representative bargaining agent. He pictured them as "extremely unjustifiable and every effort possible should be made to prevent their occurrence."[16] However, Truman voted against the Smith-Connally Act in 1943, because he thought, as he told the Senate, it was "a vicious piece of legislation . . . It would virtually repeal the Wagner Act and would not stabilize anything."[17]

Truman's most notable achievement as a Senator was his work as chairman of the Special Committee to Investigate the National Defense Program, better known as the "Truman Committee." The reports that came from that committee suggested that Truman intended to place responsibility on the labor leaders in two ways. First, the reports indicated that labor leaders should attempt to restrain workers from striking during the war. Secondly, the leaders should negotiate just wage agreements with a minimum of disturbance during the reconversion period following the war. Here again Truman stressed the idea that labor had to act responsibly. He saw wartime strikes in terms of right and wrong. Labor had its friends in Congress who were sympathetic to the causes of labor, but he felt that wartime strikes were treasonable when they threatened the welfare of the entire nation. He wrote to a union official who had threatened to strike, "The action you threaten to take and the action John L. Lewis has threatened to take is straight out and out treason."[18]

The Truman Committee reports expressed the idea that labor had come of age and the country expected union leaders to recognize that labor had its duties as well as its rights.[19] One of the Truman Committee's reports concluded by saying:

> [John L.] Lewis has hinted but not quite said that he reserves the right to determine whether Government has performed its full duty to labor . . . No citizen has the right to jeopardize the Nation's existence in wartime. The national need must be recognized as paramount.
>
> The committee urges labor leaders to make every effort to end strikes, jurisdictional disputes, and improper action of every kind. They would thereby present the most convincing answer to the enemies of labor who insist that

labor is irresponsible and must be subjected to stringent legislation. Many labor leaders have recognized this and have sought to effect it even at the danger of impairing their prestige and position with their own organizations. Such leaders are to be commended. Their example should be followed.[20]

By 1944, Truman's Senate record and reports as chairman of the Senate Committee were favorably remembered by union leaders more than anything else in his career. Organized labor generally regarded the Truman Committee's reports on war production as eminently fair. At the Democratic Convention in Chicago in the summer of 1944, the CIO Political Action Committee declared Truman acceptable as the Vice-Presidential nominee to the exclusion of all other possible contenders except one, and that was Henry Wallace. Roosevelt's fourth nomination was a foregone conclusion, but for months preceding the convention Truman had been mentioned frequently as Roosevelt's possible running mate along with William Douglas, James Byrnes, and Henry Wallace.

After arriving in Chicago, Truman had breakfast with Sidney Hillman, head of the CIO's Political Action Committee. Hillman told Truman that the CIO was backing Wallace, and that there was "only one other man he could consider supporting." Truman asked who that might be. Hillman smiled at him and said, "I'm looking at him now."[21] Truman maintained that he did not want the nomination.

Philip Murray would not support Byrnes and said that if Wallace failed to be nominated, the CIO would support Truman. On the other hand, William Green and other AFL leaders bluntly chose Truman as their first choice for the nomination. After Roosevelt eventually made it clear that Truman would make a suitable choice, all opposition to Truman faded for the most part. Truman was a man who had a number of influential friends and only a few influential enemies. He had made a reputation in the Senate by his performance as an investigator, and had come through this phase of his career without seriously alienating any large segment of the American labor movement. This was to prove to be a tremendous political asset to him by 1948, for although his postwar relationships with organized labor were extremely precarious at times, he never really lost labor's support.

When Truman became President, Eric Goldman described his political acumen with regard to the votes of large voting groups such as labor:

> The President, whatever his allergy to intellectualish New Dealers, had long leaned in the direction of wanting to use the government to help the lower economic groups. An unreconstructable Democrat, he was inclined to believe that anything a Republican Congress did was pernicious. A politician to the bone, he had an instinctive sense of the millions of votes that lay down in the row of little white houses where men worried about keeping up the payments on the car. . . .[22]

Daniel Tobin, President of the Teamsters Union, expressed what was a general feeling by labor toward Truman in 1945. He said:

> I'm asking labor in all its division to give him an honest chance to make good. Don't expect the impossible. Remember we are going into a period of perhaps serious readjustment and unemployment. All of us may have to make sacrifices. Labor will, I'm sure, understand that President Truman has a difficult task before him.[23]

In 1940, five years before he became President of the United States, Truman had said, "History is but one long record of the gigantic struggle labor has waged for its right reward."[24] These words took on an almost prophetic meaning, when, as President, Harry Truman attempted to cope with some of the most difficult aspects of that historic struggle. Truman's handling of these problems clearly mirrored the experiences from an earlier period in his public career.

Notes: Chapter 2

1. Harry S. Truman, *Memoirs* (Garden City, New York: Doubleday & Company, Inc., 1956) , Volume I, p. 495. Hereinafter cited as Truman, *Memoirs.*
2. Alfred Steinberg, *The Man From Missouri* (New York: G. P. Putnam's Sons, 1962) , p. 106.
3. *Ibid.,* p. 107.
4. *Ibid.*
5. Compilation of Information and Statements by Senator Truman, Rosenman Papers, Harry S. Truman Library. Harry S. Truman Library hereinafter cited as HSTL.
6. *Ibid.*
7. *Congressional Record,* 75th Cong., 2d Sess., pp. 6881–6882.
8. Eugene Francis Schmidtlein, "Truman the Senator" (unpublished Ph.D. dissertation, 1962, University of Missouri) , p. 219.
9. David L. Jones, "Senator Harry S. Truman: The First Term" (unpublished Master's thesis, 1963, University of Kansas) , p. 97.
10. *Labor,* July 30, 1940.
11. *Ibid.*
12. *Ibid.*
13. Harry S. Truman to Roy M. Sayers, December 22, 1941, Senatorial Files, Truman Papers, HSTL.
14. Harry S. Truman to Walter S. Johnson, December 16, 1941, Senatorial Files, Truman Papers, HSTL.
15. Harry S. Truman to Michael B. Menniges, November 27, 1941, Senatorial Files, Truman Papers, HSTL.
16. Harry S. Truman to Lloyd Weber, October 16, 1941, Senatorial Files, Truman Papers, HSTL.
17. *Congressional Record,* 78th Cong., 1st Sess., p. 7029.
18. Harry S. Truman to H. C. Newmeyer, April 29, 1943, Senatorial Files, Truman Papers, HSTL.

19. U. S., Congress, Senate, Special Committee Investigating the National Defense Program, *Additional Report*, 78th Cong., 1st Sess., April 2, 1943, pp. 2–3.

20. *Ibid.*, p. 4.

21. Steinberg, *op. cit.*, p. 210.

22. Eric Goldman, *The Crucial Decade—and After* (New York: Vintage Books, 1961), p. 65.

23. Daniel J. Tobin, "Truman is Sympathetic to Labor," *International Teamster*, OF 407, Truman Papers, HSTL.

24. Speech, Harry S. Truman, June 15, 1940, Sedalia, Missouri, Democratic National Committee Library Clipping File, Truman Papers, HSTL. Democratic National Committee Library Clipping File hereinafter cited as DNC Clipping File.

3

Reconversion Begins for Labor

WHEN THE WAR IN JAPAN ENDED IN AUGUST, 1945, ORGANIZED labor became restive under the wage stabilization program that had been developed during the war. From this restiveness grew a great number of work stoppages that were to mark the postwar reconversion period. Even at the height of the war the thing that labor leaders feared the most was that the cessation of hostilities would be accompanied by a return to large-scale unemployment. The chief concern of labor organizations was that a sudden ending of the war would catch the country unprepared and would lead to unemployment on a scale similar to that of the 1930's.[1]

The postwar strike wave was unique in many ways. Both labor and management made appeals for public support with pamphlets, news releases, magazine articles, and radio programs. During no period in the history of the United States did the scope and intensity of labor–management conflicts match those recorded in the year following V.J.-Day, August 14, 1945. During this period, the country experienced over 4,600 work stoppages, directly involving about five million workers and resulting in almost 120 million man-days of idleness. Although the number of workers that were involved in labor disputes was large, the strikes themselves were marked by a minimum of violence. Employment and production, except for temporary setbacks,

nevertheless forged ahead to establish new peacetime records.[2] Unions, for the most part, retained their several million new members recruited in the war years and kept their
organized strength at an estimated fourteen to fifteen million members.

More than ten million men and women were demobil-
ized from the armed services during this transition period,
and most of them were able to find jobs. Thousands of
factories retooled to produce the necessities, conveniences,
and luxuries for a civilian economy. Other factories, as
well as many service trades, which had been curtailed by
wartime stringencies, were returning to prewar status.
These developments, however, did not always proceed
smoothly. Shortages of materials and, occasionally, of certain kinds of skilled labor occurred. Many work stoppages,
in addition, delayed production of commodities sought by
American consumers. The direct effects of certain stoppages, particularly in the basic industries, were severe at
times. The indirect effects upon plants and industries not
involved in work stoppages were also serious, although
statistically impossible to measure.

With the end of the war, workers were faced with the
abrupt end of the production of great numbers of military
items. Many factories cut their scheduled hours from forty-
eight or more a week to forty or less.[3] Others shut down
temporarily or permanently, and wage earners, confronted
with serious losses in take-home pay, sought to maintain
their income.

Many employers, uncertain of the speed with which reconversion could be accomplished and opposed to the con-
tinuation of price and other wartime controls, expressed
inability to meet the wage proposals of organized labor.
This conflict of economic interests between labor and
management was further aggravated by the partial termination of the Little Steel formula which had held the upward
movement of the cost of living and of rates of pay within

moderate bounds during the war years.[4] Application of the Little Steel formula had done a great deal to prevent the abnormally high rates of pay which characterized some industries in World War I.

The end of the war also ended organized labor's no-strike pledge. Workers were free to exercise their traditional right to strike in order to secure what they considered their just demands. In thousands of cases adjustments were made without work stoppages, unions and management reaching agreements among themselves through direct negotiation, and often with the assistance of state and federal government conciliators. In other instances, however, the struggle reached the strike stage, with workers sacrificing savings and employers losing profits.

On the whole, both labor and management wanted to be free to bargain across the conference table and, when necessary, to submit to a test of strength. These convictions were expressed by many representatives of labor and management as the war neared its end, and were reflected in government policies as hostilities ceased. On August 16, 1945, less than two days after V.J.-Day, Truman announced that the National War Labor Board would be terminated soon after the conclusion of the forthcoming national labor–management conference.[5] During the war the NWLB had weathered numerous crises, but pressure for revision of the Little Steel formula or outright abandonment of stabilization controls over wages rose steadily in 1945.

On August 18, 1945, Truman issued Executive order No. 9599 permitting wage increases without specific government approval, provided the increases would not serve as a basis for higher prices or added cost to federal agencies purchasing goods or services from contractors.[6] The stage was then set for a return to collective bargaining within the framework of existing price levels. The NWLB indicated that it would consider only such controversies as the parties might voluntarily agree to submit to it. It was stated that

prime reliance would be placed upon a greatly strengthened United States Conciliation Service of the Department
of Labor to assist in reconciling differences between labor
and management.[7]

Despite these efforts, however, in September the postwar
strike wave began, which compounded the already high
level of public resentment against unions engendered by
wartime strikes. The work stoppage involving the oil industry which began on September 17, 1945, was the first
significant strike of the reconversion period. It reflected
most of the wage issues and led to the establishment of the
fact-finding procedures which were to characterize a number of subsequent strikes. The strike involved about 43,000
refinery workers employed in twenty states. The principal
demand of the Oil Workers International Union was for
fifty-two hours pay at straight-time for forty hours of
work, the equivalent of a thirty per cent wage increase.[8]
Direct negotiations and government conciliation were un-
successful in preventing the stoppage, and arbitration, proposed by the Secretary of Labor, was not accepted by the
oil companies, although favored by the union.

With a third of the nation's gasoline supply cut off by the
strike and shortages becoming acute, Truman on October
4, 1945, ordered the Navy Department to seize and operate the refineries.[9] Production was quickly resumed with
no change in wage rates or hours of work. Weeks of negotiations between representatives of the union, the industry,
and the government proved fruitless, and on November 27,
1945, the Secretary of Labor appointed a fact-finding panel
to review the issues and formulate recommendations for
a settlement.[10] (See later discussions of fact-finding in this
chapter and Chapter 5.)

Throughout the autumn of 1945, the number of strikes
in effect and the resulting man-days of idleness climbed
above the levels of the war years. A few days after the oil
strike began, the United Clerical, Technical, and Super-

visory Workers Union, a part of the United Mine Workers of America, struck to obtain recognition and collective-bargaining rights for mine foremen and other supervisory workers in the bituminous coalmines. During the next several weeks the strike affected more than 200,000 workers in the industry. It was terminated October 17, 1945, with a statement by John L. Lewis, President of the United Mine Workers, that "future efforts to abate this controversy will be resumed at a later, more appropriate date."[11] As later events proved, these words were an understatement of gigantic proportion.

Although the strike in the coal industry was relatively brief and did not involve the wage issues which characterized many of the major strikes, numerous other strikes continued for months despite all efforts to reach settlement. Approximately 44,000 workers represented by the Lumber and Sawmill Workers Union, a part of the United Brotherhood of Carpenters and Joiners, stopped work in the forest and sawmills of the Northwest on September 24, and many continued on strike throughout the winter before a settlement of fourteen-cents-an-hour increase was reached.[12] The Federation of Glass, Ceramic, and Silica Sand Workers of America obtained from two large glass companies a wage increase of ten cents an hour after a strike of over a hundred days. Machinists and shipyard workers in the San Francisco Bay area were idle for 140 days. Among the other large strikes from September to late November were those involving building-service employees and longshoremen in New York City, textile workers in New England, and truckers in the Middle West.[13]

Becoming aware of the growing unrest throughout the country, Truman addressed the nation by radio on October 30, on the subject of reconversion. He set forth his administration's twin objectives of price stability and higher wage rates, and declared that wage increases were necessary in order "to cushion the shock to our workers, to sustain adequate purchasing power, and to raise the national income."[14] At the same time he issued Executive Order No. 9651 amending the order of August 18, 1945, by providing that the OPA could consider for price-relief purposes unapproved wage or salary increases after such increases had been in effect, normally, for at least six months.[15]

Some strikes had been expected during the reconversion period, but the amount of labor trouble came as a surprise even to the most knowledgeable observers. There was no doubt about the impact on the economy of the extraordinary amount of labor trouble. This increase of unrest coincided with the postwar decline of the federal government's power to intervene. Sentiment for continuing the NWLB was minor compared with the rush to abandon its restraints for the freedom of unhampered collective bargaining. By autumn, 1945, the government's legislated ability to solve labor disputes was losing ground. There were many in Congress who were ready to solve any such inability with restrictive legislation. Many industry leaders were looking in that general direction for relief. None of this sentiment was favored by organized labor and the Truman administration continued its opposition to most of the labor bills which proposed compulsory changes in labor relations.

Leading the Truman administration's fight against most of the restrictive labor bills was Lewis B. Schwellenbach, the newly appointed Secretary of Labor. Schwellenbach was appointed on July 1, 1945, to succeed Frances Perkins.[16] Schwellenbach resigned a judgeship on the United States District Court in Spokane, Washington, to become Secretary of Labor. Before he was appointed as a federal judge by President Roosevelt in 1940, he had served one term as Senator from the state of Washington. In the Senate he supported New Deal legislation, voting for the Wagner Act, the Wage-Hour bill, the Wagner Housing bill, higher income surtax rates, and extension of reciprocal trade agreements. He was a member of the Committee to investigate lobbies and the La Follette Civil Liberties Committee, which spent several years studying anti-union activities.[17]

Schwellenbach and Truman had both entered the Senate in 1935 and the two soon became close friends. As Truman later wrote, Schwellenbach was "an able lawyer and federal judge, a good senator, and a real, honest-to-goodness liberal. We saw right down the same alley on public policy."[18] Schwellenbach's appointment was a popular one with organized labor. Philip Murray, William Green, and other labor leaders applauded his selection.

One of Schwellenbach's first actions concerning the reconversion crisis was in a radio address made on Labor Day.[19] In his speech he warned both labor and management that industrial peace and the creation of jobs was their joint responsibility. In this respect he wholeheartedly agreed with Truman that some positive move should be made to stop an unlimited contest between labor and management. Part of that move came in the form of the President's National Labor–Management Conference.

On July 30, 1945, Republican Senator Arthur H. Vandenberg of Michigan had suggested in a letter to Secretary Schwellenbach that a Labor–Management Conference be held in order to "lay the groundwork for peace with justice on the home front." Part of Vandenberg's letter read:

> Responsible management knows that free collective bargaining is here to stay and that progressive law must continue to support it and that it must be wholeheartedly accepted. Responsible labor leadership knows that irresponsible strikes and subversive attacks upon essential production are the gravest threats to the permanent success of Labor's Bill of Rights. The American public knows that we cannot rebuild and maintain our national economy at the high levels required by our unavoidable necessities if we cannot have productive peace instead of disruptive war on the industrial front. American Govern-

ment knows that social statutes are futile except as they largely stem from mutual wisdom and mutual consent.[20]

The question of how to deal with labor–management problems in the postwar period had been under discussion between Truman and Schwellenbach for some time, and the message from Senator Vandenberg helped to crystallize the decision to go ahead with the conference at the earliest possible opportunity.[21] Truman felt that if an agreement on peacetime procedure came out of the conference the government would have gone a long way toward assuring peaceful labor–management relations by the simplest and most direct method.

In announcing the conference, Truman appointed a special committee of representatives of the government, labor, and business organizations to serve as an agenda committee and to decide upon the scope of the conference. This committee consisted of Maj. Paul H. Douglas of the United States Marine Corps, on leave from the University of Chicago, representing the Secretary of Labor; Charles J. Symington, of Symington-Gould Corporation of New York City, representing the Secretary of Commerce; Boris Shishkin of the AFL; Ted F. Silvey of the CIO; Joyce O'Hara of the United States Chamber of Commerce; and Raymond S. Smethurst of the National Association of Manufacturers.[22] This committee drew up an agenda dealing with some of the major causes of industrial strife and the methods of reducing them. Emphasis was put on long-term, rather than short-term, remedies for labor problems.[23]

The committee proposed a series of topics for consideration by the conference. Attention was focused on the extent to which industrial disputes might be minimized by full acceptance of collective bargaining on the part of employers; full acceptance by organized labor of the right of management to direct the operation of an enterprise; the willingness of labor and management to utilize the

Wagner Act and state labor relations acts for the prompt determination of collective bargaining agencies; procedure for negotiating contracts and the possibilities of conciliation if negotiations seemed to be breaking down; and the incorporation in contracts of certain types of provisions.[24]

The possibility of improving the Conciliation Service of the Department of Labor was also suggested as a topic and it was recommended that the conference study problems arising out of jurisdictional or other inter-union disputes. The Agenda Committee recommended that the conference be composed of eighteen employer representatives selected in equal numbers by the U. S. Chamber of Commerce and the National Association of Manufacturers. Eighteen labor representatives were also proposed, eight from the AFL, eight from the CIO, one from the United Mine Workers, and one from the Railway Brotherhoods. The Secretaries of Labor and Commerce were non-voting members of the conference, which was to have as presiding officer an eminent private citizen, also without a vote. A non-voting secretary was likewise recommended. The conference met in the auditorium on Constitution Avenue next to the Department of Labor. Administrative and committee offices were set up in the Department of Labor Building. Chief Justice Walter Stacy of the North Carolina Supreme Court was selected as the chairman of the conference. Secretary of Labor Schwellenbach and Secretary of Commerce Wallace completed the small public delegation. A well known labor relations expert, George Taylor, was chosen the Secretary of the conference.[25]

President Truman stressed the importance of the conference in his radio address of October 30, a week before the conference began. Announcing the meeting, he said, "I hope the American people recognize how vital this conference actually is. Out of it can come the means of achieving industrial harmony and a new approach to human relationships in industry."[26] Truman also advocated the reconversion policy of higher wage rates with effective governmental control of prices. This policy was enthusiastically adopted by Philip Murray and pushed hard at the conferences, but it provided one of the main areas of disagreement that had not been foreseen by the Agenda Committee.

Truman spent several days before the conference interviewing the groups of delegates at the White House. He appealed for a frank discussion of difficult problems that might come up in the conference so that attention could be given to them before the first session opened.[27] It was also reported that William Green was afraid the public was being led to expect too much from the conference. From these comments, it became apparent from the outset that the conference was going to have trouble in agreeing on any major issues.

Truman opened the conference on November 5, 1945, and in his opening address called upon labor and management to recognize that they had common goals and should attempt to solve their differences in their own long-range interest. He said that the conference had been called to provide a nationwide opportunity to fulfill this objective and that representatives of management and labor had been assembled at the conference "to discuss their common problems and to settle differences in the public interest." He also made it clear that his administration was not trying to run or to dominate the conference, for it was entirely a labor–management affair. Truman spoke of the sentiment in Congress over industrial relations as expressed "in the form of all kinds of proposed legislation." He felt that it was the purpose of the conference to stop that trend, expressed disappointment over the amount of industrial strife that was developing, and said in effect that it was absolutely necessary that disagreements be resolved without stoppages in production. Truman concluded that the best way to accomplish this result was "without government directive to either labor or industry—that is your job."[28]

Philip Murray's efforts to inject the wage issue into the conference extended throughout the duration of the conference. The Agenda Committee decided the discussion of immediate bargaining issues, such as wages, were to be excluded from deliberation. But in his opening speech at the conference, Murray said that he had become convinced by recent events that the wage issue was really the main industrial relations problem of the reconversion period.[29] Moreover, he felt that he had actually acquired the strongest kind of support for his position in Truman's October 30 radio speech. Murray introduced a wage resolution which asked labor and management "to engage in genuine and sincere collective bargaining in an effort to resolve this all-important wage issue."[30] There was considerable discussion of the wage resolution. Green wanted it understood that the AFL intended to fight for higher wages, although the AFL would insist that the wage question was not within the agenda of the conference.

The AFL, supported by the mine and railroad worker representatives, joined with the employers in referring the Murray resolution to a subcommittee of the executive committee. This was done over the strong objections of Murray who refused to have anything to do with the subcommittee.

At the end of the conference William Green reported a substitute wage resolution from the subcommittee to the executive committee. The new resolution called attention to Truman's invitation to the conferees and added that "this statement makes clear the fact that this Management–Labor Conference is not a wage conference. It would be a usurpation of authority if this conference would attempt to establish a wage standard for industry throughout the nation."[31] The substitute motion received the support of industry and the labor representatives other than the CIO men. Additional parliamentary maneuvering ensued and the executive committee did not report out any wage resolution. Murray, however, brought the matter to the floor of the conference in the final plenary session. He repeated his differences with the executive committee and again made a strong plea to the conference to give consideration to the question of wage increases.[32] But the conference was adamant against discussing any short-term issues such as wages.

The procedure of fact-finding in the settlement of labor disputes, however, did become an important part of the discussions of the conference. Fact-finding in labor disputes was not a new device, and it had been resorted to informally many times as well as being an integral part of the dispute settlement procedures under the Railway Labor Act. There was a great amount of discussion at the conference about its long-term merits and the possibility of extending its use to all types of labor–management disputes. The Agenda Committee did not provide for a discussion of fact-finding procedure and when the conference opened it had no specific committee assignment. But as the conference progressed, and as more and more labor trouble appeared, the possibilities of fact-finding aroused wide interest. Under the Railway Labor Act the process of finding the facts and making recommendations by a public board in a labor dispute was coupled with a statutory waiting or "cooling-off" period. Another possibility was to have the findings and recommendations without the statutory waiting period.

The General Motors strike that began on November 21, 1945, was one of the largest of the reconversion strikes. It very dramatically demonstrated that some means of settlement was necessary even as the conference was deliberating the subject.[33] Many persons in responsible places in the administration began to give up hope that the conference could be of much help in the immediate crisis of the General Motors strike. Fact-finding as a device to fill the void created by the decline of the NWLB began to be given serious consideration in administration labor circles. A week later, on November 27, Secretary of Labor Schwellenbach inaugurated a policy of establishing fact-finding boards by appointing the first such body to consider a dispute in the oil industry.[34]

Great public interest was evident at this time in the possibility of some form of public fact-finding with compulsory "cooling-off periods" in critical disputes, but this matter was not definitely assigned to any of the working committees, and there appeared to be marked reluctance to tackle the issue. The executive committee discussed the matter at length but never reached agreement, and so made no report, and there was no conference action on the matter. Neither labor nor management seemed enthusiastic about fact-finding. Labor did not subscribe to "cooling-off" periods and management was afraid of the idea that fact-finding might include an examination of a company's records, and they also disliked the idea that fact-finders should make recommendations for settling a labor dispute.

The work of some of the committees of the conference revealed some of the basic differences betwen labor and managment. Committee I explored first, the question of minimizing industrial disputes by the full and genuine acceptance of collective bargaining on the part of management; and second, the responsibility of both parties toward their obligations in collective agreements. The labor and management members of Committee I could not agree on these points and each side submitted its own report.[35]

There was actually a good deal of agreement between the two sides but management proposed changes in existing legislation to which labor would not agree. Labor feared that the amendments to the Wagner Act and changes in the Norris-LaGuardia Act desired by the employers would threaten the existence of unions. Ira Mosher summed up management's view when he said:

> The committee on collective bargaining reached an impasse primarily because labor could not see its way clear

to agree to management's proposal for legislative changes which would make labor and management bear equal responsibilities under the law and be equally subject to legal actions for conduct in violation of contracts.[36]

The debate on this question did not die down when the conference came to an end, and the angry anti-labor sentiment of the Seventy-Ninth Congress proved that more trouble was ahead for labor in this matter.

Committee II took up the topic of minimizing industrial disputes by acceptance on the part of organized labor of management's responsibility for directing the operations of an enterprise. This question was an important subject of difference as management tended more and more to accept the unions and to bargain with them in good faith. Toward the end of the war the right to manage became one of the big issues in industrial relations. There was a good deal of agreement between the labor and management sides on this committee, but the labor group thought it "unwise to specify and classify the functions and responsibilities of management" and "because of the insistence by management for such specification the committee was unable to agree upon a joint report."[37]

There were two questions assigned to Committee III: the selection of collective bargaining representatives, and the settlement of jurisdictional disputes. Concerning collective bargaining, the two sides disagreed over management proposals for amendment of the NLRA. As the employers saw it they were only asking for equal rights with labor before the law, but the labor group replied that it did not consider "that this conference was called either to accomplish drastic revision of the Wagner Act or a drastic revision of outstanding rules of the National Labor Relations Board."[38] The labor group made a number of proposals to control jurisdictional disputes but turned a deaf ear to any management suggestion that the problem be regulated by law. Again, these conference debates were a prelude to developments in the Seventy-Ninth Congress.

The final session of the conference adopted a resolution urging tolerance and equality of opportunity in respect to race, sex, color, religion, age, and national origin in determining who should be employed or admitted to union membership. A resolution was also adopted that an informal committee of eight people be formed along the same lines as the conference membership. This group would meet as it saw fit for the purpose of creating better understanding between the labor and management factions. The group would meet as individuals and without any prepared agenda. However, this informal committee never met in the years that followed the conference. It is probable that the hostile atmosphere that arose between labor and management, partly as a result of restrictive labor bills in Congress, discouraged the sort of cooperation envisaged for the informal committee.

The Labor–Management Conference adjourned on November 30, having adopted unanimously only three committee reports, namely those on initial collective agreements, on existing collective agreements, and on conciliation services. However, the labor members of the Committee on Management's Right to Manage concluded their report in the following manner:

> It is the opinion of the labor members of this committee that if the representatives of management and labor in each industry would confer on the functions of management and labor in the same friendly spirit as the committee approached the subject assigned, industrial disputes would be minimized, production increased, and the public interest well served.[39]

Unfortunately the high hopes for the success of the conference were not realized. The conference was by no means a waste of effort, and not without some agreements; but it failed to accomplish the objective of reducing the tremendous impact of labor disputes on the economy. It became apparent that neither side was ready in 1945 to make the concessions necessary to bring about a large improvement in industrial relations.

In assessing the value of the conference, the *New York Times* reported that William Green felt that something had been accomplished but that he was disappointed over the results. Philip Murray of the CIO thought the conference had been worth holding. Daniel Tobin of the AFL-Teamsters regretted that not much had been done. Eric Johnston of the U. S. Chamber of Commerce expressed disappointment at the results of the conference but thought it was only a temporary setback. Ira Mosher of the NAM felt that too much had been expected of the conference.[40] Some leaders of both labor and management saw good coming from the fact that men sat down together and discussed their problems.

President Truman was perhaps the man most disappointed when the conference adjourned without making a sizable tangible contribution toward better labor relations. He reported to Congress immediately after the meeting ended and declared:

> The conference is now closed. The very fact that the top leaders of labor and management have met and worked together for more than three weeks is itself some progress. Some agreements on a few general principles were also reached. . . . But on all the important questions of how to avoid work stoppages, the conference arrived at no accord.[41]

He explained in this message that since the conference had failed to recommend procedures for insuring industrial peace when collective bargaining and conciliation broke down, he felt it was the duty of his administration to act. Truman then recommended that legislation be enacted extending the type of fact-finding procedure found in the Railway Labor Act to industry generally. He also announced that a fact-finding board was being appointed in the General Motors strike.[42]

The economic effects of the General Motors strike were of particular interest at this time because of the issues involved in the Labor–Management Conference. The negotiations between the United Automobile, Aircraft, and Agricultural Implement Workers of America and the General Motors Corporation that preceded the stoppage were marked by the union's demand for a thirty per cent wage increase which, the union contended, could be paid without price increases. The company insisted, however, that prices and profits be excluded from the wage discussions, and remained firm in its maximum offer of a twelve per cent wage increase, with no commitment on price.[43]

The Board appointed by the President on December 14, 1945, to investigate the dispute proceeded without the participation of the General Motors Corporation, which objected to consideration of "ability to pay" as a relevant factor. On January 10, 1946, the Board recommended a wage increase of 19½ cents and reinstatement of the contract. This the union was willing to accept. The company objected, however, and instead raised its maximum offer of a wage increase to 18½ cents. The company also objected to reinstatement of some provisions of the contract, particularly those relating to union security and seniority. Negotiations dragged on until March 13, 1946, when a national agreement was reached on a two-year contract, providing substantially for an 18½ cent wage increase and contract reinstatement. The 18½ cent wage increase ultimately became the pattern in solving later disputes involving Ford and Chrysler, as well as the steel industry. Several local issues, however, remained to be settled; and when General Motors delayed until March 26 the resumption of operations in any of its ninety-two plants until all local contracts were agreed to, the effective duration of the strike was extended further.[44] The strike was finally settled by allowing both a wage increase and a price increase.

The 113-day strike involved 200,000 workers in the 92 plants, scattered among 12 states and 46 cities. During the strike an estimated 73,000 white collar workers and 18,000 foremen, plus other maintenance employees, remained on the job. While General Motors Corporation forfeited profits and its production, and employees lost heavily in earnings and reduced savings, perhaps the public suffered most through the stimulus to higher prices resulting from the delayed appearance of automobiles in sufficient volume to meet their insistent pent-up demands. The strike was frequently estimated, in round numbers, to have cost about one billion dollars, independent of its stimulus to higher prices. The company lost about $600 million in unfilled orders, but presumably most of the sales were not lost but only postponed.

The most pronounced hardship caused by the strike was suffered by the striking workers themselves. The loss of four month's wages cut deeply into the living standard of the strikers, and wiped out a substantial part of the savings of workers fortunate enough to have that economic cushion. A few strikers found work elsewhere during the strike period, but is was generally part-time or at lower wages, and was relatively unimportant in sustaining the strikers as a group. The union provided help in certain cases, and a National Committee to Aid Families of General Motors Strikers contributed both moral and material support. But the strikers' main burden was carried through individual financial arrangements and adjustments.[45]

The economic effects of the strike should not be so construed as to exaggerate the wage issue. The demand for a wage increase was doubtless primary, but the tenacity of the union in refusing to abandon provisions relating to increased cost of living, vacations, downgrading and demotion, and union security and seniority, when only one cent separated agreement on a wage increase and when economic pressures were mounting, were indicative of the larger dimensions of labor's demands. It should also be emphasized that the substantial loss to the public from this bitter contest between labor and management was dominated as much by conflicting views of the basis and scope of collective bargaining as by any hopes of immediate economic gain.

But the effects of this strike on public reaction went beyond the fiscal losses suffered by the public. The atmosphere of tension that surrounded the Labor–Management Conference, because of this and other strikes, tended to cloud some of its very important results. The conference demonstrated for the first time in history that at a national level representatives from both labor and management could meet together without arguing as to whether or not collective bargaining was desirable. The aim of the conferees was to reach a common understanding as to how collective bargaining could function better.

The Labor–Management Conference marked the end of an era in labor–management relations. At the same time it also marked the beginning of a new era, because President Truman—although disappointed by the immediate results of the conference—ushered in a postwar labor policy in which he felt that the principal lessons learned from the conference contained latent possibilities for the possible solution of postwar labor problems.

In the years that followed the conference, Truman became more and more convinced that general procedural and policy agreements between representatives of labor and management could serve as guides in particular labor negotiations and could be significantly propounded by the use of fact-finding boards. Some of the unanimous agreements of the conference were made to appear meaningless and insignificant in relation to the pressing and critical needs of the reconversion period. When later viewed by historians, the conference was, in many instances, written off as a failure. But if the conference is viewed with an objective eye for these overall intangible results, it becomes apparent that it was not a total loss. Perhaps at any time in history other than during the trying years of labor's reconversion following World War II, it might have been applauded as a great step forward in industrial relations. The painful reconversion period for labor might have been even more painful if President Truman and his administration had not felt that reason and determination would ultimately prevail over the angry, emotional tensions that were rampant throughout the land during these postwar years.

Notes: Chapter III

1. *CIO News*, April 23, 1945.
2. Foster Rhea Dulles, *Labor in America* (New York: Thomas Y. Crowell Company, 1955), pp. 354–355.
3. "Postwar Work Stoppages," *Monthly Labor Review* (December, 1946) , p. 872.
4. *Ibid.*, p. 873.
5. *Public Papers of the Presidents: 1945*, pp. 220–222.
6. Executive Order No. 9599, OF 122, Truman Papers HSTL.
7. *New York Times*, July 31, 1945.
8. *Ibid.*, September 18, 1945.
9. *Monthly Labor Review, op. cit.*, p. 874.
10. *New York Times*, November 27, 1945.
11. *Monthly Labor Review*, op. cit., p. 875.
12. *Ibid.*, p. 876.
13. *Ibid.*, pp. 875–876.
14. *Public Papers of the Presidents: 1945*, p. 443.
15. Executive Order No. 9651, OF 122, HSTL.
16. *New York Times*, July 2, 1945.
17. *Ibid.*

18. Truman, *Memoirs*, Vol. I. p. 325.
19. Statement by Secretary of Labor Lewis B. Schwellenbach, Labor Day, 1945, Record Group 174, Records of the Secretary of Labor, National Archives, Washington, D. C. Record Group 174, Records of the Secretary of Labor hereinafter cited as Record Group 174.
20. "Labor–Management Conference on Industrial Relations," *Monthly Labor Review* (January, 1946), p. 37.
21. Harry A. Millis and Emily Clark Brown, *From the Wagner Act to Taft-Hartley* (Chicago: University of Chicago Press, 1950), p. 307.
22. *New York Times*, September 7, 1945.
23. U. S. Division of Labor Standards, *The President's National Labor–Management Conference, November 5–30, 1945*, Bulletin No. 77, U. S. Department of Labor, 1946, p. 31.
24. Thomas Holland, "The Labor–Management Conferences," Report of the U. S. Department of Labor, (mimeographed, 1950), Gibson Papers, HSTL, p. 54.
25. *Ibid.*, pp. 54–55.
26. *Public Papers of the Presidents: 1945*, p. 448.
27. *New York Times*, November 2, 1945.
28. Statement by Harry S. Truman at the Opening Session of Labor–Management Conference, November 5, 1945, Gibson Papers, HSTL.
29. *New York Times*, November 17, 1945.
30. "Report of the National Labor–Management Conference to the President" (Mimeographed, 1945), OF 407-C, Truman Papers, HSTL.
31. *Ibid.*
32. *Ibid.*
33. Holland, *op. cit.*, p. 63.
34. *Ibid.*
35. *Ibid.*, p. 65.
36. "Report of the National Labor–Management Conference to the President," *op. cit.*
37. "Labor–Management Conference on Industrial Relations," *Monthly Labor Review, op. cit.*, p. 40.
38. Holland, *op. cit.*, p. 67.
39. *Monthly Labor Review, op. cit.*, p. 40.

40. *New York Times,* December 1, 1945.
41. *Public Papers of the Presidents: 1945,* p. 517.
42. *Ibid.,* pp. 520–521.
43. "Economic Effects of the Strike of the UAW of General Motors Corporation" (mimeographed), Gibson Papers, HSTL.
44. *Ibid.*
45. *Ibid.*

4

The Fight Over Wages and Prices

PROBABLY THE MOST CRITICAL ISSUE IN LABOR RELATIONS during the first postwar year was that of wages and their relation to prices. For two decades organized labor had held to the doctrine that wages had to increase in terms of wage rates relative to the cost of living. No exception was made willingly even during a war when it was difficult to maintain the standard of living already attained. Therefore, it was clear prior to V.J.-Day that the major labor organizations would press for substantial wage advances at the conclusion of hostilities.

One element in the situation was the modification of wartime wage controls by the Truman administration on August 18, 1945. With the end of the war, comprehensive control over wage-rate changes was removed, and employers were permitted to make wage increases of any magnitude without government approval, provided such increases were not used as the basis for increases in price ceilings. Freedom of action was restored to workers and employers with respect to those upward wage adjustments that could be made within the existing framework of prices.

On August 16, 1945, two days after announcing the surrender of Japan, President Truman declared in a statement on labor policy that "with the ending of war production . . . there is no longer any threat of an inflationary bidding up of wage rates by competition in a short labor market," and indicated that a rise in wage rates was now not only permissible, but also desirable to eliminate "maladjustments and inequities" resulting from the decline in workers' "take-home" pay.[1]

On August 18, Truman issued the executive order permitting increases in wages without prior government approval "upon the condition that such increases will not be used in whole or in part as the basis for seeking an increase in price ceilings . . . or, in the case of products or services being furnished under contract with a federal procurement agency, will not increase the cost to the United States."[2]

Truman's order also provided that wage increases might be approved by the NWLB, even where they would result in price increases, if they were necessary to correct maladjustments or inequities. This was interpreted to mean that cost-of-living wage rises could be granted "where the percentage increase in average straight-time hourly earnings . . . since January, 1941, has not equalled the percentage increase in the cost of living between January, 1941, and September, 1945," or a total of thirty-three per cent.[3]

In his address delivered October 30, 1945, on the eve of the Labor–Management Conference, President Truman indicated that he believed substantial increases in wage rates could be made under his new formula without affecting prices. He pointed out that since V.E.-Day the ending of overtime pay, the downgrading of employees, and the shift from high-pay war employment to peacetime jobs and reduced total worker take-home pay by nearly one-fourth, while profits and prices had remained relatively stable.[4]

The primary assumption in the wage policy announced immediately after V.J.-Day was that many employers were in a position to grant increases in basic rates of pay within existing price ceilings and that the magnitude of these increases could be determined through collective bargaining without work stoppages.[5] Many wage-rate increases within the existing price structure were made through collective bargaining, or were granted by employers in the absence of union organization in the months that followed the end of the war.[6]

However, no agreement was reached between employers and unions on the magnitude of the wage increases that could be made under the new wage-price policy. No agency for the final determination of these peacetime disputes existed. Wage policy during the war period had been applied in dispute cases by the NWLB. However, Truman in his statement of August 16, 1945, had announced that the Board would be terminated as soon as practicable after the conclusion of the imminent Labor–Management Conference. The NWLB's wage determinations would apply only to cases begun before the end of the war. The Board was in no position to accept jurisdiction over new dispute cases between the end of the war and its termination date, December 31, 1945.[7]

The Labor–Management Conference adjourned on November 30, 1945, without agreement on machinery to effect the settlement of labor disputes in which collective bargaining and conciliation had failed. Recourse to economic power was to be expected when labor and management failed to agree on the terms of the wage bargain.

Truman, in a message to the Congress on December 3, 1945, therefore urged enactment of legislation which would give him statutory authority to appoint fact-finding boards to consider such disputes which, in the opinion of the Secretary of Labor, would seriously affect the national public interest.[8]

Truman's request for legislation to authorize fact-finding came two weeks after the beginning of what was to become one of the most prolonged and bitter stoppages of the reconversion period. The General Motors strike began on November 21. In the controversy the union contended that the corporation's ability to pay should be considered a

major factor in determining the amount of the wage adjustment and asserted that the full thirty per cent increase
demanded could be paid without price relief. Company
officials, however, insisted that prices and profits had to be
excluded from the wage discussions.[9]

Truman did not await action by Congress on his proposed fact-finding legislation and on December 14 appointed a board to investigate the General Motors dispute.
The union rejected Truman's request to return to work
pending findings of the Board, but both parties indicated
their willingness to present their case to the fact-finding
board. On the vital issue of ability to pay, Truman on December 20 declared that "ability to pay is always one of the
facts relevant to the issue of an increase in wages."[10] The
following day the board in the General Motors case announced that the ability to pay wage increases would be
considered as a relevant but not as the sole factor in its
recommendations. A week later, representatives of General
Motors withdrew from the hearing, stating that they would
refuse to participate further so long as "ability to pay is to
be treated as a subject of investigation, fact-finding and
recommendations."[11]

The demand for higher wages was also the basis for a
great number of other postwar strikes. In January, 1946,
over a million workers in steel, electrical manufacturing,
meat-packing, and farm-equipment establishments stopped
work in support of their demands for higher wages. The
nearly five thousand strikes that occurred in 1946, with
their millions of man-days lost, became the greatest number
of any previous year on record.[12] Unions considered their
demands for wage increases to maintain take-home pay, as
well as other issues involved, worth fighting for, and their
wartime treasuries were well enough stocked to make a
fight possible. Many corporations stood on principle in refusing increases of the extent demanded until price relief
was available. Moreover, they could offset losses to some

extent by refunds on portions of their wartime excess profits taxes.

The largest of these strikes over wages was in the steel industry, which was brought to a standstill when approximately 750,000 workers, members of the United Steelworkers of America, stopped work on January 21, 1946, to enforce their demands for a wage increase of two dollars a day.[13] As was true of other large stoppages in which strikes were called after the breakdown of prolonged negotiations, the steel strike followed more than three months of intermittent negotiation. The initial demand of the union for an industry-wide increase of two dollars a day, announced on September 11, 1945, was rejected by the major steel producers, who claimed that existing OPA ceiling prices for steel did not permit the companies to grant any wage increase.[14] Offers of conciliation by the Secretary of Labor were rejected by industry representatives, who insisted that further negotiations would be futile until the OPA authorized an increase in steel prices.[15]

On December 31, 1945, two weeks before the announced date of the strike, Truman appointed a three-member board to investigate the wage dispute and to determine whether an increase in steel prices would be justified.[16] In an effort to forestall a work stoppage, direct negotiations were resumed on January 10, 1946. These followed conferences between representatives of the steel industry and goverment officials over revision in steel price ceilings. The union scaled down its demand to an increase of 19½ cents an hour, the amount recommended by the fact-finding board in the General Motors case. The United States Steel Corporation, the largest employer in the industry, offered an increase of fifteen cents an hour provided price ceilings on steel were revised upward by the OPA.

At this point Truman invited union and industry negotiators to the White House, meanwhile obtaining the union's consent to a one-week postponement of the strike.[17]

On January 17, after receiving an informal report from his steel fact-finding board, Truman proposed a wage increase of 18½ cents per hour as the basis of settlement. This proposal was accepted by the union but was rejected by spokesmen for the steel industry. The strike began on January 21, 1946. For the following three weeks both parties stood their ground despite efforts by the government to find an acceptable compromise. Steel output, which had been running at eighty to eighty-five per cent of capacity, dropped to about six per cent. Other industries, dependent upon steel, were forced to curtail or suspend operations.[18]

Of the large strikes involving wages which occurred in the spring of 1946, the most significant were those involving bituminous coal miners and railroad engineers and trainmen. In soft coal, the failure of the coal operators and the United Mine Workers of America to negotiate a new agreement before the expiration of the existing contract, on March 31, 1946, resulted in an industry-wide stoppage, which continued from April 1 through May 29, except for a twelve-day truce from May 13–25 during which most of the 340,000 union miners worked.[19]

At the outset of the coal controversy, the UMWA filed a thirty-day strike notice legally required under the War Labor Disputes Act and concentrated its demand upon the establishment of a health and welfare fund to be financed by the coal operators and administered by the union. Negotiations proceeded slowly during March and April, with the effects of the coal strike on the nation's reconversion program becoming increasingly serious. A month after the strike started, Truman released a report of the Office of War Mobilization and Reconversion in which the coal dispute was termed a "national disaster."[20] When both the union and the operators rejected Truman's proposal to arbitrate, Truman on May 21, ordered government seizure of the mines and their operation under the direction of the

Secretary of the Interior. Despite this step, most miners stayed away from work and did not return until after May 29, when an agreement, to be effective during federal operation of the mines, was signed by the Secretary of the Interior, Julius A. Krug, and John L. Lewis, President of the United Mine Workers. The principal terms provided for a wage increase of 18½ cents an hour and a health and welfare fund to be financed by the levy of five cents per ton of coal produced for use of sale, the fund to be administered by three trustees—one selected by the union, one by the coal mines administrator, and the third by the other two. The settlement also served as a basis for terminating the anthracite controversy, which extended from May 31 to June 7.[21]

At about the same time that the government seized the bituminous coal mines the railroad wage controversies reached their climax. Early in 1946, two groups of railroad unions agreed to submit their wage issues to arbitration. Two other unions, the Brotherhood of Locomotive Engineers and the Brotherhood of Railroad Trainmen, declined to arbitrate. After a strike vote had been taken, Truman, in early March, appointed a fact-finding board to consider the controversy of these two unions with the railroads. On April 3, the two arbitration boards awarded the groups of railroad employees involved in the cases an increase of sixteen cents an hour.[22] The Brotherhood of Locomotive Engineers and the Brotherhood of Railroad Trainmen were not only dissatisfied over the wage awards but also felt that the recommended revisions in working rules were inadequate. These two unions planned to strike at the expiration of the thirty-day waiting period provided by the Railway Labor Act.[23]

On May 17, 1946, Truman ordered seizure of the railroads and their operation under the direction of the Office of Defense Transportation.[24] Shortly before the strike was scheduled to begin on May 18, the leaders of the two brotherhoods complied with Truman's request to postpone the threatened walkout for five days. Negotiations were resumed in Washington and on May 22, all of the rail unions except the engineers and the trainmen accepted a compromise settlement for an 18½-cent-an-hour wage increase and a one-year moratorium on changes in rules. The engineers and trainmen, however, rejected this settlement and at 4 P.M., May 23, withdrew from service, causing a complete nation-wide collapse of rail transportation, the first in the history of the industry. On the night of May 24, Truman spoke to the country by radio and requested the men to return to work. The next day he addressed a joint session of Congress seeking emergency legislation which would give him power designed to prevent strikes which might have widespread effects on the nation's economy. Almost simultaneously with his appearance before Congress, union officials signed an agreement accepting Truman's proposal of May 22, and ordered their members to return to their jobs. Service was thus restored after the two-day stoppage.[25]

The railroad controversy was the last of the wage stoppages, which involved more than 100,000 workers, that occurred during the period under survey. Another threatened transportation strike, involving nearly 200,000 members of the Committee of Maritime Unity, composed of six CIO unions and one unaffiliated union, was averted by a settlement made less than an hour before the strike deadline of June 15, 1946.[26] After negotiations had come to an impasse in this dispute, Secretary of Labor Schwellenbach summoned representatives of the unions and ship operators to meet in Washington on May 29, for further conferences under his direction. The War Shipping Administration, the government agency which owned many of the vessels, subsequently entered the negotiations and, just prior to the scheduled strike date, directed all WSA general agents or their representatives to accept proposals calling for a wage increase of $17.50 a month, certain reductions in basic hours, and arbitration of other issues. These terms formed the basis of the agreements which were adopted by the seagoing unions and their employers. The longshoremen's union, in turn, accepted the report of a fact-finding board which had recommended a wage increase of twenty-two cents an hour for West Coast longshoremen.[27]

At least one criticism can be made of Truman's V.J.-Day decision removing wage controls except where wage increases were used as a basis for seeking upward revisions in price ceilings. The Truman administration made a mistake in the combination of the decisions on wage stabilization and the abandonment of machinery to settle disputes. Had the dispute-settling machinery been extended to setting wage patterns, free collective bargaining could probably have settled a considerable proportion of other disputes and made the adjustments to a peacetime economy on a day-to-day basis more smoothly. Had stabilization controls dictated wage levels, the elimination of the dispute-settling agency would have been less serious; but it was the simultaneous restoration of collective bargaining and the removal of wage controls that produced the difficulties.

This timing was not contemplated by the Truman administration when the transition stabilization program was developed in the summer of 1945. However, it is also questionable that it could have been accurately predicted. In addition, many economists both inside and outside of the government had been for some months predicting a sharp postwar recession.

The period of transition and reconversion made the administration of any pricing standards difficult. The essence of the reconversion period in Truman's mind was readjustment and change from a wartime economy to a peacetime system. The prospective character of price standards became important and price control had to be increasingly subjective in the sense of indicating assumptions for output, productivity, and materials cost. Differences as to the business outlook made price control difficult under these circumstances. There was no clear standard or pattern to resolve such conflicts.

One of the central difficulties of the period was that uncertainty loomed particularly large in the transition from war to peace, and neither labor nor management wanted to bear the cost of uncertainty. Labor demanded immediate wage increases, and management insisted on full price offsets, since it did not desire to make wage commitments until productivity and output changes were clarified.

The cumulative effects of the stoppages and unsettled disputes involving a number of basic industries became so great that by February, 1946, the government was forced to revise its wage-price stabilization regulations. Truman, on December 31, 1945, issued Executive Order No. 9672, which had established the National Wage Stabilization Board, the successor to the former National War Labor Board. On February 14, 1946, Truman issued Executive Order No. 9697, giving the NWSB the power to approve any wage or salary adjustments consistent with the general pattern of such adjustments established in the industry or local labor-market area between August 18, 1945, and February 14, 1946.[28] Prior approval was also given to increases made in accordance with a government recommendation in a wage controversy announced before February 14, 1946.

On December 31, 1945, the NWLB ceased to exist. Its personnel and functions became the nucleus of the NWSB. The NWSB was the last official attempt by the Truman administration to stabilize wages. In the summer of 1946, Congress refused to extend the existing price control act. Since the only effective way to apply wage controls was through restrictions on the adjustment of price ceilings, the orders of the NWSB were of little real help in stabilizing wages. The NWSB continued to issue statements and to take official action, but these were of little importance, and the board came to a legal end on February 24, 1947.[29]

The NWSB actually added little of positive value to the Truman administration's program of government controls. The NWLB had come under severe public criticism, but it was nothing compared to the scorn heaped on the NWSB. Both the NWLB and the NWSB suffered from being overloaded with cases. War had been a coordinating factor of national goals for the NWLB, but with peace the degree of coordination of effort was impossible for the NWSB to maintain in such an atmosphere of political tension.[30]

From the vantage point of hindsight it can be seen that reconversion would have been smoother if controls had not been removed so soon. It was also apparent, however, that if the Truman administration was really going to achieve its aim of stabilized prices and a stabilized cost-of-living standard, there was no basis for retaining strict wartime controls over wage rates. The failure to continue adequate stabilization during the reconversion period did cause sharp public reaction, but the reaction was from the same public that had clamored for the nation and its government to return as soon as possible to "normalcy."[31]

By the end of June, 1946, the round of "reconversion" strikes, which were predominantly over the wage issue, had come to a close. The final month of the first postwar year was a period of price uncertainty characterized by numerous but relatively small disputes. During the year as a whole, the national wage-price policy was modified first in late October, 1945, and then more drastically in mid-February, 1946. Fact-finding boards as a substitute for the NWLB were found to be not always entirely successful, and government seizure by Presidential executive order had to be resorted to in certain cases as a method of resolving some conflicts.

Wage adjustments under the revised wage-price policy were far less than many unions were determined to gain.

They were also beyond what many employers were willing to give as long as they were subject to price controls. The postwar strikes that occurred in 1945 and 1946 were not merely disputes between labor and management over sharing the returns from business operations. Many of them centered about the Truman administration's determination to retain a reasonably effective wage-stabilization program. The postwar wage-price policy was a drastic shift from the wartime governmental determination of wages. Truman, however, was convinced that this policy was the only way of introducing a greater opportunity for collective bargaining while maintaining adequate controls over prices. Truman and his administration were in many instances forced by circumstances to take an increasingly active part in the settlement of labor disputes. The Truman administration's reluctant participation, therefore, at times seemed to encourage strikes rather than to avert them. Truman sought to achieve a balance between management and labor, and instead he temporarily lost the support of both. But an even "more experienced Administration would have had difficulty and might have failed in juggling the conflicting claims made upon government in this period."[32]

Notes: Chapter 4

1. *Public Papers of the Presidents: 1945*, p. 221.
2. Executive Order No. 9599, August 18, 1945, OF 407, Truman Papers, HSTL.
3. "Postwar Work Stoppages," *Monthly Labor Review* (December, 1946), p. 876.
4. *Public Papers of the Presidents: 1945*, pp. 439–449.
5. John T. Dunlop, "The Decontrol of Wages and Prices," *Labor in Postwar America*, ed. Colston E. Warne (New York: Remsen Press, 1949), pp. 7–9.

6. "Wage-Price Policy," Office of War Mobilization and Reconversion, Record Group 250, National Archives. Office of War Mobilization and Reconversion, Record Group 250, hereinafter cited as Record Group 250.
7. Executive Order No. 9672, December 31, 1945, OF 30, Truman Papers, HSTL.
8. *Public Papers of the Presidents: 1945*, p. 519.
9. "Summary of the Report of the Fact-Finding Board in General Motors Strike" (mimeographed), January 10, 1946, OF 407B, Truman Papers, HSTL.
10. "Wage-Price Policy," Record Group 250, National Archives, *op. cit.*
11. *Ibid.*
12. *Monthly Labor Review, op. cit.*, p. 876.
13. "Wage-Price Policy," Record Group 250, National Archives, *op. cit.*
14. *New York Times*, September 12, 1945.
15. "Wage Policy and the Role of Fact-Finding Boards," *Monthly Labor Review* (April, 1946), p. 539.
16. "Wage-Price Policy," Record Group 250, National Archives, *op. cit.*
17. "Wage-Price Policy," *Monthly Labor Review, op. cit.*, p. 878.
18. *Ibid.*
19. "Wage-Price Policy" Record Group 250, National Archives, *op. cit.*
20. *Ibid.*
21. *Ibid.*
22. "Railway Changes, 1941–46," *Monthly Labor Review* (September, 1946), p. 336.
23. *Ibid.*, p. 336–337.
24. *New York Times*, May 18, 1946.
25. *Ibid.*, May 23, 1946.
26. "Railway Changes, 1941–46," *Monthly Labor Review, op. cit.*, p. 336.
27. Dunlop, *op. cit.*, p. 22.
28. *The National Wage Stabilization Board, January 1, 1946–February 24, 1947*, United States Department of Labor (Washington: U. S. Government Printing Office, 1947), p. 5.
29. *New York Times*, February 25, 1947.

30. "Wage-Price Policy," Record Group 250, National Archives, *op. cit.*
31. Barton J. Bernstein, "The Truman Administration and Its Reconversion Wage Policy," *Labor History*, Vol. 6, No. 3 (Fall, 1965), pp. 214–231.
32. *Ibid.*, p. 231.

5

The Use of Fact-Finding and Mediation

ONE FACET OF PRESIDENT TRUMAN'S LABOR PROGRAM THAT HAS
been frequently overlooked was that he asked for legislation to create machinery to settle labor disputes. Truman's
overriding sense of labor's duties as well as rights in the
national interest again became evident in his policies. Truman's strong objections to later restrictive legislation, particularly the Taft-Hartley Act, clouded this fact, and the
myth arose that he was "one hundred per cent pro-labor."
The fact was that he was politically aware of not wanting
to alienate labor's votes. In times of great national stress,
however, such as during the postwar strike period, he always tried to put the national safety above any group interest, be it management or labor. His fact-finding proposals were a strong indication of this idea.

Truman first recommended the fact-finding approach
after the postwar Labor–Management Conference had
failed in November, 1945, to agree on machinery for dealing with major labor disputes not settled through collective
bargaining, mediation, or conciliation. In a special message to Congress on December 3, 1945, he outlined a fact-
finding program and expressed his belief "that the procedure should be used sparingly and only when the national
public interest requires it." He mentioned steel, automobiles, aviation, mining, oil, utilities, and communica-

tions as industries in which he felt fact-finding would be
"effective as well as fair."[1]

As he presented the program in 1945, Truman was to
appoint a fact-finding board, similar to the emergency
boards under the Railway Labor Act, within five days
after notification by the Secretary of Labor that a dispute
continued despite his efforts for adjustment and that a stoppage would vitally affect the public interest. The board
would have power to subpoena witnesses and records, and
would make "a thorough investigation of all the facts which
it deems relevant in the controversy." It would have twenty
days to deliberate and make its report. The report would
include a finding of facts and whatever recommendations
the board deemed appropriate. From the date of certification by the Secretary of Labor until five days after submission of the board's report, a total of thirty days, Truman
proposed that it should be "unlawful to call a strike or lockout, or to make any change in rates of pay, hours, working
conditions or established practices, except by agreement."[2]

While there would be no legal obligation on either party
to accept the findings or follow the recommendations of the
board, "the general public would know all the facts."[3] Truman was confident that in most cases board recommendations would be accepted by both sides. He amplified his
proposal regarding use of records in a statement December
20, 1945, by specifically including the books of the employer.

In appointing a fact-finding board in an industrial
dispute where one of the questions at issue is wages, it is
essential to a fulfillment of its duty that the board have
the authority, whenever it deems it necessary, to examine
the books of the employer. That authority is essential
to enable the board to determine the ability of the employer to pay an increase in wages where such ability is
in question.[4]

Labor's reaction to Truman's fact-finding proposal was immediate and hostile. The CIO was particularly angry. In a vitriolic speech, Philip Murray denounced the Truman administration for its "abject cowardice" in the face of industrial and management "arrogance."[5] Murray charged that the government had "embarked upon a policy of continued appeasement of American industry in the face of industry's contemptuous attitude toward the American people and the government itself." He went on to say that the proposal would result in "legislation that can have but one single purpose—the weakening of labor unions, the curtailment of the right of free men to refrain from working when they choose to do so. . . . It can be but the first step for even more savage legislative repression." Murray further stated that the CIO opposed the basic labor policy of the Truman administration "which marks a very serious departure from the policies which the people of this country have repeatedly approved . . . under the leadership of President Roosevelt."[6]

Murray's attack was one of the most bitter criticisms of a Democratic administration by a CIO leader since John L. Lewis of the United Mine Workers split with the Roosevelt administration in 1940. George Meany, AFL Secretary-Treasurer, joined the attack on the Truman proposal in a speech at Harrisburg, Pennsylvania, where he said the AFL would not accept legislation which "compels workers to work even for a minute against their will."[7]

Legislation to carry out Truman's proposals was considered by committees of both houses of Congress in the Seventy-Ninth Congress. Hearings were held in December, 1945, on the Ellender bill in the Senate, introduced by Allen Ellender of Louisiana, and the Norton bill in the House, introduced by Mary Norton of New Jersey, both of which embodied Truman's proposal.[8] Neither the House Labor Committee nor the Senate Committee on Education and Labor found that they could report their bills very quickly, and they both decided to continue hearings after the reconvening of Congress on January 14, 1946.[9]

The position of the representatives of organized labor at these hearings on the central issue of limiting the exercise of the right to strike was one of almost violent opposition. Among those labor leaders who testified at these hearings were Albert J. Fitzgerald, President, United Electrical Radio and Machine Workers of America, CIO; Thomas Kennedy, Secretary-Treasurer, United Mine Workers of America; Philip Murray, President, CIO; and Walter Reuther, Vice-President, United Automobile Workers, CIO.[10]

With reference to the specific limitation on strikes during a period of thirty days, these spokesmen for labor also said that it was impossible to frame any measure which would have the effect of limiting the right to strike to a period of no more than thirty days. They argued that the limitation was far more extensive and maintained that it would hamper the negotiations while the parties were engaged in collective bargaining, during all subsequent efforts at mediation or conciliation, during the period of discretionary uncertainty as to whether or not the President would certify the dispute, and during the deliberations of the fact-finding boards.[11]

They also argued that preparation and organization for a strike could not be developed and held static for weeks or months, built up to the point of action and let down again during the delays. During this long period of negotiation, mediation, conciliation, certification and fact-finding, strikes would have been impossible as a practical matter. In their view the strike weapon would be blunted so badly as to render it useless.[12]

Management spokesmen were not any more enthusiastic about the idea of fact-finding than the labor leaders. Ira Mosher of the National Association of Manufacturers, another witness, said that the bill went too far toward compulsory arbitration. Mosher gave a qualified and reluctant endorsement to the principle of fact-finding and said that a real need existed for legislation that would impose equal responsibility before the law on labor as well as management.[13]

William Green, AFL President, said that although the bill provided that individuals acting independently might lawfully refrain from working during the thirty-day, fact-finding period, this was merely a "window-dressing" device to help save the constitutionality of the measure. He contended that the prohibition against a concrete refusal to work for a period of thirty days "raises serious constitutional questions, for it thereby imposes upon workers involuntary servitude." Green also said the proposal would nullify a provision in the Norris-LaGuardia Act which said that no association or organization taking part in a labor dispute, and no officer or member of them, could be held liable in a federal court for the unlawful acts of individual officers or members except on clear proof of actual participation in, or authorization of, such acts.[14]

The position of the top union spokesmen remained that the proposal, if enacted into law, would condemn labor to "involuntary servitude" and that to enforce the restrictions on labor, the courts would be restored to their pre-Norris–LaGuardia Act role of issuing injunctions in labor disputes. As a waiting period, with or without fact-finding, became a common requirement in a number of other bills later to be considered, the unalterable opposition of the union spokesmen was a basic factor in the entire discussion of legislative remedies to cope with the problem of work stoppages.

The strongest support for Truman's bill came expectedly from Secretary of Labor Schwellenbach. He found a need for the measure in the breakdown of collective bargaining in some important industries and in the sharp increase in the number of strike notices filed with the NLRB under the

War Labor Disputes Act. Secretary Schwellenbach had confidence that the informed findings of a panel of public-spirited men, backed by public opinion, would generally be accepted and he based this confidence on the history of emergency boards under the Railway Labor Act. He also did not think that labor had anything to fear from the thirty-day period during which no stoppage would be lawful, which he said was also a provision included in the Railway Labor Act.

Contrasting the waiting period in the fact-finding bill with the thirty-day waiting period provided in the War Labor Disputes Act, the labor secretary pointed out that the latter was designed to be a "cooling-off" period and nothing more, while the thirty-day period provided in the new bill was to be used to secure affirmative action in the nature of hearings, fact-finding, and recommendations which would serve as a basis for the settlement of the dispute "rather than serving as a period of preparation for the beginning of a strike."[15] He also indicated that the fact-finding procedure would be used only where certification was made that government conciliation and arbitration had failed, that the parties were unwilling to submit the controversy to arbitration, and that the stoppage of work would seriously affect the national public interest.

On January 22, 1946, the House Labor Committee reported the administration bill but with amendments deleting the subpoena powers of the thirty-day cooling-off period.[16] In this form, the bill would have done little more than give legislative authorization for boards of a kind which Truman believed he already had authority to set up under his general powers. The Case bill, which Congress finally sent to the White House as a substitute for the administration measure, contained a provision which provided for Presidential fact-finding boards only in major labor disputes occurring in essential public utilities. In vetoing this bill on June 11, 1946, Truman observed: "it is difficult to understand why the Congress has applied the fact-finding principle to public utilities but has omitted it entirely in other industries of equal importance."[17]

There was, however, a certain amount of use by the Truman administration of the fact-finding procedure during the postwar years. Truman himself appointed fact-finding boards for disputes involving General Motors and United States Steel, and Schwellenbach, using his powers to provide conciliation machinery as Secretary of Labor, appointed a board in the oil dispute. He named three additional boards between mid-December, 1945, and mid-January, 1946. Six more boards were appointed in 1946, by Schwellenbach and the Director of the Federal Mediation and Conciliation Service.[18] The use of fact-finding boards during the immediate postwar period was one attempt by the Truman administration to maintain a national wage-price stabilization policy while labor and management were becoming increasingly restless under wartime restrictions. Imminent termination of the NWLB on December 31, 1945, and inability of employers and unions to resolve disputes through collective bargaining, left the administration with no machinery to cope with an epidemic of nationwide strikes.

The fact-finding boards appointed by Truman and Schwelllenbach were given the quasi-judicial function of determining the fact in each case and making recommendations for settlement within the limitations of government wage-price policy. The Truman administration expected that public opinion would force acceptance of the boards' recommendations. The boards consisted of three public members in all cases except the one involving the Greyhound Bus Lines, to which one labor member and one industry member were added. In most cases the unions and companies participated voluntarily in the hearings, but General Motors withdrew from the proceedings in its case in protest against a board decision to consider the question of ability to pay.[19]

In the United States Steel case, the board urged renewal of negotiations and settlement by collective bargaining. When a deadlock was followed by a strike, Truman intervened personally. The dispute was adjusted only when the government revised its wage-price policy and permitted an increase in prices of steel. In later cases involving Western Union and Milwaukee Gas Light, settlements were reached independently and the boards made no recommendations. After the oil and General Motors cases, the boards generally applied the "pattern" of eighteen to twenty-two cents as the basic wage settlement.[20] In all of the 1945–1946 disputes where fact-finding boards were appointed, final wage settlements closely followed board recommendations.

Even the most ardent proponents of the fact-finding procedure did not advocate it as a substitute for collective bargaining. Truman emphasized that it should be used sparingly. Experience under the Railway Labor Act indicated that the emergency boards had greater influence before the war when they were appointed less frequently.

John T. Dunlop, a professor of economics at Harvard University, felt that three conditions were necessary for successful use of fact-finding machinery:

1.) An interruption of work would significantly and immediately affect the public interest.

2.) The issues are reasonably limited in number and sufficiently nontechnical to be amenable to examination by a general panel.

3.) The issues must involve conflicting claims as to fact or emphasis upon different facts or principles rather than a single out-and-out clash of principle.[21]

Dunlop suggested that three particular types of situations might be especially suitable for examination by fact-finding boards:

1.) In the event government seizure has taken place and some method must be found to determine the appropriateness of a change in the terms and conditions of employment.

2.) In order to save face for one of the parties, particularly when the risks of arbitration may be too high.

3.) In the event that it must appear that the government is 'taking action' in a dispute in which further mediation or other plans may lead to settlement.[22]

Professor Dunlop saw the function of fact-finding boards as being closely allied to mediation. Too much use of the procedure, he warned, would constitute a threat to settlement by negotiation "whenever either party hopes for a better break from this form of government intervention than can be achieved under collective bargaining."[23] He concluded that if both unions and management were satisfied with the decisions of fact-finding boards they might become inclined to shift responsibility to the boards for difficult decisions which they should make themselves.

The simplicity and directness of Truman's fact-finding proposals became great sources of their strength with the public. Fact-finding became known as "Truman's panel technique." Although no bill was enacted into law, many people felt that the value of fact-finding lay in the reexamination of the accepted ideas of labor's unlimited right to strike.

In addition to using the fact-finding approach to industrial disharmony, the Truman administration used other means of mediation as a means of solving some of the problems of postwar labor relations. (The terms "mediation" and "conciliation" are often used interchangeably in practice, and they will be so used here.) The 1913 law that had created the Department of Labor also provided for the Secretary of Labor to mediate labor disputes and to appoint commissioners of conciliation to aid him in that task. The expansion of this work became great enough to necessitate the establishment of a special division in 1917, known as the United States Conciliation Service. The USCS regarded as its chief duty the peaceful settlement of labor disputes by informal mediation.[24] Normally, the conciliators were either labor economists recruited from universities, or ex-labor leaders.

Those conciliators assigned to a case usually arranged a meeting or a series of meetings with the parties to the dispute, as part of their attempts to mediate the disagreement. The knowledge gained at these meetings was often valuable in narrowing the whole area of disagreement that existed.[25]

When World War II ended, the bulk of the mediation in labor disputes fell upon the USCS. For about three years before V.J.-Day the overwhelming majority of serious unsettled disputes between management and labor were resolved by government directives. After January 1, 1946, no agency existed which could order changes in contracts or adjudicate disputes over grievances, and although the authority to do so existed prior to that date it was not in fact used between August 17 and December 31, 1945.

The emphasis upon direct negotiations, with a minimum of federal control, over labor controversies resulted in a tremendous increase in the obligation of the USCS to secure final settlement of conflicts on a voluntary basis, through collective bargaining between management and labor. The settlement of cases also became more difficult. During the war, increases in wages were limited by the various stabilization criteria established by the NWLB. These limitations also served as standards to be used by both management and labor in wage negotiations. Moreover, by using a uniform procedure in handling disputes over vacations with pay, night shift premiums, union security, and similar issues, the NWLB established standards which in effect set the limitations of collective bargaining on such fringe adjustments.[26]

With the end of the NWLB these standards were in great part abandoned. It was then that the task of the USCS became much more complicated. Voluntary mediation solutions, being far more difficult to achieve, required not only greater skill on the part of commissioners of conciliation, but also more time and greater energy. Previously such solutions were formulated by the NWLB and enforced under the wartime powers of the President. After the war, however, the USCS had to resort to settlements by suggestions which might or might not readily be accepted by the parties.

After V.J.-Day the two major goals of the USCS were to prevent industrial conflict and to restore peace after a work stoppage had begun. The success of the USCS in reducing the area of industrial conflict was attested to by the number of cases handled and closed by conciliators during the twelve months immediately following V.J.-Day. During that period federal conciliators aided in one way or another in the peaceful settlement of more than 12,500 industrial disputes, or ninety-one per cent of the labor–management disputes in which it participated.[27]

In 1945 the President's Labor–Management Conference had recommended that the USCS be strengthened. The role played by the USCS in assisting labor and management to achieve industrial peace was in large measure an outgrowth of the unanimous recommendations of the Labor–Management Conference. The conference had reached agreement on few points, but a principal one was that there be a "reorganization of the Conciliation Service to the end that it will be established as an effective and completely impartial agency within the Department."[28]

The conference also recommended the establishment of a Labor–Management Advisory Committee to make "recommendations to the Secretary of Labor or to the Director of the Conciliation Service with respect to the policy, procedures, organization, and development of adequate standards and qualifications for the personnel of this Service."[29] A number of other steps to extend the facilities of the USCS in assisting labor and management in their collective efforts were taken, following the unanimous recommendations of the President's Labor–Management Conference.

One of the most important steps taken by the USCS was the establishment of the Labor–Management Advisory Committee. An Advisory Committee had been established by the USCS on October 18, 1945, prior to the President's conference.[30] That committee was appointed by the Secretary of Labor. The establishment of the committee marked the first time in the history of the Department of Labor that industry and labor jointly had been given a voice in the formulation of major departmental policy.

Following the President's Labor–Management Conference, the Committee was reformed to consist of eight members selected from lists of nominees submitted by the AFL, CIO, United States Chamber of Commerce, and the NAM. The committee met once every month. All contemplated major policy or procedural changes were submitted to the committee for approval prior to their adoption, and the committee actively participated in the policy-making process. The arbitration policies were worked out with the committee, including the discontinuance of a permanent staff and the substitution of an approved arbitration panel, the use of regional labor–management committees for screening the names for this panel, and the limited use of arbitration paid for by the government.

The committee reviewed and approved the organizational policies of the USCS, including the increased salary scale for conciliators and their field supervisors, the further development of branch officers, and staff reductions made necessary by budget stringencies. The committee reviewed and approved the training, informational, and planning activities of the Program Division referred to below. The committee, in addition to its regular function of advising the USCS, was particularly helpful in serving as a clearing house for criticisms that might be made by labor or management on the functioning of the USCS. The opportunity thus created to air these criticisms on a constructive basis was of great assistance in promoting the acceptability of the USCS among labor and management.[31]

In the reorganization of the USCS that followed World War II a number of divisions were created each with special functions to aid in the settlement of labor disputes. The Program Division was a direct outgrowth of the unanimous report of the President's Labor–Management Conference, which specifically recommended:

> Provision should be made for practical training for newly appointed conciliators. During such training, the newly appointed conciliators should be assigned as observers in the course of actual conciliation of a variety of cases. Adequate facilities should be made available to assure thorough knowledge on the part of conciliators of the policies of the Service, techniques of conciliation, labor laws, and industrial relations practice. Information services should be made available to all conciliators to keep them currently abreast of developments in the Conciliation Service, and to provide them with up-to-date information on current labor law and industrial relations practice. In addition, periodic refresher courses should be conducted in the interest of maintaining high standards of service.[32]

By the end of the war collective bargaining had become a highly complicated process. Industry and labor began to train their representatives in personnel and industrial relations practices. Industry conducted training courses for its supervisory staffs, and labor organizations conducted shop stewards' classes to instruct their representatives in the handling of grievances and in the process of collective bargaining. Industry and labor both took steps to train their representatives in the field of labor law. Many universities recognized the need by labor and management for trained representatives and instituted industrial relations schools to provide trained leaders in the field. It was apparent that, with highly trained people representing industry and labor on both sides of the collective bargaining table, government representatives would have to be at least equally as well trained. Persuasion alone was no longer a sufficient qualification for a good conciliator. The good conciliator had to be a labor relations expert as well as a man of tact and persuasiveness.

Labor and management both looked to the government after World War II to provide leadership by providing competent and impartial conciliators to assist the parties in the resolution of their disputes. In September, 1945, there were few facilities in the USCS for intensive training or refresher courses and there were no staff functions relating to basic planning of the operations of the agency. The Program Division, therefore, was established to accomplish these objectives.[33] This division planned and conducted an in-service training program through periodic courses in Washington and through two-day regional conferences. The Washington conferences, known as Current Problems Conferences, ran for a period of one week and were held approximately once every six weeks.

At these conferences basic labor laws, contract clause problems, and techniques of conciliation were discussed; leading representatives of labor and management attended these sessions and frequently acted as discussion leaders. The area conferences generally had the participation of local labor and management representatives, and labor relations problems—particularly as they concerned the local area—were discussed.

The Program Division was also responsible for compiling and making available to the field staff new information on laws and regulations, labor-contract provisions, and summaries of current wage data. This information was designed to keep commissioners abreast of current developments that directly affected the disputes that they were working on in the field.

Another division of the uscs was the Technical Division.[34] The role of the Technical Division was well established before 1946. Its work was related to disputes between labor and management involving incentive plans, job evaluations, merit-rating systems, work-load studies, and related questions. The uscs provided trained specialists in the field of industrial engineering and personnel management to assist both companies and unions in resolving disputes of those kind. The President's Labor–Management Conference unanimously recommended that "The Technical Service Division be reorganized. It should operate with the advice and counsel of a Technical Advisory Committee."[35] In compliance with these recommendations, a Technical Advisory Committee was appointed by Secretary of Labor Schwellenbach, consisting of leaders of industry and labor. This committee made recommendations of specific methods of operation that were adopted by the Technical Division.

The Labor–Management Technical Advisory Committee reviewed the work of the Technical Division and then set up standards for its performance. These standards included the requirement that the technical commissioners could not enter any dispute for the purpose of making a factual study unless both parties requested such a study, and that the findings of the technician were final so far as he was concerned in his further meetings with the disputants. The committee also reviewed the types of reports that had been made and suggested changes in them. The members of the committee discussed the procedure in handling textile disputes over work loads and set up a definite procedure for studying and reporting such cases. The method of working with an arbitrator as a technical advisor was amplified, and definite rules were established.

Another important division of the USCS that was reorganized was the Arbitration Division. Until September, 1945, the Arbitration Division of the USCS provided arbitration services without cost. One of the first recommendations of the Labor–Management Advisory Committee was that free arbitration be discontinued; the Committee held that such a practice encouraged its premature use. Consequently in reorganizing the USCS, the staff of full-time paid arbitrators was eliminated. Parties to disputes were required to pay for their arbitration costs, except in cases of hardship. Protesting this change, the President of the Confederated Unions of America urged Congress to continue free arbitration for unions.[36] He contended that small unions could not afford the expense of arbitration and that consequently employers could refuse to negotiate grievances or to bargain fairly.

The Arbitration Division of the USCS was retained, but its function was chiefly that of submitting to labor–management representatives the names of individuals acceptable as arbitrators. With the aid of the regional labor–management advisory committees, the USCS prepared a national roster of two hundred arbitrators, all of whom were screened for competence and impartiality. When it was decided to arbitrate, the USCS, upon request, provided a panel of five to seven names from which the parties made their selection of arbitrators.

In addition to the reorganization of the USCS, the Taft-Hartley Act of 1947 dealt further with the conciliation of labor disputes. The law declared that it was to be the policy of the United States Government to enhance collective bargaining by providing facilities for mediation, arbitration, and conciliation. Although Truman had many reasons for wanting to veto the Taft-Hartley Act, it was not because of any opposition that he had for this portion of the law. The law created an independent Federal Mediation and Conciliation Service outside the Department of Labor whose duty was "to assist parties to disputes in industries affecting commerce to settle such disputes through conciliation and mediation. . . ."[37] The FMCS could offer its services in any dispute upon its own motion or upon the request of either of the parties. If unable to bring the parties to agreement by conciliation within a reasonable time, the director would submit to the employees in the bargaining unit the employer's last offer of settlement for their approval or rejection in a secret ballot.

A postwar trend which disturbed many thoughtful students of labor problems was the tendency of the President to assume the role of mediator and arbitrator in the settlement of labor disputes. Harold W. Metz noted that this was a trend which had been started by President Roosevelt in 1934 and continued throughout the 1930's.[38] In the reconversion strikes of late 1945 and early 1946, Truman also participated actively in labor disputes. In his rail strike message to Congress on May 25, 1946, Truman said:

> For months, publicly and privately, I have been supervising and directing negotiations between the railroad operators and the twenty different railroad unions. I have been doing the same with respect to the pending labor disputes in the coal mines. Time and again I have seen the leaders of the unions and the representatives of the operators. Many hours have been spent by me personally, and many days have been spent by my representatives in attempting to negotiate the settlement of these disputes. . . .[39]

Participation of the President in labor disputes was criticized on the ground that it diminished the prestige of his office. The view that the disputants would increasingly become inclined to bypass the regular machinery in the belief that they might as well go promptly to the highest authority was even more serious. Such a practice was thought to weaken the processes of collective bargaining and was one of the strongest objections to compulsory arbitration.

Since conciliation referred to the government's acting as a disinterested third party trying to get labor and management disputants together, some observers of the postwar strike scene began to look beyond both conciliation and fact-finding as the most satisfactory means of solving labor disputes. The Seventy-Ninth Congress, reflecting the mood of a distressed public, began to move in the direction of a more compulsory form of "getting something done" about the rash of labor disputes.

Some of the strongest reasons for wanting to enact restrictions on union activities could be found in the existence of certain abuses by the unions themselves. Included among these abuses were jurisdictional strikes; examples of failure to bargain in good faith; coercion of employers to recognize a union despite the wishes of the employees; abuses under closed-shop agreements such as collusive contracts, unreasonable expulsions, and refusals of membership; and unjustifiable boycotts.

Although responsible union leaders were aware of these abuses, they were unable in many instances to correct them because of the autonomy of individual unions and disunity in the entire labor movement. Another strong factor in the public's exasperation with organized labor was the rigid attitude adopted by labor leaders toward modifying the supposed imbalance created in favor of organized labor by the Wagner Act. This exasperation showed itself in a number of bills in Congress that provided for compulsion where conciliation had failed in labor relations. There arose a general feeling in the months after the end of World War II of wanting to teach undisciplined labor unions, and particularly their leaders, a lesson. That lesson proved to be a painful one for labor.

Notes: Chapter 5

1. *Public Papers of the Presidents: 1945*, p. 520.
2. *Ibid.*
3. *Ibid.*
4. *Ibid.*, p. 563.
5. *Washington Daily News*, December 5, 1945, DNC Clipping File, HSTL.
6. *Ibid.*
7. *Ibid.*
8. Gustav Peck, "Industrial Relations Policy," Library of Congress Legislative Reference Service, *Public Affairs Bulletin No. 48* (Washington, January, 1947), p. 41.
9. *Ibid.*, p. 42.
10. U. S. Congress, Senate, Committee on Education and Labor, *Hearings on A Bill to Provide for the Appointment of Fact-Finding Boards*, 79th Cong., 2d Sess., 1946.
11. Peck, *op. cit.*, p. 42.
12. *New York Times*, December 13, 1945.
13. *Ibid.*
14. *Ibid.*
15. "Proposed Reorganization of Federal Labor Functions," Bureau of the Budget (July, 1945), Record Group 250, National Archives.
16. *New York Times*, January 23, 1946.
17. *Public Papers of the Presidents: 1946*, p. 293.
18. "Proposed Reorganization of Federal Labor Functions," *op. cit.*
19. *Ibid.*
20. *Ibid.*
21. John T. Dunlop, "Fact-Finding in Labor Disputes," *Annals of the American Academy of Political and Social Science*, CCXLIV (May, 1946), p. 73.
22. *Ibid.*
23. *Ibid.*, p. 74.
24. "Proposed Reorganization of Federal Labor Functions," *op. cit.*
25. *Ibid.*
26. *Ibid.*
27. *Ibid.*

28. *Report of the National Labor–Management Conference to the President* (mimeographed, 1945), OF 407–C, Truman Papers, HSTL.
29. *Ibid.*
30. Edgar L. Warren, "The Conciliation Service: V.J.-Day to Taft-Hartley," *Industrial & Labor Relations Review*, I (April, 1948), p. 353.
31. *Ibid.*, p. 354.
32. *Ibid.*
33. *Ibid.*, p. 355.
34. *Ibid.*, p. 356.
35. Leland J. Gordon, "Recent Developments in Conciliation and Arbitration," *Labor in Postwar America*, ed. Colston E. Warne (New York. Remsen Press, 1949), p. 227.
36. *Ibid.*
37. *Ibid.*, p. 236.
38. Harold W. Metz, *Labor Policy of the Federal Government* Washington: Brookings Institution, 1945), pp. 249–254.
39. *Public Papers of the Presidents: 1946,* p. 278.

6

Labor Proposals from an Angry Seventy-Ninth Congress

BY 1946 THE STRIKE SITUATION IN THE UNITED STATES WAS AT
its most crucial, the legislative attempts at achieving labor
peace were at their most numerous, and government participation in industrial disputes was at one of the highest
points in history. Solutions to labor relations problems
were advanced from many sides, including management,
labor, educators, government officials, and the press. It was
also while the American labor movement was at the peak of
its numerical strength after World War II that the most
restrictive measures limiting its activities were advanced
to try to bring about more friendly relations between labor
and management.

Many of the proposed solutions concerned amendments
to the Wagner Act. The objectives of the Wagner Act in
1935 were to equalize bargaining power between management and labor. It did not purport to regulate the abuses
of union activities. After World War II this omission was
seized upon by those who, branding the law as unfair and
one-sided, wanted to change it.

In 1946 there was much to that charge. It was claimed
that the law regulated the activities of employers in the collective bargaining relationship but neglected to deal with

101

many union practices. Many observers still felt that there was a great need for the Wagner Act, but also were convinced that its defect lay in the fact that it was not broadened from time to time in order to regulate labor's abuses of its responsibilities.

Had the unions shown more of a willingness to reform themselves, then perhaps the remedies that were so restrictive would not have been offered or would have at least been of a milder nature. However, as Joel Seidman stated, "while offering no guarantees that they would stamp out offensive behavior on the part of their affiliates, labor leaders attacked every proposed regulatory measure in extreme terms." At the same time they offered no positive program for righting the evils that even they admitted did exist. Therefore, the unions created a climate of opinion in which they ultimately paid the penalty for their shortsightedness with the passage of the Taft-Hartley Act.[1]

The compulsory nature of the measures suggested in the Seventy-Ninth Congress cut across party lines as both Republicans and Democrats brought forth proposals for restricting the activities of unions. And from President Truman there came suggestions for labor legislation that made it evident that he too had lost patience with labor's actions. Those who advocated compulsory arbitration proposed its use in a limited area of labor conflict and only as a last resort. Their generally cautious attitude reflected a natural dislike for anything involving what could be considered the equivalent of forced labor. It was recognized as well that compulsory methods were easier to prescribe than to enforce and were in practice less effective than voluntary methods. There was further opposition to compulsory arbitration because it took control over wages out of the hands of those directly concerned and tended to place it, directly or indirectly, in the hands of the government. All of these factors entered into the long-standing opposition to compulsory arbitration in this country, an opposition voiced by labor and management alike.

Organized labor's antagonism to compulsory arbitration stemmed from the fact that the right to strike was a basic element of union bargaining power. In countries where labor organization was in its infancy, or at times when unions were weak and had little hope of staging successful strikes, labor might have stood to gain under a system where it could bring employers before an arbitration court. But at the postwar stage of labor development in the United States compulsory arbitration had no such attraction. Unions accordingly regarded all plans of this sort as attacks upon labor and its jealously guarded right to strike. In the opinion of the AFL:

> Compulsory arbitration means compulsory labor. Compulsory labor means involuntary servitude, which is forbidden by the 13th Amendment to the Constitution of the United States . . . Compulsory arbitration implies compulsory compliance with the award made. This would compel the employees to work against their will. If they rebelled, they would be fined, sent to prison or both. Such a law would be repugant to all justice-loving and freedom-loving Americans.[2]

In 1947, before the House Labor Committee, AFL President William Green defended the right to strike as an "unlimited right," although he held that American workers should not exercise it to the point of menacing the public health and welfare. Before the Senate Labor Committee, John L. Lewis, President of the UMW, declared that "Whenever the Congress enacts a bill for compulsory arbitration, then the end of the republic is right there."[3]

In addition to denouncing compulsory arbitration as undemocratic, labor spokesmen insisted that it would not promote industrial peace. Edward Keating, editor of the railway brotherhoods' newspaper, *Labor,* observed that "Proponents of anti-strike legislation fail to understand that it is one thing to outlaw strikes and quite another to compel free men to labor under conditions which they regard as grossly unfair."[4] Keating further pointed out that experiments with compulsory arbitration demonstrated "that in every instance a departure from the processes of democracy has provoked bitter class feeling but has utterly failed to end strikes."[5] Industry members of the Labor–Management Advisory Committee of the United States Conciliation Service joined with the labor members on December 15, 1946, in stating that "any form of compulsory arbitration . . . of labor disputes may frustrate rather than foster industrial peace."[6]

During the war, if not earlier, public reaction as reflected in public opinion polls and in editorial opinion was hostile to the increase in the power possessed by unions to disturb or upset the economy.[7] One poll conducted by the American Institute of Public Opinion in 1945 illustrated the strong public feelings against labor's actions. When asked what they thought that the government should do if the coal miners were to go on strike in the spring of 1945, seventy-four percent of those polled indicated that they thought the government should use force and take over the mines.[8] Proposed labor legislation, which had previously taken the form of assisting labor organizations to increase their power and influence, began to take the form of controlling union activities and setting bounds to collective bargaining. The emerging ideas of restricting labor activities developed more sharply in the Seventy-Ninth Congress in 1945 and 1946 when strikes reached an all-time high, and when it appeared that reconversion to peacetime production was being seriously interferred with by the persistent inability of one key industry after another to continue in production because of the failure of management and unions in that industry to come to terms satisfactory to both sides.

The growing realization that the onset of widespread collective bargaining was not promoting industrial peace but was in fact being accompanied by increasing strikes and work stoppages intensified the search for remedies. Editorial discussion became more widespread and intense. Union control bills were introduced in Congress in increasing numbers by both Republicans and Democrats. Union spokesmen who had always wanted more labor legislation now feared it.

Several days after the adjournment of the Labor–Management Conference in November, 1945, Truman issued a statement in which he said:

> The American people have been patient. They have waited long in the hope that those leaders in labor and management whose business it was to handle this problem would be able to do so in agreement. The Federal Government declined time and again to make any suggestion to the conference as to proper machinery. All that the Government did was to point out the objective which the American people expected it to attain.
>
> Now that the conference has adjourned without any recommendations on the subject, it becomes the duty of the Government to act on its own initiative. Therefore, I now suggest to the Congress that well-reasoned and workable legislation be passed at the earliest possible moment to provide adequate means for settling industrial disputes and avoiding industrial strife.[9]

During the life of the Seventy-Ninth Congress, 1945–1947, and in the first four months of the Eightieth Congress, there were seventy-three bills relating to labor policy introduced in the House. More than two-fifths of the seventy-three bills were from Republicans who had never introduced labor bills prior to 1945. Most of these bills were sponsored by representatives from the Northeastern states, and were restrictive of labor's activities. Some of these measures, however, were also sponsored by Democrats. The Democratic bills were in general less restrictive and were mainly introduced by Southern members.[10]

In the Senate the postwar years saw an increased concern for labor matters. From January, 1946, until April, 1947, forty-five bills, almost twice the number of the previous eight years, were proposed in the Senate. The increasing amounts of amendatory proposals reflected in general the attitude of a growing number of Republicans who were elected to the Senate. Some of the newer Republicans in the Senate were Irving Ives of New York, Wayne Morse of Oregon (Morse changed parties in the 1950's and became a Democrat), Joseph Ball of Minnesota, Homer Ferguson of Michigan, and Joseph McCarthy of Wisconsin, who all felt disposed to take an active part in shaping postwar labor policy.[11]

During the course of the Seventy-Ninth Congress the legislative proposals that were intended to lessen strikes differed greatly in their attitude toward unions and toward the effective participation of unions in the economy. Some Congressmen, like Democrat Howard Smith of Virginia, were hostile to the extension of union conditions and power in industry, and to the Communist influence that was evident in some labor organizations. Others, like Democrat Jerry Voorhis of California, were friendly to the aspirations of the unions in playing their part in developing joint and mutually satisfactory relations in industry. One thing that was agreed upon was that good industrial relations flowed from mutual trust and cooperation.

Some Congressmen, however, looked upon the volume of strikes in the postwar years as evidence of the periodic breakdown of collective bargaining, and as proof that the national labor policy of encouraging the growth of unions and the extension of collective bargaining was not really achieving the beneficial results anticipated by its friends. Democratic Senator Carl Hatch of New Mexico said during one debate in Congress that although legislation was needed to control union activities, no one was proposing "to break down the rights of the individual workers."[12]

Nearly all of the authors of proposed additional legislation to lessen strikes emphasized the conclusion that strikes were practically always an inconvenience to the public and that strikes in key industries involved great losses to innocent parties and jeopardized the health, safety and welfare of many individuals. Some were convinced that many strikes were called or continued for trivial reasons or to serve private ends and that most strikes could have been avoided if a legal obligation to come to agreement were imposed and proper alternative facilities provided. By 1946, however, a majority of Congressmen in both parties were convinced that it had become necessary to bring the weight of public opinion to bear upon the postwar strike problem as a whole in order to protect all the interests involved.

The labor relations remedies proposed in the Seventy-Ninth Congress differed greatly in content. A number of the mildest bills contained the imposition of only a moral obligation on the part of unions not to strike in important industries while the facts and recommendations of a disinterested panel were published. Examples of this type of bill were introduced in the Senate by Democrats Alben Barkley of Kentucky and Harley Kilgore of West Virginia.

Other proposals were for compulsory waiting periods and closer implementation of collective bargaining with more effective machinery and voluntary arbitration. Sponsors of bills of this type included Democrats Allen Ellender of Louisiana and Carl Hatch of New Mexico, and Republican Joseph Ball of Minnesota in the Senate. The same sort of legislation was introduced in the House by Democrats Jerry Voorhis of California and Mary T. Norton of New Jersey and Republicans Christian Herter of Massachusetts and Clare Hoffman of Michigan.

The most extreme position of any of the bills called for the prohibition of strikes, at least during certain periods or in certain industries and services upon which the health and welfare of the community depended; severe penalties would be imposed for illegal strikes. The authors of bills of this type included Republican Ellsworth Buck of New York in the House and Democrat W. Lee O'Daniel of Texas in the Senate.

Most of the bills introduced in the Seventy-Ninth Congress to regulate the activities of unions were never reported out of committee. But among them there were basically six major bills warranting closer examination in order to understand the mood of the Congress. The six were the Ball-Burton-Hatch bill, McMahon bill, Smith bill, Ball-Hatch amendment, Case bill, and the Hobbs Anti-Racketeering Act. The first four will be considered in this Chapter.

On June 20, 1945, a bill was introduced to provide various procedures for federal assistance in the settlement of labor disputes.[13] Although the bill never emerged from committee, its bipartisan authorship displayed the general feelings in Congress toward the actions of organized labor. The new legislation, known as the Federal Industrial Relations bill, was sponsored by a Democrat (Senator Carl Hatch of New Mexico) and two Republicans (Senators Joseph Ball of Minnesota and Harold Burton of Ohio), all of whom were considered friendly to labor. They said it was designed "to avert the serious danger of a knock-down, drag-out fight between management and labor in the postwar period" and to bring permanent peace to "the last surviving field in which civil war is tolerated."[14] The bill proposed to: 1.) Place all Federal conciliation and mediation activities under control of a new five-man Federal Labor Relations Board. This board, with authority to supervise compulsory arbitration in cases affecting the public welfare, would have replaced the National Labor Relations Board, the National War Labor Board, and the Conciliation Service of the Labor Department. 2.) Establish an Unfair Labor Practices board of three members

to hear and rule on all complaints by either management
or labor. The decrees of this tribunal would have been
enforced through the federal courts.   3.) Make the closed
shop illegal except when the union was "the freely chosen
representative of seventy-five per cent of the employees
involved," when its agreement with management was endorsed "by sixty per cent of the employees," when union
membership was open to anyone hired by management
and when members were removable only on written
charges after a hearing.   4.) Amend the Wagner Act to
make its compulsion equally applicable to employer and
employee.   5.) Make arbitration compulsory for all grievances arising out of contract interpretation and for all disputes arising in public utilities or in industries dealing in
essential commodities such as coal.   6.) Direct the new
Federal Labor Relations Board to study the need of legislation to insure "democratic control and operation of labor
organizations engaged in collective bargaining."[15]
In presenting the bill to the Senate, Hatch said:

It is the imperative obligation of managers and workers in every major industry to use every reasonable effort
to maintain peaceful and just labor relations and settle
their differences by negotiations, or through arbitration,
without resort to coercive measures and stoppages or
production by either party. . . . This obligation should
be written into Federal Law. This obligation to the
public interest is the underlying principle of the bill
we introduce today.[16]

Senator Ball, in urging adoption of the bill, said he had
been told by many employers that federal labor policy
made postwar industrial expansion hazardous, if not impossible. He said he had been told "by many leaders of
organized labor" that they feared a management campaign
to destroy labor unions. He continued by saying, "I have
seen some indication that a few of our large corporations

are preparing for some such campaign." Ball also laid particular emphasis on the closed shop provisions of the bill. He said:

The closed shop contract, in various forms is deeply imbedded in the whole structure of American labor relations. To tear it out might easily result in chaos. On the other hand, if the Government is to see to it that job opportunities are open to all who want to work, it cannot permit those opportunities to be monopolized by labor organizations whose leadership and policies do not represent at least a substantial majority of their membership and which deny membership on an arbitrary basis.[17]

Philip Murray, speaking for the CIO, said the bill would enslave labor and characterized it as a "bald-faced attempt to destroy labor unions and nullify the basic constitutional rights of workers." A statement by the CIO said in part:

The proposed bill tears the heart out of the Wagner Act, the Magna Charta of labor. Under the guise of affording equality of protection to employers, the rights now guaranteed to workers by the Wagner Act are practically eliminated. . . . Labor can do nothing to protect itself against the most arbitrary and destructive actions of the employers. Thus, the constitutional and fundamental rights of free men to organize into unions to exercise their freedom of speech and assembly and to refrain from working if they so desire in order to remain free, are destroyed.[18]

William Green, of the AFL, called the bill a "straitjacket."[19] The union issued the following statement:

The bill proposes compulsory arbitration. This is a restriction upon their freedom that the wage earners of America will never accept. Organized labor has fought compulsory arbitration since its earliest days as the first step toward involuntary servitude. We will not give up that fight now. . . . In sum, this measure seeks to establish government regimentation of labor and industry in normal times to a degree that would gravely undermine free collective bargaining.[20]

The United Mine Workers issued a statement describing the measure as "a scheme blueprinted to rob the poor and further enrich the rich."[21] The UMW also called the measure ". . . A cleverly designed ripper bill which would decapitate and rape the Wagner Act, the Norris-LaGuardia Act, and regiment American workers through the medium of compulsory arbitration, and is more than we can understand."[22]

Senator Ball, asked to comment on the labor leaders' reaction to the bill, said he would have had more respect for their viewpoint if it were based on a study comparable to the time put in by the committees which drafted the bill and the Senators who proposed it.[23]

The Ball-Hatch amendment, introduced on December 10, 1945, was a somewhat reduced and toned down version of the Ball-Burton-Hatch bill originally introduced in June, 1945. When the Senate Committee on Education and Labor held hearings on Truman's fact-finding proposal embodied in the Ellender Bill, it permitted discussions of the Ball-Hatch amendment as part of the overall effort to find a satisfactory method of handling industrial disputes. However, the Ball-Hatch amendment made no effort to amend the National Labor Relations Act or to make illegal certain labor practices by labor organizations, which were the most criticized provisions of the original Ball-Burton-Hatch bill. In place of these there was a provision that a Federal Industrial Relations Board created under this amendment "shall take no action which will interfere in any way with the consideration or determination of complaints of unfair practices by the National

Labor Relations Board in accordance with the provisions of the National Labor Relations Act."[24] Thus, the Wagner Act was left untouched.

The major problem which the Ball-Hatch amendment tried to solve was how to make collective bargaining function to settle the issues between management and labor fairly but without work stoppages. It sought to restore to the parties and to the government a sense of the public necessity to settle collective bargaining issues amicably and to make collective bargaining work as the national labor relations policy. It did so by imposing upon all parties the duty to make and maintain agreements, while it provided detailed orderly government settlement procedures for controversies which threatened to provide a substantial interruption of commerce.

The Ball-Hatch amendment provided for a Federal Industrial Relations Board of five members which was given comprehensive power to mediate and attempt to settle disputes. The United States Conciliation Service was to be transferred to this Board and was also to have the power to utilize the services of other agencies deemed helpful in its settlement efforts. If the Board was not successful in its efforts at mediation and conciliation, it was obligated to use its offices to induce the parties to agree to submit their controversy to arbitration. Pending the exhaustion of settlement efforts, existing conditions had to be maintained by the parties to the dispute. If a fact-finding commission was appointed as a last step in the government's settlement efforts, no strike or change in conditions by employers was to be made until thirty days after the report was made. It was a violation to strike or lockout until every reasonable effort had been made to settle controversies by the formal procedures established for collective bargaining, conciliation, mediation, fact-finding, and voluntary arbitration.

The right to strike was specifically impeded under this

amendment by the imposition of the duty imposed on both parties to make and maintain agreements, to settle controversies by the procedures provided, and to maintain conditions pending exhaustion of settlement efforts, including a thirty-day period following the report of a fact-finding commission, if one was appointed.[25]

The Ball-Hatch amendment, like the Ellender bill, also provided that nothing in it should be construed to require an individual employee to render labor or service without his consent. The goal in this and other bills seeking to provide additional conciliation and mediation machinery was to fill what was felt to be a postwar need to improve collective bargaining as a technique of arriving at joint agreements.

The Ball-Hatch amendment would have made the supplementary mediation and arbitration processes integral parts of the collective bargaining process, and it endeavored to make collective bargaining itself less of a burden upon commerce. It would not have prohibited strikes or lockouts but it was not expected that strikes and lockouts would be as inevitable or as numerous if both sides accepted the duty to maintain agreements, and made use of the settlement machinery provided. The amendment, however, was never reported out of committee.

Democratic Senator Brien McMahon of Connecticut, after making extensive investigations as a member of the Interstate and Foreign Commerce Committee and holding a number of informal hearings in the summer of 1945, sponsored a labor relations bill which aroused less criticism than many of the other bills introduced in the Seventy-Ninth Congress. The McMahon bill was also not reported out by the Committee on Education and Labor. This bill, however, was much milder in the restraints imposed than the other bills considered and consequently received the least criticism from labor sources, which opposed any labor legislation.

The McMahon bill was introduced on September 20, 1945, by Senator McMahon, for himself and for three other Democratic Senators: Carl Hayden of Arizona, Elbert Thomas of Utah, and James Tunnell of Delaware.[26] It provided for the creation of special Boards of Inquiry to hold hearings on the issues of a labor dispute and to make "the factual argument of each party to the controversy available to the public." Nothing was said about recommendations to be made by Boards of Inquiry which would bring objective thinking to bear upon the contesting arguments and help to crystallize public opinion of the issues involved. The bill provided that the appointment of such Boards of Inquiry "shall not otherwise interfere with an action undertaken or to be undertaken by either party."[27]

In this bill, unlike the Ellender bill and the Ball-Hatch amendment, no recommendations were to be made by the fact-finding boards. Strikes or lockouts would be legal before the appointment of such boards, while the board was conducting hearings, or any time after the board made available to the public "the factual argument of each side of the controversy."[28] The other provisions of the Mc-Mahon bill dealt with the centralization of labor functions in the Labor Department, the creation in the Department of Labor of a Conciliation and Mediation Division which would take over the functions of the Conciliation Service and any other conciliation and mediation functions in the Department, and the establishment of an independent United States Board of Arbitration to handle arbitration voluntarily requested by both sides.

The administrator of the Conciliation and Mediation Division would have had the duty under this bill of encouraging representatives of employees and employers to make and maintain agreements and to settle all differences that might arise. The services of the Division would have been employed in mediation and conciliation efforts to bring the parties to agreement in any labor controversy involving or threatening an immediate and substantial interruption in the free flow of commerce.[29]

The independent arbitration agency created was to be known as the United States Board of Arbitration. It was to be composed of three members appointed by the President with the advice and consent of the Senate for overlapping terms of three years. This Board was to cooperate with the parties in forming a board of arbitration when requested to do so, but "the failure or refusal of either party to agree to arbitration shall not be construed as a violation of any legal duty or other obligation imposed by this Act."[30]

The Board was to establish a roster of fair and competent arbitrators familiar with the industrial and employment problems in the region where the controversy existed. Arbitration awards were to be transmitted and filed with the District Court of the United States and with the United States Board of Arbitration. Boards of Arbitration were to have the power to require the attendance of witnesses and the production of necessary books and records that were necessary to a just determination of the matters submitted for arbitration. For this purpose the Board could have requested the District Court to issue the necessary subpoenas.

Under the McMahon bill the Bureau of Labor Statistics of the Department of Labor was authorized to maintain a file of copies of agreements reached as a result of mediation, conciliation, and of arbitration agreements made and awards rendered by the Act; of all statements and summaries of fact issued by the Board of Inquiry; and of any other collective labor agreements submitted by the parties. Such files were to be opened to inspection for the guidance and information of interested representatives of employers, employees, and the general public. The Bureau of Labor Statistics was authorized to be equipped to furnish factual information which might aid in the settlement of any labor controversy. It was also provided that nothing in the bill

should be construed as in any way interfering with, imped-
ing, or diminishing the right to strike, or as amending or
modifying the provisions of the National Labor Relations
Act.

The McMahon bill, which was submitted after the original Ball-Burton-Hatch bill, contained substantially the
same arbitration provisions and was motivated by the same
aim as the Ball-Hatch proposal to prolong the process of
collective bargaining before such bargaining broke down
in a work stoppage. But it differed from the Ball-Hatch
amendment particularly in that it provided for no such
compulsory duty on both parties to make and maintain
agreements and to use the settlement facilities of the government, no recommendations by the fact-finding board,
no obligatory waiting period, and no sanctions.

The AFL was quoted in the press on January 5, 1946, as
saying that the McMahon bill did not contain the "objectionable features" of Truman's proposal for a "fixed waiting period" and "for recommendations by the fact-finding
board." The AFL added that "we possibly should have indicated that fact-finding in and of itself is not harmful to
labor even though we are not convinced that it can do
much good."[31] The McMahon bill, which representatives
of both the AFL and the CIO found "least objectionable"
because of its moderate tone, was never reported out by
the Senate Committee or debated on the floor. Later, even
though the representatives of organized labor opposed the
fact-finding bills based on Truman's proposals, union
spokesmen referred to the acceptance of the principle of
these proposals by the unions involved in ways which im-
plied that they had no objections to such procedures if
their freedom of action was not impaired. The McMahon
bill was generally regarded as the one that was more acceptable to organized labor than any bill introduced during the Seventy-Ninth Congress.

The Smith bill of the Seventy-Ninth Congress was introduced by Democratic Congressman Howard Smith of Virginia, a member of the powerful House Rules Committee, two days after the adjournment of the President's Labor–Management Conference and was referred to the Committee on Labor.[32] It contained a number of provisions for the direct regulation of union conduct. One would have deprived any labor organization of its status under the National Labor Relations Act if it knowingly or negligently permitted members of Communist organizations, Nazi organizations, or felons to hold office. This bill was an indication of the strong anti-Communist reaction in the United States after World War II.

Another provision required the registration of unions, including the furnishing of detailed information on their organization, membership, and finances. With respect to collective bargaining, the Smith bill provided for the maintenance of the status quo by making it unlawful to conduct strikes or lockouts until after thirty days' written notice, filed with the employer and the Secretary of Labor, of both the intention of striking and the reasons for doing so.

There were also a number of specific provisions regarding violence and intimidation in industrial disputes. These made it unlawful for any person to use or threaten force or violence in an attempt to prevent another person from working in a struck plant, to picket the homes of workers, to picket a place of business unless before the strike or lockout the picket was himself in the employ of the company. On the other hand, employers were enjoined from employing any person for the purpose of obstructing or interfering by threats or force with peaceful picketing or with the exercise by employees of their rights of self-organization or collective bargaining.[33]

The Smith bill also made it unlawful for workers to engage in sympathy strikes, jurisdictional strikes or to refuse to work on articles produced by any person in an attempt to induce such persons to recognize, comply with

the demands of, or to employ members of any labor organization. Federal District Courts were given jurisdiction
to enjoin any of the above acts, and persons committing
them were to be liable to civil suits for damages. Individuals committing any of these acts lost their rights under
the National Labor Relations Act, and employment and
other benefits under any act making appropriations for
relief purposes or any unemployment compensation benefits under the Social Security Act. If a trade union or an
officer of a union was guilty of any of the violations, the
union would cease to have the status of a labor organization under the National Labor Relations Act and lose the
protection of the Norris-LaGuardia Act, which prohibited
the issuance of injunctions against certain acts of labor
organizations.[34]

The Smith bill also declared it to be the policy of the
government that labor disputes affecting the public interest should be settled fairly and without interruption or
delay in the production necessary in the public interest.
Additional facilities were created for the voluntary settlement of such disputes that could not be settled expedi-
tiously by collective bargaining and by existing conciliation
and mediation procedures. There was to be created in the
Executive Offices of the President a National Mediation
Board composed of an equal number of representatives of
employers, workers, and the public to have jurisdiction
over labor disputes which were not adjusted by collective
bargaining or other conciliation and mediation procedures.
The Board was empowered to set up panels of employer-
employee-public representatives or exclusively of public
representatives who would make every reasonable effort to
settle the dispute.[35]

Other provisions of the Smith bill—dealing with the
purging of unions of leaders that were Communists, Nazi
sympathizers, or racketeers or criminals, and the elaborate
provisions regarding the registration of unions and the

publication of the basic facts regarding their organization, jurisdiction, fees, dues, assessments, limitations, on membership, paid-up membership, election of officers, constitution and by-laws, and financial statements—had as their purpose the cleansing of unions of internal abuses, the elimination of subversive purposes in the conduct of unions and of strikes, and the protection of both the membership and the public from irresponsible control by selfish or vicious union leaders.[36]

Union leaders such as William Green, Philip Murray, and John L. Lewis pointed to the severe penalties imposed on union activities, including what they felt to be the practical repeal of the Norris-LaGuardia Act, and which they said would result in the return to the destructive and immoral doctrine of conspiracy under which men were not permitted to do in association what was perfectly legal for them to do as individuals. Labor's leadership pointed to the withdrawal of all unemployment compensation and relief benefits as measures which were sure to destroy unions as well as to intimidate the rank and file of union members. The reactions of union spokesmen to the remedies proposed in the Smith bill were bitter. They charged that those who supported these proposals were either naïve individuals who did not know much about the struggles of labor in the past to obtain its present position of near-equality with management, or that they were anti-union spokesmen who used fair words to destroy the American labor union movement and wished to return to a condition where it would be impossible, if not illegal, for workers to organize for mutual aid and protection and for effective bargaining with large aggregations of capital.

Nearly all of the union leaders who spoke on the issue of strike limitation contained in all of the above bills argued that any limitation concerning the right to strike was an interference with freedom to work or not to work and was a return to feudal or slave conditions. Their argument rested on the conviction that under modern conditions workers did not have real industrial freedom except in association. In turn the association of workers in trade or industrial unions derived its strength from the power to strike, which gave them a weapon to be used in negotiations with employers to force the best terms and conditions which the economic situation could afford. Any limitation on the time or place of attack limited the union that much in its strategic campaign to bring the employer to accept the terms and demands of the union by giving him time to prepare to counteract the pressure of the union or to nullify its effects.

The AFL expressed its position regarding a thirty-day waiting period while a fact-finding report was to be prepared, in the following manner:

> Whether it is designated as 'cooling off' or given some other term or designation, it amounts to the same thing, involuntary servitude. Its effect would be to compel employees to work against their will for a period of at least thirty days. Now, involuntary servitude is prohibited by the Thirteenth Amendment to the Constitution of the United States. It does not matter whether one is compelled to work against his will for thirty days, thirty hours, thirty minutes, or thirty seconds—it is still involuntary servitude. It is a violation of the constitutional guarantee against slavery.[37]

In nearly all postwar union releases and publications and in the speeches of union leaders, the bills were all blanketed as anti-labor measures. The position of the unions was that they did not want to strike but that they had to retain the strike weapon. They argued that workers risked much in going out on strike. They were not paid for time lost and they ran the risk of losing the strike as well. There might be no financial gain at all, and strikes were also ordered to prevent reductions in pay or standards. They asserted that in a profit-seeking, competitive, industrial economy the strike and the threat to strike were the time-tested means by which free men attempted to improve their economic position.

Concerning the public interest, labor spokesmen said that the workers were largely the public and, anyway, what was to the workers' interest was always in the public interest. Limiting the freedom of unions to strike, when they judged it was to their long-time interest to do so, would weaken all unions by dulling the edge of their most effective weapon. They also contended that it would lower efficiency and morale, lessen the pressure on management, reduce general purchasing power, and expose all workers to irresponsible employers. For these reasons union spokesmen opposed all legislative measures which had as their objective the limitation in any way on their freedom to resort to a strike in furtherance of their aims at any stage in their dealings with employers.

Despite the almost hysterical union charges, there is little evidence to support most of them if all of the bills concerning labor relations are examined carefully. Congressmen, with the exception of Congressman Smith, who introduced postwar labor legislation in the Seventy-Ninth Congress, wanted to postpone, in one way or another, the use of the strike weapon or to make its use rarely necessary in order to obtain a form of justice in industry. Nearly all of the bills in the Seventy-Ninth Congress provided machinery for delay and friendly mediation. They more often sought to reduce the necessity for work stoppages than to prohibit or strangle the right to strike. Most of the bills stated that it was the duty of public authority to develop effective machinery for peaceful and fair settlements of labor disputes and to prevent the development of conditions which made strikes easy. The strike might be the final resort in an industrial dispute, but it did not have to be the only solution. The preambles of most of the bills stated as their purpose the encouragement of peaceful settlements of industrial disputes and the minimizing of industrial strife and work stoppages. The spirit of the bills, however, sought to insure the responsible actions of unions by law.

With these ends in mind, it was the Case bill and the Hobbs Act that contained the embodiment of the pent-up feelings toward labor in the Seventy-Ninth Congress. It was these measures to which Congress gave its most sympathetic attention, and to which organized labor summoned all of its strength to defeat.

Notes: Chapter 6

1. Joel Seidman, *American Labor From Defense to Reconversion* (Chicago: University of Chicago Press, 1953), p. 254.
2. American Federation of Labor, "Compulsory Arbitration," (Washington: Mimeographed, n.d.) Record Group 174, National Archives.
3. B. W. Patch, "Compulsory Arbitration," *Editorial Research Reports*, Vol. II, No. 7, 1947, p. 593.
4. *Ibid.*
5. *Ibid.*, p. 594.
6. *Ibid.*
7. Sanford Cohen, *Labor in the United States* (Columbus, Ohio: Charles E. Merrill Books, Inc., 1960), p. 505.
8. Hadley Cantril (ed.), prepared by Mildred Strunk, *Public Opinion, 1935–1946* (Princeton, New Jersey: Princeton University Press, 1951), p. 824.
9. *Public Papers of the Presidents: 1945*, pp. 518–519.
10. Harry A. Millis and Emily Clark Brown, *From the Wagner Act to Taft-Hartley* (Chicago: University of Chicago Press, 1950), p. 343.
11. *Ibid.*, pp. 344–345.
12. *Congressional Record*, 79th Cong., 2d Sess., p. 4910.
13. Informal Digest of Bills Introduced in the 79th Congress to

Regulate Industrial Labor Relations, (typed), Gardner Papers, HSTL.

14. *Philadelphia Inquirer*, June 21, 1945, DNC Clipping File, HSTL.
15. *New York Herald Tribune*, June 22, 1945.
16. *Ibid.*
17. *Ibid.*
18. *Philadelphia Inquirer*, June 21, 1945.
19. *New York Herald Tribune*, June 22, 1945.
20. *New York Times*, June 22, 1945.
21. *Ibid.*
22. *New York Herald Tribune*, June 22, 1945.
23. *Ibid.*
24. Informal Digest of Bills Introduced in the 79th Congress to Regulate Industrial Labor Relations, *op. cit.*
25. *Ibid.*
26. *New York Times*, September 21, 1945.
27. *Ibid.*
28. *Ibid.*
29. Millis and Brown, *op. cit.*, p. 357.
30. Informal Digest of Bills Introduced in the 79th Congress to Regulate Industrial Labor Relations, *op. cit.*
31. *New York Times*, January 5, 1946.
32. Gustav Peck, "Industrial Relations Policy," Library of Congress Legislative Reference Service, *Public Affairs Bulletin No. 48* (Washington: January, 1947), p. 50.
33. *Ibid.*, pp. 52–53.
34. *Ibid.*, p. 54.
35. Informal Digest of Bills Introduced in the 79th Congress to Regulate Industrial Labor Relations, *op. cit.*
36. Millis and Brown, *op. cit.*, p. 360.
37. Peck, *op. cit.*, p. 34.

7

The Struggle Over the Case Bill and the Hobbs Act

DESPITE THE ANGER DIRECTED TOWARD ORGANIZED LABOR, the Hobbs Anti-Racketeering Act and the Case bill were the only important pieces of labor legislation passed by both Houses of the Seventy-Ninth Congress. The Case bill was introduced by Republican Congressman Francis Case of South Dakota on January 29, 1946, as a substitute measure for President Truman's fact-finding proposals embodied in the Norton and Ellender bills.

The Case bill passed the House on February 7, 1946, by a vote of 258–155.[1] After the measure went to the Senate, the Committee on Education and Labor held extensive hearings, where union leaders spoke out vehemently against the bill. William Green, President of the AFL, declared that it was in violation of the Thirteenth Amendment, which forbade slavery. The final decision on the bill by the Senate came at the height of the controversy surrounding the nationwide railroad strike. On May 25, 1946, a few hours after Truman's speech to Congress, the Senate adopted the Case bill by a vote of 49–29.[2] The House accepted the Senate version on May 29.[3]

In its final form, the Case bill contained two broad categories of provisions. One group, sections one through six, dealt with the basic collective bargaining relationship and had as its purpose the lessening of work stoppages, and another group, sections seven through eleven, dealt with what were regarded as specific abuses of union activity. The bill ended with some miscellaneous provisions regarding the duties of the Bureau of Labor Statistics and the Office of the Solicitor of the Department of Labor and the authorization of funds for carrying out its provisions.

The version of the Case bill that was finally passed by the Senate and accepted by the House was clearly a reflection of the earlier postwar labor relations bills. This could be seen in the main points of the bill:

1.) Creation of a Federal Mediation Board to encourage the making and maintenance of agreements and to aid the parties in settling disputes.

2.) Provision for a sixty-day cooling-off period.

3.) Provision for enforcement of the cooling-off period by administrative remedies against employers and deprivation of Wagner Act rights for employees.

4.) Provision for fact-finding commissions in major labor disputes involving public utilities, to make recommendations, and with extension of the cooling-off period until five days after the report of the commission.

5.) Imposition of stringent penalties against "whoever" interferes by violence or extortion, or conspiracy to do so, with the movement of goods in interstate commerce.

6.) Proscription of employer contributions to welfare funds administered exclusively by unions.

7.) Exclusion of "supervisor" from the Wagner Act's definition of "employee" but not prohibiting union membership of them.

8.) Provision for damage suits against unions for violation of contract.

9.) Provision for action against "wildcat" and rival union violations of collective bargaining contracts by deprivation of Wagner Act rights for employees involved.

10.) Outlawing of secondary boycotts by making them unlawful under the antitrust laws and removing the limitations of the Norris-LaGuardia Act on the use of injunctions in labor disputes in such cases.[4]

The Case bill was not passed, however, without a great deal of extensive and informed, though sometimes bitter, debate in both the House and Senate. Congressman Case repeatedly denied that the bill had been drawn up in haste and without proper consideration. Case said that the bill sought to:

> Strengthen and continue the processes of collective bargaining. It seeks to provide an opportunity for the process of negotiation and mediation to be completed without resort to strikes or lockouts, without costly interruptions in wages and production.[5]

Some of the attacks on the bill by its enemies were vigorous. Democrat Emanuel Celler of New York said that the bill was "applauded by that type of industrialist who might have the best mind of the eighteenth century."[6] Democrat Ray Madden of Indiana called the bill "the most bitter anti-labor legislation which has been presented in the history of the Congress."[7]

In the Senate, Democrats James Murray of Montana, Joseph Guffey of Pennsylvania, Claude Pepper of Florida, Elbert Thomas of Utah, and Robert Wagner of New York led the attack against the bill. Some of the defenders of the bill included Democrats Allen Ellender of Louisiana, Carl Hatch of New Mexico, Scott Lucas of Illinois, and J. William Fulbright of Arkansas. Among Republican leaders in pushing for passage were Robert Taft of Ohio, Joseph Ball of Minnesota, Arthur Capper of Kansas, H. Alexander Smith of New Jersey, and Leverett Saltonstall of Massachusetts.

Despite the protestations against it, the miscellaneous

provisions of the Case bill represented legislative proposals which had been pending in Congress in various forms for some time. Much of the blame that both labor and Truman later placed on the Eightieth Congress regarding the restrictions placed on unions was in reality preceded by the strong feelings in the Democratic-controlled Seventy-Ninth Congress. The Case bill sharply pointed out that circumstances were ripe for a substantial alteration in national policies concerning labor relations. The Case bill, when examined in detail, showed that in many important respects it foreshadowed the restrictions on unions by the Taft-Hartley Act of 1947.

As previously stated, the Case bill, in its final form, fell into two parts. The first contained provisions relative to the mediation of labor disputes, through the creation of a Federal Mediation Board. The second consisted of sections relative to robbery, extortion, unauthorized welfare funds, prohibitions against the organization of supervisory employees, and union liability in the courts, as well as providing criminal sanctions, injunctive remedies, and suits for damages against unions engaging in secondary boycotts and jurisdictional disputes.

The provisions relative to mediation differed from the fact-finding proposals endorsed by Truman only in the following ways:

1.) A new board would have been created not responsible to the President or the Secretary of Labor.

2.) A longer cooling-off period would have been provided and instead of thirty days the period would have been sixty days in most industries, ninety-five days in public utilities.

3.) Heavy penalties would have been imposed on employees who engaged in strikes during the cooling-off period.[8]

After Congress passed the Case bill, a tremendous amount of mail immediately began to arrive at the White

House from labor organizations that urgently asked Truman to veto the bill.[9] Undecided whether or not to veto it, Truman sought the advice of various members of his administration for their opinions of the bill.

Secretary of Labor Schwellenbach replied to Truman's request for a personal reaction to the Case bill by saying in part that:

> The Act takes away from the Secretary of Labor all authority to have anything to do with a labor dispute until the time has come when a strike is inevitable, and then the Act authorizes the Board to dump the controversy into the lap of the Secretary of Labor and places upon him all the responsibility at the time when the real trouble arises. . . .[10]

He concluded his analysis by stating:

> We are faced with a serious emergency. This emergency requires emergency legislation. . . . The fact that we are faced with the emergency does not justify us, however, in the adoption of permanent legislation without the study that such permanent legislation needs. . . .[11]

Schwellenbach, as well as Truman, felt the need for some kind of legislation concerning labor's activities. It was, however, in the degree as to what constiuted "emergency legislation" that the Truman administration and the Congress disagreed.

Secretary of the Interior J. A. Krug surmised that:

> The bill is a heterogeneous collection of separate proposals to regulate labor relations. I believe it is fair to comment that they have in common only an anti-labor approach. I believe that it is bad statesmanship to link them together in an omnibus anti-labor measure. The truism that all laws must rest on the consent of the governed is notably the case with respect to legislation

Herbert L. Miller, White House Record Clerk, leaves the
White House for Congress with the vetoed Case Bill, June 11,
1946. (United Press International Photo)

United Mine Workers President John L. Lewis and Bituminous Operators Group Chairman Ezra Van Horn had two
lengthy conferences with Secretary of Labor Lewis B. Schwellenbach in the Labor Department, October 6, 1945. (United
Press International Photo)

President Truman opens the Labor and Management Confer-
ence at the Department of Labor Auditorium. Photo shows
President Truman and Judge Walter P. Stacy of the North
Carolina Supreme Court. Date is November 5, 1945. (United
Press International Photo)

During a campaign swing through Pennsylvania, President Truman is shown laying a wreath at the statue of the late John Mitchell, one-time President of the United Mine Workers Union. October 23, 1948. (United Press International Photo)

President meets with reconversion advisory board—August 20, 1945, President Truman (seated center) laughs as he talks with a member of the Office of War Mobilization and Reconversion advisory board as he met with the group in his office. Standing (l to r) are Albert S. Goss, national Grange master; George H. Mead, War Labor Board member; James G. Patton, Farmers Co-operative Union; Edward A. O'Neal, chief of American Farm Bureau; Nathaniel Dyke, Jr., Small War Plants corporation; Anna M. Rosenberg, member of the Social Security board; O. Max Gardner, board chairman and former North Carolina governor; John W. Snyder, director of OWM; William Green, AFL president; T. C. Cashen, Buffalo, N.Y., International Switchmen's president; Holt McPherson, assistant secretary of board, Shelby, N.C.; Philip Murray, CIO president; William Davlin, executive secretary of board; William H. Davis, economic stabilization chief. (World Wide Photos)

The four editorial cartoons of the period depict some of the frustrations faced by Truman.

Note the elephant figure under Knecht's signature in #1.

Note James Berryman's encouragement to Truman under his signature in #2.

1

(Karl Kae Knecht in the *Evansville Indiana Courier*)

2

PRE-THANKSGIVING DREAM

(*The Washington Star*)

Note monkeywrench in "Labor's" back pocket in #3.

Note signature of Cliff K. Berryman in #4. Berryman was the father of James Berryman.

3

(The Washington Star)

4

(The Washington Star)

President Truman speaking to the Communications Workers Convention at the Davenport Hotel, Spokane, Washington, June 9, 1948. (The Harry S Truman Library Still Collection)

Presidential trip and speech in Gary, Indiana, October 25, 1948. (The Harry S Truman Library Still Collection)

in the delicate and often turbulent field of union rights
and union activities.[12]

However, Truman's closest associates were not in unanimous agreement over whether he should veto the Case
bill. Against a veto were such men as John W. Snyder,
Truman's old friend and Director of War Mobilization
and Reconversion, and George E. Allen, a director of the
Reconstruction Finance Corporation. Allen and Snyder
sought to convince Truman that politically labor had no
other place to go than to the Democratic Party. That, even
if he accepted the bill, labor could not shift to the Republicans. They argued that only one of every five workers
was organized and Truman needed to gain strength with
the 40 million unorganized workers instead of the 14 million organized. They felt that these independents and
"middle-of-the-roaders" would be lost if the President
vetoed the measure.[13]

By the first week of June, there was a great deal of public conjecture over whether Truman was going to sign the
bill or veto it. In a public letter addressed to Truman on
May 31, urging the veto of the Case bill, Philip Murray,
President of the CIO, stated that far from removing the
causes of labor disputes, the Case bill would in fact encourage and increase labor disputes.[14] Murray said that
since the policy of encouraging trade unionism and promoting collective bargaining had been adopted, it had always been under attack by those who had opposed the
policy. He offered in support of his views the large number
of unfair labor practice charges being filed regularly with
the National Labor Relations Board, the issuance of injunctions against peaceful picketing in many jurisdictions,
and the alleged maltreatment of union organizers.

He also listed and classified a large number of labor
bills introduced in the Seventy-Fifth Congress and suc-
ceeding Congresses and characterized them all as having

as their "sole purpose the weakening of labor and the undermining of its bargaining strength." Murray's letter was largely an attack on the motives and sincerity of "the antilabor legislative crusade" of which the Case bill was regarded as the latest phase. In the letter Murray went on to say that the Case bill was drawn from pieces of previous "anti-labor" bills, and maintained that some of its provisions had not even been discussed by the Labor Committees of the Congress. He concluded the letter by saying that the Case bill "must be smashed because a free labor movement is a vital part of a free America."[15]

On June 8, 1946, a few days after the appearance of Murray's letter to the President, with its accompanying analysis of the Case bill by the General Counsel of the CIO, a bipartisan group of six Senators issued a public statement of reply. The six were Democrats Harry Byrd, Allen Ellender, and Carl Hatch, and Republicans H. Alexander Smith, Joseph Ball, and Robert Taft.[16] The bipartisan nature of the letter was quite significant. These men represented political views that ranged from being quite conservative in regard to labor problems to being considered among the defenders of labor's rights.

The Senators criticized the "many exaggerations as to the nature and effect of the bill." They said that Murray's position would be tenable only if one could agree with the basic premises of his criticism that there could be no restraints of any sort on the right to strike even if it deprived the public of transportation, fuel, light, and water; that labor organizations should be immune from laws prohibiting robbery and extortion and from the anti-trust laws, even though the purpose and effect might be the same when done by labor organizations as when done by others; that unions should not be held responsible for the acts of their agents; and that there shall never be injunctive relief against wrongs committed by labor organizations even if no other adequate remedy was available. The Senators in this affirmative argument for the Case bill pointed out that if it would not have prevented or shortened any of the recent strikes, it could not at the same time have been described accurately as an anti-strike measure.[17]

The Senators felt that the Case bill was not an emergency measure to deal exclusively with current strike situations, but permanent legislation calculated over the years to improve industrial relations by facilitating genuine collective bargaining, minimizing the necessity of using the strike weapon and eliminating abuses which had caused strikes to develop. The Senators' statement admitted the charge that Congress had struggled with these problems for years and that there had been numerous bills and hearings on most of the provisions which were finally embodied in the Case bill.

The Senators also maintained that the argument that Congress was conspiring to throttle labor unions was hardly consistent with the fact that for over a decade the Congress had endured the excesses of labor until the nation was virtually brought to its knees and Congress was finally compelled by the pressure of public opinion to remove labor's complete legal immunity from doing public harm. The statement went on to say that except for its provisions with respect to improving collective bargaining procedures, the Case bill, like the Wagner Act itself, sought to eliminate some of the demonstrated abuses which lead to labor disputes and strikes. The Senators said that while the Wagner Act dealt with employer practices, the Case bill made a beginning toward equal treatment of unions and employers under the law and thus tended to restore the equality at the bargaining table which had been destroyed by the Wagner Act as interpreted and applied.[18] This was strong language from both Democrats and Republicans who sought to reestablish responsible action on the part of organized labor.

In a last-minute appeal for the bill's approval, Charles

E. Wilson, President of the General Electric Company, wrote to Truman on June 5, a few days before Truman was scheduled to make his decision, saying:

> You have a long and consistent record as a friend of organized labor. I urge you to now continue as such a friend and champion by allowing this remedial legislation to save labor from its own excesses—excesses which if unrestrained will in the long run be injurious to labor itself.[19]

After considering all the arguments both for and against the bill, Truman, on June 11, 1946, vetoed the bill.[20] He stated that the Case bill would defeat the objectives for curbing strikes and lockouts and cause them to increase. Further, he said, it would encourage, by its sixty-day-"cooling-off" period, a resort to "quickie" strikes. He argued that under the measure employees would face penalties more severe than those for employers; and by its terms it would make workers feel free to strike, once the waiting period was over, "with the sanction of the Congress."

The proposed Federal Mediation Board, Truman said, could take jurisdiction "to outlaw" strikes under prescribed circumstances, then wind up with "the anti-climax of nothing." He also stated that, "Not one of the major disputes which have caused such great public concern during the past months would have been affected in any way by this bill had it been the law at the time."[21]

Truman also felt that the Mediation Board would have been inconsistent with the principles of good administration and would take on responsibilities which should be reserved for Cabinet members who in turn are responsible to the President. He continued by saying that provisions of the measure which would authorize Presidential appointment of emergency commissions would permit the extension of cooling-off periods to ninety-five days with an additional thirty days on the approval of the parties to the dispute.

The application of fact-finding to disputes involving public utilities while omitting other industries was also criticized. While the President was in full accord with the objective of the anti-racketeering provision of the bill, it was lacking the safeguard of the original anti-racketeering act against impairment of the rights of labor organizations lawfully to carry out their "legitimate" objectives.

Truman agreed with the principle that a union should be held responsible for a violation of its contract, but said that the Case bill went much further than that and largely repealed the Norris-LaGuardia Act. He also asserted that a way "must be found" to prevent the jurisdictional strike, but not through the anti-trust laws. He suggested that a comprehensive study of the problems which Congress sought to meet with the Case bill should be made and "based on a realization that labor is now rapidly 'coming of age' and that it should take its place before the bar of public opinion on an equality with management."[22]

The House at once sustained Truman's veto when 135 members supported Truman, and 255, with 260 needed to override, voted to pass the bill over the veto.[23] It was not necessary for the Senate to go on record after the House failed to override, so no vote was taken there. In the voting, the House divided as follows: To override: 159 Republicans and 96 Democrats, with 80 of the latter from Southern States who were joined by 16 from Maryland, Kentucky, Missouri, Oklahoma, and California. To sustain: 118 Democrats, 15 Republicans and 2 minor party members.[24] Five Southern Democrats who had originally voted for the bill changed their position and voted to sustain the veto. If they had voted the way they had previously, the Case bill would have become law.

But it soon became apparent that labor's troubles were

not over. There was talk among those members who supported the Case bill that its provisions would be introduced in other bills to be presented in the Eightieth Congress in January, 1947. There were, however, some concrete results from the legislative efforts concerning labor in the Seventy-Ninth Congress. The angry mood of the Congress continued to grow even after Truman's veto of the Case bill. This became clear three months after the veto when Truman approved the Hobbs Act.[25]

The Hobbs bill stemmed from a Supreme Court interpretation of the Anti-Racketeering Act of 1934. Some union teamsters had been charged with stopping trucks at the Holland Tunnel in New York, and giving the drivers one of three choices: paying a union driver to take the truck to its destination in the city, paying a fixed sum without a driver, or being beaten up. The Supreme Court, in 1942, in the case involving AFL-affiliated New York Local No. 807 of the International Brotherhood of Teamsters, Chauffeurs, Stablemen and Helpers of America, held that Congress did not intend to apply the 1934 act to labor unions. The majority opinion, written by Associate Justice James Byrnes was accompanied by several dissenting opinions[26] favoring the application of the law to such union abuses.

In a sharply worded dissent, Chief Justice Harlan Stone said that a truck owner who paid New York teamsters to take over his vehicle because of threats could not be considered their "bona fide employer." Nor could the extortionists be considered "bona fide employees." He said that the majority decision would "make common-law robbery an innocent pastime." The Supreme Court majority, in arguing that Congress meant to exempt such labor practices from the 1934 Anti-Racketeering Act, observed: "This does not mean, however, that such activities are beyond the reach of Federal Legislative control."[27]

From this interpretation Democratic Congressman

Samuel Hobbs of Alabama drew up his anti-racketeering bill, and on April 9, 1943, the House passed it by 270–107. The Senate, however, refused to act on the bill and continued to bottle it up even after the House passed it again on December 12, 1945. Then came the postwar uproar over strikes and the Hobbs bill was written into the Case bill. Truman, however, did not disapprove of the anti-racketeering provision of the Case bill.[28] After Truman vetoed the Case bill, the Senate Judiciary Committee approved the Hobbs bill as a separate measure, and upon the recommendation of Democratic Senator Carl Hatch it was passed unanimously and without debate on June 21, 1946.[29]

The bill made it a criminal offense, punishable by imprisonment for not more than twenty years or a fine of not more than $10,000, or both, to obstruct, delay, or affect interstate commerce, or the movement of any article or commodity in interstate commerce, by robbery or extortion. The term "robbery" was defined as the unlawful taking or obtaining of personal property from another, against his will, by means of actual or threatened force, or violence, or fear of injury, immediate or future, or to property in his custody or possession, or to the person or property of a relative or a member of his family or to anyone in his company. The term "extortion" was defined as the obtaining of property from another with his consent, induced by wrongful use of actual or threatened force, violence, or fear, or under color of official right. Conspiracies, attempts, and acts in furtherance of a plan or purpose to do anything prohibited by the legislation were also made unlawful.[30]

The bill incorporated, in almost identical terms, section seven of the Case bill, the anti-racketeering section, not because it was related or connected in any way with the purposes or objectives of the Case bill, but merely as an expedient to secure early enactment of its provisions into law. In his message of June 11, 1946, withholding approval

of the Case bill, Truman expressed the view that he was
in full accord with the objectives which the Congress had
in mind in enacting section seven, but that it would be
well to provide in express terms "that section seven does
not make it a felony to strike and picket peacefully, and
to take other legitimate and peaceful concerted action."[31]
While the bill was being debated in the House of Representatives considerable discussion was devoted to these effects. Congressman Hobbs made the following observa-
tions:

> Title III of this bill exempts from the operation of
> this law any conduct under the antitrust statutes, under
> the NLRB Act, under the Norris-LaGuardia statute, the
> Railway Labor Act, the Big Four that have been termed
> the Magna Carta of Labor. . . . Let me point out that
> when you are striking, when you are picketing, when you
> are organizing a labor union, or engaging in any legiti-
> mate labor function, then you are operating under some
> one of these four laws. . . . Aside from that there is abso-
> lutely nothing farther from the mind of any proponent
> of this bill than to hurt labor. . . .[32]

Congressman Hobbs further remarked that representatives
of organized labor appeared before the House Committee
on the Judiciary, of which he was a member, and stated
that organized labor would have no objection to the enactment of a bill outlawing robbery or extortion in interstate
commerce provided the bill preserved the rights of labor
under the four branches of labor's Magna Charta.[33]

While the legislation was on Capitol Hill, William
Green of the AFL and Philip Murray of the CIO denounced
it as a direct attack on labor's legitimate rights. Green said
it contained no guarantees that the right to strike and
picket peaceably would not be outlawed. He said further
that it would cause widespread labor unrest.[34]

On July 3, 1946, in a special message to Congress delivered just before he left for an extended holiday, Truman explained that he had approved the measure and felt justified in doing so. He said he had been advised that the act in no way denied to labor organizations their rights "in carrying out their legitimate objectives," and this was the reason for his approving attitude.[35] Truman also asserted that he had been advised by Tom C. Clark, Attorney General, that nothing in the bill could be construed "to repeal, modify or affect" provisions or protective features of such other major pieces of labor legislation as the Railway Labor Act, the Norris-LaGuardia Act, the Wagner Act, and some sections of the Clayton Act. Truman described those measures as "the great legislative safeguards which the Congress has established for the protection of labor in the exercise of its fundamental rights." Truman said that Clark had also informed him that the bill was not intended to deprive labor of any of its recognized rights, "including the right to strike and to picket, and to take other legitimate and peaceful concerted action."[36] Truman declared that he had approved the terms of the bill only after they had been separated from the Case bill. He recalled that in vetoing the Case bill he had stated that he was in full accord with the objectives of section seven, which embodied the provisions of the Hobbs bill.

The Hobbs Act thus became the first labor bill to become law during the Truman administration. Although the legislative attempts of the Seventy-Ninth Congress to limit the union's strike activities were seriously thwarted, organized labor was not going to be able to exhibit such disregard for all types of governmental control as it had in the past. As later events proved, the defeat of the Case bill was to become a hollow victory for labor. Not only Congress, but Harry Truman as well, was convinced that labor was going to act responsibly in its actions. And during the next few years they both went to considerable lengths to back up that conviction.

Notes: Chapter 7

1. Digest of Pending Legislation, Legislation File, Record Group 250, National Archives.
2. *New York Times*, June 1, 1946.
3. *Congressional Record*, 79th Cong., 2d Sess., p. 5739.
4. *Labor Relations Reporter*, June 3, 1946.
5. *Congressional Record*, 79th Cong., 2d Sess., p. 838.
6. *Ibid.*, p. 685.
7. *Ibid.*, p. 780.
8. Memorandum, Richard B. Keech to the President, May 30, 1946, Truman Papers, OF 407–B, HSTL.
9. Case Bill File, Truman Papers, OF 407–B, HSTL.
10. Lewis B. Schwellenbach to the President, June 4, 1946, Truman Papers, OF 407–B, HSTL.
11. *Ibid.*
12. J. A. Krug to the President, June 4, 1946, Truman Papers, OF 407–B, HSTL.
13. *United States News*, June 14, 1946, p. 22.
14. Philip Murray to the President, May 31, 1946, Truman Papers, OF 407–B, HSTL.
15. *Ibid.*
16. Statement on H. R. 4908 by Senators Joseph H. Ball, Harry F. Byrd, Allen J. Ellender, Carl A. Hatch, H. Alexander Smith, and Robert A. Taft. Truman Papers, OF 407–B, HSTL.
17. *Ibid.*
18. *Ibid.*
19. Charles E. Wilson to the President, June 5, 1946, Truman Papers, OF 407–B, HSTL.
20. *Congressional Record*, 79th Cong. 2d Sess., pp. 6674–6678.
21. *Ibid.*, p. 6675.
22. *Ibid.*, p. 6676.
23. Digest of Pending Legislation, *op. cit.*
24. *Ibid.*
25. *Public Papers of the Presidents: 1946*, p. 336.
26. Analysis of the Hobbs Bill, Record Group 174, National Archives.
27. *Ibid.*

28. *Public Papers of the Presidents: 1946*, p. 336.
29. *New York Times*, June 22, 1946.
30. Analysis of the Hobbs Bill, *op. cit.*
31. *Public Papers of the Presidents: 1946*, p. 336.
32. *Congressional Record*, 79th Cong. 2d Sess., p. 12085.
33. *Ibid.*, p. 12086.
34. Analysis of Hobbs Bill, *op. cit.*
35. *Public Papers of the Presidents: 1946*, pp. 336–337.
36. *Ibid.*, p. 337.

8

Presidential Action in Postwar Labor Disputes

THE MOST CRITICAL ASPECTS OF THE POSTWAR STRIKE PERIOD were not solved by the legislative attempts of the Seventy-Ninth Congress. There was another method which Harry S Truman used as a somewhat effective means of controlling the serious strike situation. This was the seizure by Presidential Executive Order of certain industries in which strikes had threatened the national safety. It was during these seizures that Truman came into bitter conflict with some of the most willful of labor's leaders, namely A. F. Whitney and Alvanley Johnston of the railroad brotherhoods and John L. Lewis, the leader of the nation's coal miners.

From August 17, 1945, to June 14, 1946, the government exercised its seizure powers under the War Labor Disputes Act in nine instances. Though actual hostilities had ceased, the plant seizure provisions of that law remained effective until six months after the President's proclamation of December 31, 1946, ending hostilities.

In the postwar seizures no single method for settling the underlying controversy was followed. It was also difficult to analyze with any degree of accuracy the extent to which seizure helped to settle the disputes. If the settlement procedures followed during any of the seizures had been utilized without it, the result might have been the same. On

140

the other hand, the fact that both management and the workers desired the termination of government possession was possibly an element in compelling acceptance of the final settlement. In almost all of the seizure cases, the business facility was operated under the terms and conditions of employment in effect at the time of seizure.

The nine situations involving seizure were as follows by the date of the Executive Order authorizing possession: the Illinois Central Railroad, August 23, 1945; a variety of oil refining and pipeline properties, October 4, 1945; the Capital Transit Company, November 21, 1945; the Great Lakes Towing Company, November 29, 1945; the "Big Five" and certain other meatpacking companies, January 24, 1946; the New York harbor tugboat companies, February 5, 1946; the railroads, May 17, 1946; the bituminous coal mines, May 21, 1946; and the Monongahela Connecting Railroad, June 14, 1946.[1]

When the seized company accepted the government's settlement proposal, as in the oil seizure, no problem was encountered. But where—as in the Great Lakes Towing Company and the bituminous coal mines seizures—the company refused to accept the proposal, the government was obliged, at the risk of a strike, to effect these proposals without the owner's consent.

Seizure was always regarded by the Truman administration as a temporary measure. An unsigned memorandum was found at the Harry S Truman Library among the papers of John W. Gibson, Assistant Secretary of Labor, that shed light on this aspect of the Truman administration's policies. The memorandum stated:

The most fundamental principle that will be followed by the Government is that seizure will be employed only as a last resort. Management–Labor problems should be solved by management and labor. The Government should provide the most favorable climate possible within which management and labor can work out their own differences. . . .[2]

The memorandum also maintained that the government was not equipped to manage enterprises and that seizure should be considered only in labor disputes in transportation, mining of basic materials, food processing, public utilities, or "such others as the President may find are or will impede reconversion from the war effort."[3]

The seizures of the coal industry and the railway system in the spring of 1946 were the most important of these postwar seizures. These were the two disputes that put the final touches on the acute case of nerves from which the public and the administration were suffering.

The bituminous coal agreement made in 1945 by the United Mine Workers of America and the Coal Operators' Negotiating Committee of the Appalachian Joint Conference terminated March 31, 1947. However, this agreement contained a clause which provided that at any time after March 1, 1946, either party could give ten days' notice asking for a joint conference to consider changes in wages and working conditions. Both parties obligated themselves to attend such a conference. If they did not reach an agreement on changes in fifteen days, either party could give notice that the agreement would terminate in five days.[4]

Prior to asking for changes in wages and working conditions the miners' National Scale Committee, composed of the presidents of the various coal districts, met on February 20, 1946, considered the economic outlook affecting the industry, and directed the union's National Policy Committee and executive officers to negotiate the best wage contract obtainable as instructed by the union's national convention. On March 2 the union notified Secretary of Labor Schwellenbach and the National Labor Relations Board, in accordance with the War Labor Disputes Act, that the agreement with the coal operators might be terminated on March 31, unless changes therein were negotiated satisfactorily, and that the union had asked for a conference with the Operators Negotiating Committee on March 12.[5]

Although the miners indicated that they expected a considerable increase in wages and a decrease in hours of work, they did not state how much they expected. The miners had had no increase in wage rates since 1941, but their take-home pay had increased greatly because of their working longer daily and weekly hours. Furthermore, the increased take-home pay was continuing because of the great demand for coal in the postwar years. The operators were willing to grant an increase "necessary to meet the requirements of the government's wage-price policy."[6] The operators expected price increases which would offset the wage increase.

The miners, however, put the greatest stress on the creation of a health and welfare fund primarily for retired miners to be supported by a tonnage tax on coal. This idea was first presented in connection with the negotiations of the 1945–1947 agreement. It was regarded by many at that time as mere "window dressing" because the miners did not fight for it to the finish. When the proposal was advanced this time the miners pointed out that the operators themselves had used such a tax to furnish armed guards in districts where they sought to prevent the miners from organizing. They felt that they should have no objection to that form of tax as such even if it was used for welfare purposes. Either way, the consumer would pay the tax if the operators could add it to the price of coal. Nevertheless, the operators opposed such a tax and were doubtful that it would be used purely for welfare purposes.[7]

Because of the high accident rate and the extensive loss of life among the miners, they demanded not only laws and measures for the relief of the unfortunate, but better safety measures (in the framing of which they would have a part), federal inspection of the mines, and compulsory introduction of precautionary methods and facilities. They also demanded better sanitation in connection with their working conditions, such as wash houses for bathing and change of clothing, and in connection with living conditions in and about the company houses, such as water supply, toilets, and garbage disposal. When patronizing the company store the miners requested a discount of ten per cent on all goods purchased and twenty per cent on work clothing and other equipment which miners had to buy in order to work in the mines. They also expected the companies to furnish, at cost, coal used in their homes. They demanded a change in the leasing system of company houses so that a miner could not be evicted from his house within thirty days after formal notification. This was regarded as particularly important during a strike.[8]

The United States Conciliation Service on April 1, 1946, appointed a conciliator familiar with the industry to participate in further conferences. These meetings continued until April 10, when the miners led by John L. Lewis told the operators, among other things, "our effort to resolve mutual questions has been vain; you have been intolerant of suggestions and impatient of analysis—to cavil further is futile. We trust that time, as it shrinks your purse, may modify your niggardly and anti-social propensities."[9] Thereupon the miners withdrew from the conference.

On April 11, Secretary of Labor Schellenbach called the operators and the miners into separate sessions. Although nothing seemed to have been accomplished he asked the parties to return on April 17, which they did. In the meantime some of the operators indicated they would oppose all demands except for wages and hours, while others favored bills which made it illegal for any union to demand a levy or excise tax on the product of any industry and which eliminated supervisory employees from the provisions of the National Labor Relations Act. On April 29, however, the miners and operators were persuaded to resume their talks. Because of the lack of progress in reaching an agreement, Truman, on May 10, asked representatives of the miners and operators to come to the White House for a conference.[10] Truman's invitation pointed up the importance placed on coal in the nation's economy by his administration.

Prior to attending the conference the miners had been instructed by their Policy Committee to relieve the existing tight market for coal by agreeing to begin production of May 13, and to continue until May 25, to supply hospitals, utilities, railroads and other essential industries. During that period they would work at the old wage rates on condition that any increases agreed upon would be retroactive. However, work would cease on May 25 if no agreement had been made. During the discussion of the demand for a health and welfare fund it appeared that Truman had gained the impression that the operators would agree to such a fund in principle.

The White House then issued a statement that the operators had agreed to "the acceptance of a health and welfare fund in principle."[11] Five days later the operators issued a statement that they had not given any such understanding. During this five-day period the miners had indicated at the joint conference a willingness to substitute for a tax per ton on coal a seven per cent assessment on payrolls which would be added to the cost of production. The operators indicated they were as much opposed to this form of tax, regardless of the percentage used, as they were to a tax per ton on coal.

On May 4, a report was issued by the Office of War Mobilization and Reconversion which concluded that the coal strike had developed into a "national disaster."[12] The OWMR report, based on data gathered by the Civilian Production Administration, said the effects of the strike will "spread rapidly through the economy and the damage to reconversion progress will take months to mend."[13]

The report was preceded by an angry discussion of the strike in the Senate, where Democratic Senator Scott Lucas of Illinois, who was to become the Democratic Senate Whip in the Eightieth Congress, condemned John L. Lewis as "drunk with power" and termed the strike, a movement that could "easily become an insurrection, against the Government."[14] Truman was called upon to seize the idle mines unless Lewis "bows to reason," and there was talk of action by Congress itself. Although there was no public indication on May 4 that Truman was about to act decisively, one report credited to a high business authority stated that Truman had a "revolutionary" idea which he might act upon later.[15] Reports from all over the nation indicated the gravity of the crisis induced by the strike. Telegrams and messages to members of Congress contained frantic appeals for help in ending the coal strike.

Meanwhile William Green of the AFL wrote to Lewis that "we of the AFL stand with you, by you, and beside you in the noble fight you are making."[16] Green said that there was a lack of public understanding of the merits of the controversy, but that "the ranks of labor hail the courage, the spirit, and the determination with which you are fighting for adequate health and safety for the miners and for welfare provisions for their dependents. . . . Your struggle deserves the cooperation and support of all classes of people." Green concluded that:

> The 7,000,000 members of the AFL will fight with you, will resent the unjustifiable attacks which are being made upon you and will insist and demand that the mine workers as freemen in a free America shall be accorded the right to mobilize and use their economic strength in order to secure justice, security, and protection.[17]

On May 15 and 16, the representatives of the miners and operators were again called to the White House for conferences. As a result of the failure to bring about an agreement, Truman issued Executive Order No. 9728 on May 21, authorizing the Secretary of Interior to take possession of the mines.[18] The actual seizure took place on May 22. On May 23, the railroad strike began, although the railroads had already been seized on May 17. On May 25, Truman asked Congress for legislation designed to enable him to cope with such an unprecedented situation. The Secretary of Interior was ordered to permit the managers of the mines "to continue with their managerial functions to the maximum degree possible consistent with the aims of this order."[19] On May 29, the miners and the operators reached an agreement and the seizure ended.

The *United Mine Workers Journal* called the agreement the "greatest economic and social gains registered by the UMWA in a single wage agreement since the birth of the union in 1890."[20] The contract called for an increase of the basic hourly wage of 18½ cents, introduced a number of other improvements, and established a health and welfare fund financed by a five-cent-a-ton royalty for each ton of coal mined. Secretary of Interior Krug signed an agreement for supervisors, a sore point with the private coal operators, who were not in control of the mines at the time. After making the agreements, the government wanted to return the mines to the private owners. A conference was called on September 11, by the Coal Mines Administrator, in the hope that an agreement could be reached for returning the mines. But before a satisfactory arrangement could be devised, a second dispute involving monthly vacation payments to miners began.[21]

When Secretary Krug had refused to yield to the miner's demands relating to the Coal Mines Administrator's interpretation of vacation payments, Lewis said that the contract had been breached. On October 19, Lewis demanded the attendance of government representatives at a joint conference "for the purpose of negotiating a new arrangement affecting wages, hours, rules, practices, differentials, inequalities, and all other pertinent matters affecting or appertaining to the national bituminous coal industry."[22] When the request for a conference was rejected, Lewis announced that the miners would go on strike on November 20. The government sought and obtained an order from the U. S. District Court instructing the miners to return to work on the grounds that the UMW could not unilaterally terminate its contract. When the court order was ignored, the union was fined $3,500,000 and Lewis himself $10,000 for contempt of court. Lewis thereupon ordered the miners back to work.[23] After the fines were announced, a flush of optimism over the strike situation resulted in a sharp rise in prices on the New York Stock Exchange.

The personal clash between Truman and Lewis was sharp. Truman called Lewis's conduct during the 1946 strike crisis "a new grab for more power on the part of the miners' boss."[24] Truman also was convinced that Lewis wanted to be sure that he had placed the President "in the most embarrassing position possible for the Congressional election on November 6."[25] Secretary of the Interior Krug told Truman that "Lewis had boasted he would get Krug first . . . and that he would wait until 1948 to get the President."[26]

At the UMW convention in October, 1946, Lewis denounced Truman in bitter terms:

> He is a man totally unfitted for the position. His principles are elastic, and he is careless with the truth. He has no special knowledge of any subject, and he is a malignant, scheming sort of an individual who is dangerous not only to the United Mine Workers, but dangerous to the United States of America.[27]

When D. B. Robertson, President of the General Grievance Committees of the Brotherhood of Locomotive Firemen, wrote to Truman complaining of his actions toward the miner's strikes, Truman replied in terms equally as emphatic as those of Lewis. His reply said in part:

> There should be, however, a sense of shame in all the hearts of all the leaders of labor for the manner in which Mr. Lewis attempted to defy the Government. His action is in line with the action of Whitney and Johnson last fall and does labor no credit.
>
> Lewis had the best contract he ever had in his life. I myself forced him to take the safety measures in that contract for which he had never fought before. . . . He attempted to pull a dirty political trick and it backfired; but he succeeded in giving labor generally a black eye, which will do labor no good in the new Republican Congress.
>
> We used the weapons that we had at hand in order to fight a rebellion against the Government, and I am here to tell you that I expect to use whatever powers the President and the Government have, when the law and the Government are defied by an arbitrary dictator, such as Lewis. . . .[28]

Truman concluded the letter by warning that, "When Murray and Green and able leaders, like yourself, condone the action of Lewis you are not helping yourselves either with me or with the Congress."[29]

Apart from Truman's struggle with the coal miners perhaps the most significant trend during 1946 was the progressive decline of good labor relations in the railroad industry under the Railway Labor Act. The Railway Labor Act had come to be regarded as the model upon which to base good labor relations in other industries. Consequently the unexpected failure of its mediation machinery to prevent a nationwide rail strike in May, 1946, came as a shock to many people.

A. F. Whitney, leader of the Brotherhood of Railway Trainmen, and Alvanley Johnston, leader of the Brotherhood of Locomotive Engineers, chose this moment to force the Truman administration's hand, and as a result reaped much of the resentment which Lewis had aroused. Their complaint was an old one. As early as July, 1945, all of the brotherhoods had expressed serious discontent as the backlog of cases before the Railroad Mediation Board. They demanded a wage increase of $2.50 per day, and a revision of working rules. Eventually eighteen of the railroad unions had agreed to submit their case to arbitration. But the Trainmen and Engineers issued a strike call for March 11, 1946. Truman averted an immediate tieup of rail transportation by appointing a fact-finding board.[30]

The Emergency Board reported on April 18, 1946. The engineers and the trainmen rejected the recommendations of the Board in their entirety and set 4 P.M. May 18, as the date to strike unless a settlement satisfactory to them was made prior to that time. On May 17, Truman issued Executive Order No. 9729 taking possession of all the transportation properties involved in the strike threat.[31] The Executive Order also included authority for the Director of the Office of Defense Transportation to take possession of any other properties if he found it necessary. The order applied specifically to 337 listed railroads.

The order, however, contained definite instructions requiring the Director to permit the managements of the carriers "to continue their respective managerial functions to the maximum degree possible consistent with the purposes of this order."[32] This included all financial and contractual dealings and operations, collective bargaining with the employees, and conformity with Interstate Commerce Commission regulations. The Director was also given the powers and duties vested in the Secretary of War to utilize the railroads for the transportation of troops, war material, and equipment to the exclusion of all other traffic. He could also call upon the Secretary of War for protection of facilities and persons employed or seeking employment therein.

On May 18, a few minutes before the strike was to go into effect, the leaders of the engineers and trainmen postponed the strike for the period of five days. This was done in response to Truman's request for the resumption of negotiations. In this connection Truman suggested that, as a compromise, all of the railroad unions should accept the sixteen cents per hour and $1.28 per day increase suggested by the fact-finding board.[33]

Truman's compromise was acceptable to all of the unions except the engineers and trainmen and the strike of these two unions went into effect at 4 P.M. on May 23. However, the strike lasted only two days. On May 24, Truman made a radio appeal to the striking brotherhoods to return to their jobs and threatened that if they had not gone back to work by 4 P.M., May 25, he would call out troops to stop the strike.[34]

Truman said: "I shall call upon the Army to assist the Office of Defense Transportation in operating the trains and I shall ask our armed forces to furnish protection to every man who heeds the call of his country in this hour of need."[35] Truman said the emergency caused by the railroad strike was so acute that he had requested Congress to assemble in joint session at the time of his deadline for resumption of operations in order to hear his address. Repeatedly, Truman stressed that the current country-wide railroad strike was no contest between labor and management, but one between a small group of men and their government. He felt that "The railroads are now being operated by your Government and the strike of these men is a strike against their Government . . . The fact is that the action of this small group of men has resulted in millions of other workers losing their wages."[36] Addressing his remarks directly to Alvanley Johnston, head of the loco-

motive engineers, and A. F. Whitney, leader of the trainmen, Truman said that he had warned both union chiefs
repeatedly of the tragic consequences that would follow
a strike call and added: "It is inconceivable that in our
democracy any two men should be placed in a position
where they can completely stifle our economy and ultimately destroy our country."[37]

The strike came to an end a short time after 4 P.M. May
25, while Truman was addressing Congress and requesting
drastic legislation to deal with the strike situation. The
engineers and trainmen accepted Truman's compromise,
and on the next day the railroads were restored to their
owners.[38] The leaders of the two striking brotherhoods
signed the memorandum of agreement in a hotel room as
Truman was about to begin his address to a joint session of
Congress. Dr. John R. Steelman, the President's consultant,
who assisted him in the settlement of labor disputes, witnessed the signing and telephoned the news to the Capitol
in time for Truman to make an extemporaneous announcement of the settlement to the legislators.

In his speech to Congress on May 25, 1946, Truman also
proposed a Temporary Disputes Settlement Bill which contained some drastic provisions. The bill stated that "It is
the policy of the United States that labor disputes inter-
rupting or threatening to interrupt the operation of industry essential to the maintenance of the national economic structure and to the effective transition from war to
peace should be promptly and fairly mediated. . . ."[39] It was
then provided that whenever the United States Government had taken possession of a plant, mine or facility, the
existence of a national emergency could be declared if a
strike, lockout, or slowdown occurred. In proclaiming such
an emergency, the President could put it into effect at
once and was empowered to call upon all employees and all
officers of the employer to return to their jobs. All union
officials and officers of the employer were required to take

positive action to recall employees. The bill also provided that fair wages and conditions of employment should be established by the government. After such a proclamation had been issued, affirmative action to rescind or terminate the stoppage was required of officers of the union and officers of the employer. Continuance of the stoppage would be unlawful and subject to penalty of fine and imprisonment. The Attorney General was empowered to obtain injunctions in any district court, while the President was given the power to draft strikers into the army. Any employee who failed to return to work would be considered to have quit voluntarily and would lose his rights under the National Labor Relations Act. Any profit resulting from operation by the United States Government was to be turned over to the Treasury of the United States.[40]

The Temporary Disputes Settlement bill was passed by the House by an overwhelming vote of 306–13 with practically no debate. The measure had been introduced by Democratic Congressman John McCormack of Massachusetts and it also provided that it was to expire six months after the cessation of hostilities as proclaimed by the President or by passage of a concurrent Congressional resolution, whichever was earlier. McCormack included the latter proposal concerning Congressional termination at the suggestion of Republican Congressmen Clarence Brown of Ohio and Francis Case of South Dakota. The temporary nature of the bill was thus emphasized and in addition bipartisan support of Truman's proposal was revealed.

However, the bill failed to pass the Senate. After House passage, the measure was referred to the Senate Committee on Interstate Commerce. Debate on the bill was lively. Senator Robert Taft felt that it was ridiculous in nature and violated "every principle of American jurisprudence."[41] In the meantime the railroad strike was settled, and Republicans, led by Taft, got the bill recommitted to committee. Taft felt that the bill gave the President too much power and that those provisions concerning the powers of the President could only be rewritten in committee. Taft voiced the idea in debate that if the railroad strike had not been settled he would have voted for Truman's bill.[42]

From Taft's attitude an interesting imponderable emerged. By the Senator's reasoning it could easily have been seen that prevailing circumstances were felt to be the test of the correctness of labor proposals. This also showed that the dispute between Truman and his opponents on the Republican side came down to a difference of opinion over the *degree* of a labor emergency and not over principles.

In the meantime, labor leaders were stunned by Truman's sweeping proposal. They felt that Truman had turned his back on them. Philip Murray sent a telegram to every member of the Senate which read in part:

> In a moment of wild hysteria an attempt is being made to stampede through Congress legislation which has as its sole aim the destruction of the labor movement of this nation.[43]

William Green bitterly declared that "to compel free workers to remain on the job against their will by drafting them into the armed forces and making them subject to court martial if they refuse is slave labor under Fascism."[44] Seldom has a President of the United States been spoken of in such a manner.

Truman's justification of this action was that he was concerned for the nation as a whole and would not allow the special interests of a single economic group to prevail. After three conferences at the White House with the leaders of the railroad brotherhoods, who threatened to continue the strike action, Truman saw things in black and white terms. He later wrote:

I saw that this was no contest between labor and management but one between a small group of men and their government. Johnston and Whitney said, despite my appeals to them, that they were determined to strike.

"You are not going to tie up the country," I told them. "If this is the way you want it, we'll stop you."[45]

On November 5, 1945, Truman had said:

When industrial strife becomes widespread, all of us lose the things we need—the wages that labor wants, the earnings and dividends that businessmen and investors want, the products that the consumers want. . . . Continued production and an expanding industry—unhampered as far as humanly possible by stoppages of work—are absolutely essential to progress.[46]

As for limiting labor's activities he had said in a radio broadcast on January 3, 1946, from the White House concerning his plea for fact-finding boards in handling strikes:

In the setting up of fact-finding boards, there is nothing harmful to labor. There is no reason why a strike cannot be postponed for thirty days. Nor is there any intention of taking away labor's right to strike. That right remains inviolate. There is no effort to shackle labor. There is only an effort to find the truth, and to report it.[47]

Truman pointed out that the parties to a dispute would not be legally bound to accept the findings or recommendations of the fact-finding board. But he was confident that, because "the general public would know all the facts," it would follow that "in most cases both sides would accept the recommendations, as they have in most of the railway labor disputes." The procedure, he said, "should be used sparingly and only when the national public interest requires it."[48]

No matter what his critics said, Truman never really lost sight of the fact that the general right of workers to strike against private employers had to be preserved. But by the end of 1946 he also was adamant in stating that "the paralyzing effects of a nation-wide strike in such industries as transportation, coal, oil, steel or communications, can result in a national disaster."[49]

On May 26, 1946, Whitney declared that his union would use the $47 million in its treasury if necessary to defeat Truman if he should seek reelection in 1948. Whitney was in a bitter mood as he and Johnston left their hotel suites and headed for their headquarters in Cleveland. Whitney denounced Truman as a "political accident." He also asserted that his union had authorized him to spend $2.5 million to defeat every member of Congress who voted for the restrictive labor legislation requested by Truman in his address to Congress.[50]

Truman's success in ending the railroad strike brought strong commendation from a wide segment of the nation's press, little of which would normally praise him. Many papers also gave approval editorially to the emergency labor legislation requested by Truman in his message to Congress. The *Philadelphia Record* stated that, "Harry Truman met magnificently one of the greatest tests of courage ever to face an American President. . . . If there was surprising power and eloquence in President Truman's address to Congress; if he rose to heights of greatness in the critical hour—it was because he spoke from the heart of the American people."[51]

The *Philadelphia Inquirer* echoed the same sentiment by saying, "It was a novel and refreshing experience for his millions of listeners to hear a President of the United States, after all these years, take a militant stand against the rapidly accumulating encroachments on the people's rights by labor bosses."[52] The *Los Angeles Times* editorialized that, "There appeared to be something of Grover

Cleveland in the President that spoke to the nation Friday and Congress Saturday. . . . In the White House we need Cleveland's capacity to hew to line and insist upon rightness of his course."[53]

The *Pittsburgh Post-Gazette* said: "The issue has been put squarely up to Congress" by the President and added that Congress "can no longer evade its responsibility to the people" with respect to enactment of new labor legislation.[54] The *Atlanta Journal* asserted that, "Lawlessness personified in two labor dictators has surrendered to the principles and the public for whom the President spoke and acted."[55]

But organized labor continued to react to what it felt to be an unfair attack upon its ranks. When the House Committee on Labor opened hearings on the causes of industrial unrest in June, 1946, the labor spokesmen almost seemed to be suffering from a persecution complex. Philip Murray insisted that the nation had just witnessed a "big-business plot" to undermine unions. In essence his contention was that management had deliberately fostered and prolonged strikes in order to create a public demand for anti-labor legislation. In support of that charge he pointed out that in each case it had been management and not labor that had refused to accept the recommendations of Truman's fact-finding Boards.[56] His chief explanation of management's ability to hold out centered around the rebates upon wartime excess profits payments, which the 1942 Tax Law granted to corporations whose incomes fell below a specified level. Specifically, he cited the example of the J. I. Case Company and Allis Chalmers, which had drawn tax rebates over a period of several months while consistently rejecting all terms even after the union was more than willing to scale down its demands. Secretary of Labor Schwellenbach concurred in the opinion that management had deliberately avoided an early settlement of wage contracts.[57]

The theory that there was a plot by "big business" in causing industrial disputes was completely rejected by management spokesmen and particularly by the National Association of Manufacturers. But they created their own counterpart which rested upon the conviction that the "irresponsible acts of arrogant union leaders" constituted the primary cause of strikes.[58] They assumed that the strikes had been personal rather than economic in character. Eventually the whole debate began to revolve around the merits of the union wage demands. Not only the cio but all other labor groups insisted that the loss of overtime pay, transfer to lower paying jobs, plus serious inflationary tendencies had subjected the worker to an intolerable economic situation.

In his appearance before the House Labor Committee, William Green argued the simple fact was that wages had been the major factor in only about twenty-six per cent of the strikes in 1939, but that the proportion had risen to more than forty-two per cent in 1945, and to seventy-five per cent in the first quarter of 1946 was a good indication that the reconversion strikes had been normal adjustments to a period of great economic uncertainty.[59]

On behalf of the cio, Murray presented abundant statistical evidence which was designed to show that the workers' standard of living had been at stake in the postwar strikes. In addition, he refused to countenance the notion that unions were irresponsible or that strikes had reached the proportions of a national emergency. To support his contention he called attention to the general effectiveness of conciliation, and to the fact that strikes were more numerous among unorganized workers than among those who belonged to unions.

One of the most interesting aspects of the testimony of some of the labor spokesmen was the extent to which it revealed deterioration in their relations with the Truman administration. Murray sharply attacked the Truman proposal that a sixty-day cooling-off period in strikes and compulsory fact-finding should be written into law. He contended that there was no need for a cooling-off period, because most wage contracts already required thirty to sixty days of negotiation prior to expiration, and that compulsory fact-finding would establish a dangerous precedent of federal interference in the collective bargaining process. The feeling that the welfare of the workers was being sacrificed to political expediency was evident in much that he said. Dan Tobin, of the AFL Teamsters, expressed political fears when he warned the Democratic Party that it had lost the confidence of labor and would face defeat in both 1946 and 1948, unless it changed its course.[60]

In many ways, therefore, the strikes largely destroyed for the moment the mutual trust between labor and the Truman administration. Truman's patience was completely exhausted, and he came to believe that labor would have to be brought under firmer control. Labor, in turn, had become suspicious of the Truman administration's intention and had lost confidence in its ability to provide a solution to economic problems. But labor had only begun to face some of the opposition it would encounter before the end of 1948. The actions of the Eightieth Congress soon made it forget most of its bitterness against Truman and his policies.

Notes: Chapter 8

1. Arthur E. Suffern, *Labor–Management Disputes, Subsequent to August 17, 1945 Involving Possession of Properties by the Federal Government*, U. S. National Wage Stabilization Board (Washington, 1946), p. 2.
2. Presidential Seizure in Labor Disputes, Gibson Papers, HSTL.
3. *Ibid.*
4. Suffern, *op. cit.*, p. 43.
5. *Ibid.*

6. *Ibid.*
7. *Ibid.*
8. *Ibid.*, p. 44.
9. *Ibid.*, p. 47.
10. *Ibid.*
11. *Ibid.*
12. Postwar Labor Disputes File, Record Group 250, National Archives.
13. *Ibid.*
14. *New York Times*, May 5, 1946.
15. *Ibid.*
16. *New York Times*, May 7, 1946.
17. *Ibid.*
18. Suffern, *op. cit.*, p. 48.
19. *Ibid.*
20. Philip A. Taft, *Organized Labor in America* (New York: Harper & Row, Publishers, 1964), p. 574.
21. Suffern, *op. cit.*, p. 49.
22. Taft, *op. cit.*, p. 574.
23. *Ibid.*
24. Truman, *Memoirs*, Vol. I, p. 502.
25. *Ibid.*, p. 505.
26. Suffern, *op. cit.*, p. 49.
27. *New York Times*, October 21, 1946.
28. Truman, *Memoirs*, Vol. 1, pp. 504–505.
29. *Ibid.*, p. 505.
30. Suffern, *op. cit.*, p. 15.
31. Executive Order No. 9729, Truman Papers, OF 407–B, HSTL.
32. *Ibid.*
33. Suffern, *op. cit.*, p. 21.
34. *Public Papers of the Presidents: 1946*, pp. 274–277.
35. *Ibid.*, p. 277.
36. *Ibid.*
37. *Ibid.*, p. 275.
38. *New York Times*, May 27, 1946.
39. *Public Papers of the Presidents: 1946*, p. 279.
40. *New York Times*, May 28, 1946.
41. *Congressional Quarterly*, Vol. II, 1946, p. 300.
42. *Ibid.*

43. Joel Seidman, *American Labor from Defense to Reconversion* (Chicago: University of Chicago Press, 1953) , pp. 236–237.
44. *Ibid.,* p. 237.
45. Truman, *Memoirs,* Vol. I, p. 501.
46. *Public Papers of the Presidents: 1945,* pp. 462–463.
47. *Public Papers of the Presidents: 1946,* p. 4.
48. *Ibid.*
49. Postwar Labor Disputes File, *op. cit.*
50. *New York Times,* May 27, 1946.
51. *Philadelphia Record,* DNC Clipping File, HSTL.
52. *Philadelphia Inquirer,* DNC Clipping File, HSTL.
53. *Los Angeles Times,* DNC Clipping File, HSTL.
54. *Pittsburgh-Post-Gazette,* DNC Clipping File, HSTL.
55. *Atlanta Journal,* DNC Clipping File, HSTL.
56. Postwar Labor Disputes File, *op. cit.*
57. Secretary of Labor Schwellenbach's Testimony Before House Committee on Labor, June, 1946, Record Group 174, National Archives.
58. U. S. Congress House Committee on Labor, *Investigation of the Causes of Labor Disputes,* Hearings before the Subcommittee, June 7–June 25, 1945, 79th Cong., 2d Sess.
59. *Ibid.,* p. 191.
60. *Ibid.,* p. 226.

9

The Eightieth Congress and the Taft-Hartley Act

WHEN THE SEVENTY-NINTH CONGRESS ADJOURNED IN AUGUST, 1946, the strike situation was relatively quiet, but it became active again in September, when stoppages by various maritime unions tied up the nation's ports. The maritime strikes continued in parts of the country through the autumn and were followed toward the end of November by another bituminous coal strike. Strike activity declined in December and there was no further major stoppage until April, 1947, when the telephone workers walked out in a strike that lasted more than a month. Despite the labor calm in the first quarter of the year, the Eightieth Congress, which had come to Washington in January, was determined to impose curbs on unions and their activities.

The Congressional election results of 1946 had been in part a confirmation of the angry mood of much of the electorate toward labor's actions in the months after the war's end. In the elections the Republicans won control of both houses of Congress. The Republicans had a 249–185 majority in the House and also held 51 of the 96 seats in the Senate. Much of the Republican success was attributable to things other than the issue of labor-relations legislation. There was also a backwash of resentment in a public that had grown tired of inflation, price controls, shortages of consumer goods, housing shortages, and all of the general discomforts of postwar adjustments. The Republicans thus used the campaign slogan "Had Enough?" to great effect.

But the leadership of organized labor had contributed its share to the public's resentment, according to one author, by permitting "labor's shortcomings to be painted in loud, unattractive colors."[1] In the eyes of much of the public the arrogance and stubbornness of a few labor leaders had clouded the honorable actions of many unions and their leaders. Although the election campaign was fought on a broad front, the postwar strike wave served to fan tensions that already existed. One poll conducted by the American Institute of Public Opinion revealed that sixty-eight per cent of those polled approved of the possibility of Congressional action to limit strikes.[2] The Communist influence in labor organizations, particularly in some of the CIO affiliates, also damaged labor's image with the electorate.

The results of the election revealed a crushing defeat for organized labor. Few labor stalwarts in Congress survived the storm of ballots. Six Democratic Senators were defeated who seldom opposed legislation which labor favored or who seldom supported legislation which labor opposed. The six were James Tunnel of Delaware, Hugh Mitchell of Washington, Frank Briggs of Missouri, Abe Murdock of Utah, Joseph Guffey of Pennsylvania, and James Mead of New York. The band of House members who generally took the lead in supporting organized labor's cause was almost destroyed. They included Democrats Frank Hook of Michigan, Hugh DeLacy of Washington, Michael Bradley and John Sheridan of Pennsylvania, Andrew Biemiller of Wisconsin, James Geeland of Connecticut, and C. M. Bailey of West Virginia.

Attempts to restrict labor's actions became evident again

soon after the election. In his January, 1947, message to Congress on the State of the Union, President Truman referred to the turmoil that had characterized labor relations in 1946, but said that "we must not, however, adopt punitive legislation."[3] Truman felt that it had to be realized that "industrial peace cannot be achieved merely by laws directed against labor unions."[4] But in order to correct certain abuses and to provide additional governmental assistance in the bargaining process, Truman said *some* sort of legislation was needed. He said that attention should also be given to finding the causes of labor–management difficulties. Truman suggested that a four-point program to reduce industrial strife be enacted as follows: 1.) The early enactment of legislation to prevent certain unjustifiable practices; 2.) the extension of facilities within the United States Department of Labor for assisting collective bargaining; 3.) the broadening of social legislation to alleviate the causes of workers' insecurity; and 4.) the appointment by Congress of a temporary joint commission to inquire into the entire field of labor–management relations.[5]

Truman recommended legislation to prevent jurisdictional disputes when the public and the employer were injured because of "a collision between rival unions," which be called indefensible. He also felt legislation was desirable to prevent strikes by minority unions to compel employers to deal with them, in spite of the legal requirement under the National Labor Relations Act that employers had to bargain with the majority union. It was further suggested that provisions be made for peaceful and binding determination of questions as to labor-union jurisdiction in the performance of particular tasks.

Any secondary boycott which was used to further jurisdictional disputes or to compel employers to violate the terms of the NLRA was pointed out as being unjustifiable. Truman stated, however, that not all secondary boycotts were unjustifiable and that there should not be a blanket prohibition against them. He wanted legislation that would prohibit secondary boycotts when they had unjustifiable objectives, but not impair the right of unions to preserve their existence and their gains made through collective bargaining.[6]

Lack of clear understanding by labor and management as to their responsibility for settling disputes through their own negotiations was cited by Truman as one obstacle to the avoidance of labor strife. Extension of facilities within the Department of Labor for aid in the collective-bargaining process, and integration of government machinery which would facilitate and expedite the settlement of disputes was suggested.

A commission to inquire into labor–management relations was recommended by Truman, its membership to consist of twenty persons of whom twelve were to be chosen by Congress from the members of both parties in the House of Representatives and the Senate, and eight to be appointed by the President to represent the public, management, and labor. The commission would be charged with investigating and making recommendations upon the special and unique problem of nationwide strikes in vital industries affecting the public interest. It was also to search for the best methods and procedures for carrying out the collective bargaining process, and the underlying causes of labor–management disputes.[7]

Other members of Truman's administration suggested some form of labor legislation. Paul M. Herzog, a member of the National Labor Relations Board, confidentially drafted an editorial for the January 14, 1947, issue of the *Washington Post*. He probably chose this method of expressing his ideas in order to escape the charge of not being impartial as a member of the NLRB. At one point he stated:

Legislation, to repeat, is necessary. But it would compound an ancient fallacy to assume that labor problems,

> which are problems of human relations, can all be
> solved by passing laws or creating new government in-
> strumentalities. There are other methods, effective al-
> though admittedly not infallible. Stronger mediation
> machinery is the first requirement. . . . Public utility
> strikes cannot be tolerated, and more than mediation
> may be required to prevent them.[8]

Herzog, like Truman, believed that anti-labor legislation
would only stimulate labor disputes. It was significant,
however, that the Truman administration was advocating
a legislative program of its own concerning the restriction
of labor union activities.

Efforts to persuade labor to act responsibly were, therefore, not exclusively Republican in nature. Many of the
Democrats held over from the Seventy-Ninth Congress were
again going to give powerful support to regulatory labor
legislation, and in a Republican-controlled Congress. The
Eightieth Congress saw the introduction of an avalanche
of restrictive labor measures. A number of bills for compulsory arbitration of labor disputes threatening the public
health and safety were introduced during the 1947 session
of Congress. Although most of the measures received no
consideration on the floor, their terms indicated the type
of legislation that was being suggested and were indicative
of the Congressional mood toward labor.

Seventeen bills to amend the Wagner law or otherwise
to deal with unions or collective bargaining were introduced in the House of Representatives on January 3, 1947,
the first day of the opening session of the Eightieth Congress. In the following week fifteen such bills were introduced by members of the Senate. By the end of January
forty-eight bills dealing with unions and collective bargaining were before the two houses. There were sixty-five bills
introduced by the end of February.[9]

Of the seven labor bills introduced by Democratic Senator W. Lee O'Daniel of Texas on January 8, five dealt

with the National Labor Relations Act. Four of these assumed its continuance and offered amendments. The fifth proposed its repeal altogether. Two days later the same Senator, according to one author, "either forgetting his efforts of the day before yesterday, or in the belief that two bills are better than one,"[10] introduced another bill, in identical language, again to repeal the National Labor Relations Act.

The most detailed, and in some respects the most moderate, of the bills was the so-called "Public Rights in Labor Disputes" measure, offered on the first day of the session by five Republican members of the House.[11] They were Congressmen James Auchincloss and Clifford Case of New Jersey, Christian Herter and John Heselton of Massachusetts, and Robert Hale of Maine.

The bill would have set up a federal system of compulsory arbitration along lines suggested by economist Sumner H. Slichter. It was based on the theory that it was necessary for the government to intervene to protect the public when a labor dispute affecting interstate commerce resulted in, or threatened to result in, substantial curtailment of transportation, public utility, or communications services, or substantial curtailment of supplies or articles or commodities essential to public health or safety.

The bill would also have set up a Labor Disputes Conciliation Administration to offer conciliation services where helpful in such disputes. A Labor–Management Advisory Committee composed of seven labor representatives and seven business representatives also would have been created to advise on administration of the act and to recommend persons for appointment to a panel of arbitrators to be maintained by the Conciliation Administration. At any time a labor dispute threatened to endanger the public health or safety, the President could issue an order, enforceable by court injunction, and therefore prohibit the strike.[12]

Another general labor bill was offered by Democratic Congressman Howard Smith of Virginia to make it an unfair labor practice for employees or their representatives to interfere by strike or otherwise with the operation of public utilities whose rates were fixed by government authority, or with the operation of any plant, mine, or facility whose continuous operation was essential to public health or safety.[13] No formal system of arbitration was proposed, but collective bargaining contracts in such industries would not be enforceable unless they contained anti-strike provisions and provisions for submission of disputes to "voluntary" arbitration. This bill was similar to one that Smith had introduced in the Seventy-Ninth Congress.

On January 10, 1947, Republican Representative Margaret Smith of Maine introduced a bill "to provide a basis for the settlement of industrial disputes vitally affecting the national health, security or economy."[14] The bill authorized the President to declare the existence of a national emergency and order seizure by the government whenever he determined that a labor dispute was of sufficient magnitude to interrupt or threaten to interrupt operation of an industry essential to public health or security and the national economic structure.

Congresswoman Smith maintained that the bill covered "emergency situations affecting or threatening to affect vital industries and grants to the Congress a check against Presidential abuse of power."[15] She added that the crux of the matter was "abuse of power,"[16] and accordingly the bill was composed of interlocking checks against all parties who were involved in a dispute: employers, employees, and the government itself. Like other proponents of labor legislation Mrs. Smith favored authorizing the President to step in where interruptions affected the national economy. However, her proposal was unique in that the Congress was permitted to veto Presidential action whenever it deemed "that existing conditions do not warrant the determination made by the President."[17]

Republican Congressman Gerald Landis of Indiana introduced a bill to require arbitration of industry-wide labor disputes which the President and the Secretary of Labor, or the President and the Govenor of any affected state, declared to be a threat to the national health and safety. Arbitration boards were to be made up of two employer representatives, two employee representatives, and a fifth member selected from a panel of federal arbitrators. Either side could reject the award, but in that case the government was authorized to seize the plants or facilities and operate them until the award was accepted or the parties reached an independent settlement. If neither event occurred within one year, the properties were to be returned to the private owners.[18]

Several other House bills were introduced which would have required submission of major disputes to arbitration and allowed the parties to reject the award, with no provision for government seizure in the latter eventuality. A different approach to the problem, however, was contained in a bill offered by Republican Senators Homer Ferguson of Michigan and H. Alexander Smith of New Jersey.[19] It would have divided the country into eleven labor court districts, each with a three-judge district labor relations court. These courts would have had original jurisdiction over all disputes regarding the interpretation of existing labor contracts that covered workers in industries affecting interstate commerce. Decisions of these courts were to be binding on the parties, subject to an appeals procedure. Although the bill did not give the labor courts jurisdiction over disputes involving negotiations of new contracts, Senator Smith voiced the opinion in Senate debate that the proposed system would "take care of at least three-quarters of all disputes between management and labor."[20] Both

Smith and Ferguson expressed the hope that "national paralysis" strikes could be included eventually.

Although none of the above bills ever reached the floor of the Eightieth Congress, they were significant for several reasons. Despite the hectic rush to introduce bills restricting union activities, there was strong evidence on the part of many Congressmen that they were not trying to destroy unions but were seeking to promote the public welfare in times of emergency caused by union abuses. To think otherwise would be to impugn the integrity as well as the intelligence of a large proportion of the members of the Eightieth Congress. But this evidence did not always lie on the surface. Easier to see was evidence of haste and carelessness in draftsmanship by legislators who were eager to obey what they considered the "mandate" of the 1946 election.

Labor opposition to these bills was delayed too long after the election and was too dispirited to be effective. During the Congressional hearings on these bills, labor witnesses made an unfavorable impression. Neither the AFL nor the CIO was willing to offer any concrete amendments to the Wagner Act or to admit that there was room for improvement. Both limited themselves to a generally negative policy. They feared that once they had consented to some minor revisions the Wagner Act would be destroyed by those who had always been hostile to it. Both union groups believed that, no matter what suggestions might be made by labor, the Congressional leaders would disregard them just the same and carry out their own predetermined program. It was also possible that both factions of labor believed that even this new Congress would not dare to change the Wagner Act. On the other hand it might also have been that the "do-nothing" policy was due to the fact that neither the AFL nor the CIO really had any constructive suggestions to offer.[21]

The behavior of some unions supplied additional ammunition for anti-labor legislation. John L. Lewis in particular contributed his share. Almost immediately after the Republican victory in November, 1946, the miners walked out on a strike, declaring the Krug–Lewis agreement at an end. The nation's newspapers carried the news on the front pages and their editorial comments reflected on the arrogance and abuse of labor's power. The contempt proceedings against the union and against Lewis personally kept the news in the public's mind. During the postwar years the public was emotionally more aroused by the potential abuse of power by labor than by any misgivings concerning the principle involved in the government's use of the injunction in labor disputes.

In addition, the Republican-controlled Congress was in no mood to conciliate labor. Its leaders were aware that the electorate was psychologically ready for some changes in the Wagner Act. The legislation that finally emerged from the Eightieth Congress was a law blended from the Hartley measure in the House and the Taft measure in the Senate, titled the Labor-Management Relations Act of 1947, or more popularly known as the Taft-Hartley Act.

However, from the beginning of the session it was evident that a split existed among Republican legislative leaders. Senator Taft claimed that the "Republican Party has frequently declared its belief that the solution of employer–employee relationships rests on a sound system of collective bargaining. . . . It means that the Wagner Act should be retained."[22] He was supported by Senators Wayne Morse of Oregon and Irving Ives of New York. On the other hand, leaders of the majority in the House such as Fred Hartley of New Jersey and Clare Hoffman of Michigan expressed opposition to Taft's position and favored stiffer restrictions.

The differences between leaders of both the House and Senate were evident in their respective hearings as well as in their reports and the bills they initially passed. The witnesses before the House Committee on Education and Labor were almost all hostile to organized labor. Many favored the repeal of the Wagner Act, the application of the anti-trust laws to labor organizations, and restrictions on industry-wide bargaining and union security. The few labor representatives who attended the hearings held by the House Committee were sharply questioned by its members.[23]

The hearings of the Senate Committee on Labor and Public Welfare, presided over by Taft, heard almost an equal number of representatives from each side. Taft and other members of the Senate committee showed a readiness to listen to and consider the arguments presented by both labor and employer witnesses. Democratic Senator Allen Ellender of Louisiana told William Green, when he objected to restrictions on jurisdictional strikes, that "Congress is going to do something to stop jurisdictional strikes and secondary boycotts and we want your assistance."[24]

Senator Taft was not the legislative ogre that he was later represented as by both organized labor and Truman in the 1948 election campaign. He was a man, however, who was committed to the idea that organized labor had accumulated far too much power. In this sense, he differed little from a majority of the members of both the Democratic-controlled Seventy-Ninth and the Republican-controlled Eightieth Congresses. Taft's handling of the committee displayed an objectivity in his approach to the problem of postwar labor relations for which he was seldom given credit by later observers.

In the press, the House bill introduced by Congressman Hartley, was often referred to as a "tough" bill, while the Senate bill was described as "mild." In conference, it was the Senate version that dominated. Taft's great prestige was probably responsible for the elimination of the House bill's provisions that placed limitations on industry-wide bargaining, a ban on mass picketing, and a detailed regu-

lation of internal union activities. Even with these modifications, the provisions of the Taft-Hartley bill bore a
substantial similarity to the Case bill passed by the previous Congress.

The House approved the conference measure on June 3
by a vote of 320–79, with 217 Republicans and 103 Democrats in favor of the bill. There were 66 Democrats, 12
Republicans and one American Labor Party member who
voted in opposition. In the Senate on June 6 the vote was
54–17 for passage with 37 Republicans and 17 Democrats
voting in favor and 15 Democrats and 2 Republicans opposed.[25] While the sentiment for the Taft-Hartley Act
was stronger among Republicans, it was a significant fact
that a majority of Democrats in both houses supported the
measure. The votes in both Houses were almost identical
to the original approval of the separate Hartley and Taft
bills. After approval by both Houses of Congress the bill
was sent to the White House.

On June 16, 1947, Truman received a letter from his
Council of Economic Advisors expressing its objections to
the bill. The Council took the following position:

> The fatal defect in the present Labor Bill as we view
> it is twofold. First, it provides no genuine solution for
> those industrial conflicts which threaten to paralyze
> the economy because of their size or the vital points at
> which they strike. Second, it would, however, inject
> the Government into almost innumerable details in the
> internal affairs of labor organizations of all sizes and in
> the collective bargaining process. . . .[26]

On June 20, 1947, when Truman vetoed the Taft-
Hartley bill, he said he still shared with Congress "the
conviction that legislation dealing with the relations between management and labor is necessary," but asserted
that the measure presented to him was "far from a solution" of the problems in that field.[27] He went on to say:

The bill taken as a whole would reverse the basic direction of our national labor policy, inject the government into private economic affairs on an unprecedented scale and conflict with important principles of our democratic society.[28]

Truman also maintained that the bill constituted "a long step toward the settlement of economic issues by government dictation," that it would "time and again . . . remove the settlement of differences from the bargaining table to courts of law," that it would "prove to be unworkable" and that it was unfair to labor. He contended that, despite the claim that the measure would simply equalize the positions of labor and management, "many of the provisions . . . considered in relation to each other reveal a consistent pattern of inequality."[29]

Organized labor denounced the act as a "slave-labor" measure and pledged itself to work for its repeal. With that purpose primarily in mind, the AFL at its October, 1947, convention set up Labor's League for Political Education.[30] At the same time, the CIO's Political Action Committee announced plans to organize a get-out-the-vote campaign in 1948 in order to defeat candidates regarded as unsympathetic to the cause of labor.[31]

Both Truman and Taft gave radio speeches on June 20, following the veto. Truman told radio listeners that it was "a shocking piece of legislation" that was "bad for labor, bad for management, and bad for the country."[32] He went on to say:

A bill which would weaken unions would undermine our national policy of collective bargaining. The Taft-Hartley bill would do just that. It would take us back in the direction of the old evils of individual collective bargaining. It would take bargaining power away from workers and give more power to management.[33]

Taft declared in his radio address that Truman's recommendation for a Congressional committee to study the whole labor question was "the standard plan of those who want to delay." Taft said that the bill "in no way" authorized government interference except in the case of the eighty-day injunction provision covering "national paralysis" strikes.[34] In regard to Truman's objection to the section of the bill authorizing the government to seek injunctions against national emergency strikes, Taft reminded his listeners that only a short time ago the government had obtained a court order to block the coal strike called by John L. Lewis. He also pointed out that Truman had recommended the drafting of striking railroad workers into the Army in 1946. Taft declared that the only new thing among Truman's objections was his reference to too much government interference.[35]

Truman's veto was easily overridden in both houses of Congress and the measure became law. Labor's last efforts to save the situation consisted of a deluge of mail to the White House supporting the President's veto.[36] Rallies were staged throughout the country, but all to no avail. The House voted to override the veto, 331–83. The Senate overrode the veto by six votes more than the required two-thirds majority, 68–25. There were 48 Republicans and 20 Democrats who voted to override.[37] More Representatives and Senators voted to override the veto than had voted for the original version compared to the additions to the ranks of those opposing it.

The law as it was finally passed provided for changes in administration, retained the unfair labor practices provisions from the Wagner Act, and introduced several regulations governing the conduct of unions. The unions were forbidden to coerce employees in their choice of collective bargaining representatives, discriminate or cause employers to discriminate against employees, cause payment for services not performed, or engage in jurisdictional strikes or secondary boycotts.

The closed shop was outlawed, and the union shop allowed, if approved by a majority in the bargaining unit. Thirty per cent of workers in a bargaining unit could petition the Labor Board for a decertification election, and if a majority of the voters approved, the union forfeited the right to act as bargaining representative. Damage suits against employers and unions were permitted for violation of contracts. A procedure to be used in emergency strikes was established, and the government was given the right to seek a postponement or suspension of such walkouts for a limited period through an injunction in the Federal District courts. Unions and corporations were forbidden to contribute to candidates for federal political office.

Supervisory employees were denied protection under the statute. The Federal Conciliation Service was made into an independent agency, unions seeking the service of the National Labor Relations Board were required to file their constitutions, bylaws, and financial statements with the U. S. Department of Labor, and their officers had to file an affidavit declaring they were not members of the Communist party or any organization supporting it.[38]

After its passage one of the first instances of labor resistance to the Taft-Hartley Act resulted from the effort of the International Typographical Union of the AFL to circumvent the law's provision banning the closed shop. Just before the act went into effect, the ITU adopted a "no-contract" policy under which union members, upon expiration of existing contracts, were to accept employment only under posted "conditions of employment" requiring a closed shop or under a special contract which in effect imposed closed shop conditions.[39] In November, 1947, the American Newspaper Publishers Association filed charges with the NLRB which in turn issued a complaint accusing the ITU of violating various sections of the new law.

At the end of November printers on Chicago's five major dailies, rejecting the publishers' demands for the customary annual contract, started a strike which lasted for more than a year. The NLRB then brought the ITU into court, and in March a Federal District Judge issued a temporary injunction restraining the union from continuing in effect or permitting any of the following acts:

(1). Demanding unilateral "conditions of employment," a closed shop, or a 60-day contract cancellation clause.

(2). Observing union rules which discriminate or cause employers to discriminate against non-Union employees in regard to hire or tenure of employment.

(3). In any manner supporting, authorizing, sanctioning, or encouraging subordinate local unions and ITU members to engage in or to continue to engage in any strikes, slow-downs, walkouts, or other disruptions of any kind to the business operations of newspaper publishers which are attributable to conduct banned by the order.[40]

Even though the union officials indicated that they would comply with the terms of the order, the judge held the ITU and its four top officials in contempt of court. He said he was convinced that they had "deliberately attempted since the issuance of the injunction to accomplish the objective against which the injunction was directed, namely, the continuance of closed shop conditions in the newspaper industry." Instead of assessing penalties, the judge ordered the ITU officers to file sworn statements "showing in detail the steps taken by them to comply with the decree."[41]

Labor was more successful in its opposition to the Taft-Hartley restriction on political expenditures. The CIO invited a test of the validity of that section of the law by publishing an editorial in the *CIO News* endorsing the candidacy of E. A. Garmatz of Baltimore for a vacant House seat to be filled at a special election in July, 1947.[42] Indictments against Philip Murray and the CIO itself were dismissed in March, 1948, by a federal district court, which held the pertinent provision of the act unconstitutional insofar as it prohibited any expenditure of a labor organization in connection with an election for federal office.

The Supreme Court, reviewing the decision on June 21, refused to rule on the question of constitutionality, but it held that the law was not intended to apply to political articles in regular union periodicals even when the expenses of such periodicals were met from union funds. In a concurring opinion, four members of the Court voiced the opinion that the political-expenditures ban was a clearly unconstitutional encroachment upon the freedom of speech and the press.[43]

A number of unions indicated that they would forego use of NLRB procedures rather than comply with the anti-Communist affidavit provision of the Taft-Hartley Act. Prominent labor leaders, notably Philip Murray of the CIO and John L. Lewis, a Vice President of the AFL and President of the UMW, refused as a matter of principle to sign affidavits. The situation was complicated when NLRB General Counsel Robert Denham ruled on August 19, 1947, that the requirement applied to officers of the parent labor bodies, the AFL and CIO, as well as to officers of individual unions.[44]

The NLRB reversed Denham's ruling in October, 1947, but this did not solve the problem for the AFL. Its thirteen vice-presidents not only were officers of international unions, but as AFL officers were officers also of more than a thousand directly chartered local trade and federal labor unions. In order to leave them free to follow the policies of their own unions on the affidavit question, and at the same time not deprive the federal labor unions of NLRB service, the AFL in October amended its constitution to make its president and secretary-treasurer the organization's sole officers and designate the vice presidents simply as members of its executive council. This action was taken over the opposition of Lewis, who vacated his seat on the executive council in protest, and two months lated "disaffiliated" the UMW from the AFL.[45]

By the end of August, 1948, a year after the Taft-Hartley Act had gone into effect, anti-Communist affidavits had been filed by over 81,000 union officers, including the officers of 89 of the AFL's 102 international unions, of 30 of the CIO's 41 international unions, and of 45 independent unions. Conspicuous among the holdouts, one or more of whose officers had not filed, were those of the UMW. Failure to sign anti-Communist affidavits led to a number of formal rulings by which the NLRB refused to place non-complying unions on the ballot in collective bargaining elections and sustained employers who refused to bargain with such unions.

Truman in his Taft-Hartley veto message had declared that "The so-called emergency procedure for critical nation-wide strikes would require an immense amount of government effort but would result almost inevitably in failure."[46] Pointing out that a Presidential board of inquiry "would be specifically forbidden to offer its informed judgment concerning a reasonable basis for settlement" of a dispute, he concluded that "Such inquiry, therefore, would serve merely as a sounding board to dramatize the respective positions of the parties." And he predicted that the required poll of employees on the last offer of an employer, prior to dissolution of the eighty-day anti-strike injunction for which the act provided, "would almost inevitably result in a vote to reject the employer's offer, since such action amounts to a vote of confidence by the workers in their bargaining representatives." The effect would be to reinforce the union "by a dramatic demonstration . . . of its strength for further negotiations."[47]

Despite this attitude at the time of the veto, however,

Truman had invoked the Taft-Hartley Act's "national emergency" provision in seven critical labor disputes by September, 1948.[48] Eighty-day injunctions were issued in connection with four of the disputes. In every case where employees were polled on the employer's last offer, the offer was overwhelmingly rejected. The injunction cases, however, did not all end either in stalemate or in settlement. Atomic energy workers at Oak Ridge, Tennessee, turned down the employer's final offer, but when the injunction expired, negotiations were resumed and the dispute was settled a week later without a strike. Bituminous coal miners on strike went back to work a few days after the injunction was issued, although not until after the union and its president had been found guilty of contempt for violation of an earlier restraining order.[49] An agreement was reached in an East Coast maritime dispute in August, 1948, two weeks before scheduled expiration of the eighty-day injunction. On the West Coast, however, the employer's final offer was voted on and rejected and five unions went on strike when the injunction expired at the beginning of September, 1948. One of the unions settled two months later, but an agreement achieving full settlement of the strike was not reached until November 25, at approximately the time of the first East Coast longshoremen's strike. The shipping association's final offer was rejected a few days before the injunction expired on November 9. Settlement of the strike that followed was announced on the same day that peace came into view on West Coast waterfronts.[50]

By 1948, those early experiences with the national emergency procedure were neither wholly encouraging nor wholly discouraging. In some instances employment of this procedure accomplished no more than postponement of a critical strike, but in others the enforced cooling-off period may have been helpful in promoting settlement.

In the cases where injunctions were not issued, the threat of injunctive action may have contributed to settlement.

The volume of NLRB cases and the volume of court cases involving unions increased under the Taft-Hartley Act, but there was no increase in the number of strikes. The fact was that the number and extent of strikes actually declined. During the first eight months of 1948, there were only 2,130 work stoppages, as against 2,958 in the first eight months of 1947, and 3,458 in the first eight months of 1946. The relative strike impact, moreover, was heavier in 1946 and 1947. The number of workers involved in stoppages in the first eight months of the year dropped from 8,228,000 in 1946 to 1,932,600 in 1947 and to 1,525,-000 in 1948; and the number of man-days of idleness from 96,850,000 in 1946 to 29,390,000 in 1947 and to 25,775,000 in 1948.[51]

The charge that the underlying purpose of the Taft-Hartley Act was to undermine organized labor did not seem to be borne out by events. There were few major provisions in the Taft-Hartley Act which did not have counterparts, with strong bipartisan support, in legislation previously introduced. The assumption of the Wagner Act had been that once unions were permitted to organize on an equal basis with employers, collective bargaining would be capable of solving most major problems of industrial disputes without government intervention except in the form of conciliation or mediation. The assumption of the Taft-Hartley Act was that in order to maintain industrial peace and protect the rights of employers, individuals, and the public as well as those of unions, government regulation had to extend to the procedures of collective bargaining. The fact that the unions did not suffer inordinately did not lessen the vigor of labor's denunciations of the act. One of the purposes of the law was to loosen the grip of union officials over the rank and file of union membership. By 1948, however, there was no appreciable relaxation of the hold that such leaders as John L. Lewis had on their unions. This aspect of the Taft-Hartley Act could have accounted at least in part for the fact that the drive for its repeal came more from union leaders than from the rank and file membership.

Despite the effects of the act, real and imagined, by the end of 1948 it had provoked a sufficient uproar among organized labor to provide Truman with an excellent political issue—one that was to prove to be the deciding factor between victory and defeat in his bid for reelection. President Truman's actions with regard to the passage of the Taft-Hartley Act were later criticized by Harry Millis and Emily Clark Brown, authors of *From the Wagner Act to Taft-Hartley*. Dr. Millis was a former Chairman of the NLRB. They theorized that:

> Possibly the President should have been somewhat more conciliatory toward a Congress which had exhibited such majorities in favor of the vetoed bill. Perhaps he could have achieved the better legislation he ostensibly sought by recognizing and complimenting the work Congress did on the measure and by pointing out the good or better aspects of the bill and indicating that such legislation, despite his specific January proposals, he would have accepted.[52]

But the political connotations attached to the Taft-Hartley Act by Harry Truman were more difficult to calculate. Truman shrewdly realized that the passage of the Taft-Hartley Act by a Republican-controlled Congress could be politically exploited in the 1948 election. He felt that the Taft-Hartley Act, at least in part, had destroyed Republican chances for a national victory in 1948. Truman politically was never more correct.

Notes: Chapter 9

1. John A. Fitch, "The New Congress and the Unions," *Survey Graphic* (April, 1947), p. 231.
2. Hadley Cantril (ed.), prepared by Mildred Strunk, *Public Opinion 1935–1946* (Princeton, New Jersey: Princeton University Press, 1951), p. 826.
3. *Public Papers of the Presidents: Harry S. Truman,* 1947 (Washington: U. S. Government Printing Office, 1963), p. 3.
4. *Ibid.,* p. 4.
5. *Ibid.,* pp. 4–5.
6. *Ibid.*
7. *Ibid.,* pp. 5–6.
8. *Washington Post,* January 14, 1947, Herzog Papers, HSTL.
9. Fitch, *op. cit.*
10. *Ibid.*
11. *Congressional Record,* 80th Cong. 2d Sess., p. 3081.
12. *Ibid.*
13. *Ibid.,* p. 42.
14. *Ibid.,* p. 47.
15. Memorandum, J. Donald Kingsley to Dr. John R. Steelman, April 4, 1947, Truman Papers, HSTL.
16. *Ibid.*
17. *Ibid.*
18. Digest of Labor Bills in 80th Congress, Record Group 174, National Archives.
19. *Ibid.*
20. *Ibid.*
21. Joel Seidman, *American Labor from Defense to Reconversion* (Chicago: University of Chicago Press, 1953), pp. 254–255.
22. Philip Taft, *Organized Labor in America* (New York: Harper & Row, Publishers, 1964), p. 579.
23. *Ibid.,* p. 580.
24. U. S. Congress, Senate, Committee on Education and Labor. *Labor Relations Program,* Hearings, 80th Cong., 1st Sess., p. 993.
25. *New York Times,* May 30, 1947.
26. Council of Economic Advisors to the President, June 16, 1947, Truman Papers, OF 407–B, HSTL.

27. *Public Papers of the Presidents: 1947*, pp. 288–289.
28. *Ibid.*, p. 289.
29. *Ibid.*, pp. 290–297.
30. Philip Taft, *The A. F. of L. from the Death of Gompers to the Merger* (New York: Harper & Brothers, Publishers, 1959), p. 311.
31. John H. Leek, *Government and Labor in the United States* (New York: Rinehart & Company, Inc., 1952), p. 298.
32. *Public Papers of the Presidents: 1947*, p. 298.
33. *Ibid.*, p. 299.
34. *New York Times*, June 21, 1947.
35. *Ibid.*
36. Taft-Hartley File, Truman Papers, OF 407, HSTL.
37. *Washington Post*, June 24, 1947, DNC Clipping File, HSTL.
38. Memorandum, Paul M. Herzog to the President, June 11, 1947, Truman Papers, OF 407, HSTL.
39. "Labor Disputes: 1947–1948," (typed), Record Group 174, National Archives.
40. *Ibid.*
41. *Ibid.*
42. *New York Times*, June 22, 1948.
43. *Ibid.*
44. *Ibid.*, August 20, 1947.
45. "Labor Disputes: 1947–1948," *op. cit.*
46. *Public Papers of the Presidents: 1947*, p. 295.
47. *Ibid.*, pp. 295–296.
48. National Emergency Disputes in 1948, Gibson Papers, HSTL.
49. *Ibid.*
50. "Labor Disputes: 1947–1948," *op. cit.*
51. *Ibid.*
52. Harry A. Millis and Emily Clark Brown, *From the Wagner Act to Taft-Hartley* (Chicago: University of Chicago Press, 1950), p. 392.

10

Toward a Full and Fair Employment Economy

IN THE POSTWAR PERIOD THE UNITED STATES WAS FACED BY
the threat of widespread unemployment. Nearly twelve
million men and women who had been in the armed forces
were released from duty and sought civilian jobs. The sudden termination of war production also threw millions of
war workers on the labor market. Prompt action by the
Truman administration was therefore needed in order to
devise and implement a comprehensive program to prevent a possible depression and the labor relations turmoil
that would accompany it.

Under the pressure of war demands, American industry
had enormously increased its production, not only of war
materials, but of civilian products as well. President Truman became convinced that the industrial machine in the
United States was obviously able to satisfy individual material wants, and that some means had to be found to assure
a full employment and sustain the purchasing power in
order to make it possible to utilize total industrial capacity
and raise the general standard of living.

Much of the thinking and discussion about the employment problem during the war and early postwar periods
came to center around the proposal that government
should assume responsibility for providing employment
opportunities for all persons able and willing to work. The

first point in President Roosevelt's "Economic Bill of Rights," which was contained in his State of the Union message to Congress in January, 1944, was ". . . the right to a useful and remunerative job in the industries or shops or farms or mines of the nation."[1] To make the right a reality, the idea was advanced that the federal government should estimate how much spending by all groups in the country would be necessary to achieve full employment, with the understanding that the government would make up whatever difference in total outlays might develop between actual and required levels.

It was impossible to say where this proposal originated. The concept was an outgrowth of the experience of the 1930's when the government was obliged to formulate a number of measures to cope with the unemployment problem. The basis for this approach to this problem could be found in the writings of John Maynard Keynes in England and of Alvin Hansen, an economics professor at Harvard University, in the United States.

Hansen was an advocate of what was called the "compensatory fiscal policy." He contended that if the government was firmly committed to compensatory action to guarantee employment, industry would have no occasion to fear loss of business, nor consumers loss of jobs. The resulting increase in confidence would tend to keep up demand and prevent the usual cyclical influences from checking investment and expenditure. A minimum of compensatory government spending then would suffice to overcome any unfavorable influences that should appear. He also asserted that, in any case, the cost of applying the policy did not compare with the cost to the nation of a major depression. This compensatory fiscal policy followed the policy of timing public works to take up slack in employment.

It also represented a more direct and comprehensive effort to plan for full employment. It sought to attack the

weak point in the private enterprise system, which sometimes had difficulty in assuring widespread and uninter-
rupted distribution of the products which the nation was
capable of producing. Hansen maintained, "Private business can and will do the job of production. It is the responsibility of government to do its part to insure a sustained
demand. We know from past experience that private enterprise has done this for limited periods only."[2] Opponents
of a compensatory fiscal policy feared that it would involve
a degree of government planning which would eventually
be fatal to private enterprise. Hansen, on the contrary,
held that "A positive governmental program looking toward full employment would greatly vitalize and invigorate
private enterprise."[3]

Additionally, in postwar America, the acceptance of the
famous "Beveridge Report" in Great Britain undoubtedly
contributed to the atmosphere favoring the passage of
legislation establishing new social security plans and the
extension, improvement, and revision of existing plans
with regard to full employment.

When President signed the Employment Act of 1946,
he committed the federal government to a similar policy
when he committed his administration to take "measures
necessary for a healthy economy, one that provides opportunities for those able, willing, and seeking to work."[4]

The law contained the following "declaration of policy."

It is the continuing policy and responsibility of the
Federal Government to use all practicable means consistent with its needs and obligations and other essential
considerations of national policy, with the assistance and
cooperation of industry, agriculture, labor, and state
and local governments, to coordinate and utilize all its
plans, functions, and resources for the purpose of creating and maintaining, in a manner calculated to foster
and promote free competitive enterprise and the general
welfare, conditions under which there will be afforded

useful employment opportunities, including self-employment, for those able, willing, and seeking to work, and
to promote maximum employment, production, and
purchasing power.[5]

Under the Act the President had the duty of formulating
programs to carry out the purposes of the law. To facilitate
cooperation between the Executive Branch and the Congress in fulfilling the objectives stated, provision was made
for the establishment of a joint Congressional Committee
consisting of seven members each of the Senate and the
House of Representatives. A Council of Economic Advisers was also provided for and was to be in the Executive
Office of the President. The Employment Act's provisions
naturally brought it into close contact with the postwar
problems of organized labor.

After the war spokesmen for labor, almost without exception, voiced the belief that the problems of unemployment were an immediate and serious danger. In his testimony before a subcommittee of the Senate Committee on
Banking and Currency in 1945, Philip Murray stated:

I come to your committee today as spokesman for
millions of American workers and veterans who need
above all else to have continuing employment at good
wages. . . . For all these people and their families the
hourly burning question is whether they can expect
soon to be gainfully employed—or for how long if they
do get a job. This doubt darkens their view of the
world ahead. They and the whole country need some
immediate concrete evidence that their elected representatives understand the needs of today as they understand them.[6]

An editorial in the September, 1945, issue of the *American Federationist,* the AFL monthly publication, stated:

Within ten days of the Japanese surrender at least

2,700,000 had been let out of their war jobs. Some found new jobs promptly, but most did not. Additional workers are slated for dismissal in the next few weeks. Meanwhile, the armed services are returning men to civilian life at an accelerated pace. Millions of jobs must be provided for these veterans.[7]

The editorial went on to observe that the AFL anticipated a total of eight million unemployed persons by the spring of 1946. The postwar legislative programs of the AFL, CIO, and Railroad Brotherhoods, formulated at the end of the war in 1945, all contained provisions designed to stop a decline in job opportunities or to check unemployment when and if it occurred. The AFL recommended to Congress legislation to stimulate the planning and construction of community facilities such as hospitals, schools, roads and airports, a national housing program designed to assure high and sustained levels of public and private construction, and more liberal unemployment-compensation legislation as requested by Truman in 1945. The CIO's legislative program included similar measures, as well as increased help to veterans, and a broader program of social insurance. Underlying most of labor's demands during the immediate postwar period was the fear that sooner or later widespread unemployment would reappear.

One answer to some of the problems of postwar employment was that of a guaranteed annual wage. Its advocates said that its adoption would not only put the responsibility on employers to provide regular work through slack seasons of normal years, but would go a long way toward eliminating cyclical depressions by assuring the steady mass purchasing power needed to sustain continuous production. They conceded, however, that year-round wage guarantees involved substantial risks for employers and that no one plan could be devised that would fit all cases.

The stated aim of responsible labor leaders was to win management cooperation in studying the possibilities of annual wage guarantees in individual companies and industries. The CIO, and to a lesser extent the AFL, carried on educational campaigns to acquaint union members with the advantages of the guaranteed annual wage and to prepare for new contract negotiations in the autumn of 1947, and the spring of 1948. Joseph Snider, an expert in labor–management relations, predicted that the guaranteed annual wage would become "the battle cry of labor in this generation, as the eight-hour day was in the last."[8]

Public interest in the annual wage was stimulated by the release by the White House on May 14, 1947, of a report made to the President at the end of February, 1947, by the Advisory Board of the Office of War Mobilization and Reconversion.[9] The OWMR report was the result of a two-year study of guaranteed wage plans made by a special research staff under the direction of Murray Latimer, former chief of the Railroad Retirement Board. It was supplemented by special studies carried out by the Bureau of Labor Statistics, and by Alvin Hansen of Harvard University and Paul Samuelson of the Massachusetts Institute of Technology. The studies were originally recommended to the President by the War Labor Board as a result of the steelworkers' 1944 demands, and the spending of $200,000 for the project was authorized by Congress in 1946.[10]

The most significant finding of the Latimer Report was that guaranteed annual wage plans were feasible in a "large variety" of industrial establishments, including those with considerable seasonal and cyclical fluctuation in production and employment. In transmitting the report to Truman the OWMR Advisory Board said: "The study shows clearly that the plans guaranteeing wages and employment, when suitably adapted to the needs and conditions of the industry or establishment, are valuable to the entire nation and afford a wholesome and desirable means for improving both worker and employer security."[11]

The report made no suggestion of action by the government to impose guaranteed wages on industry, emphasizing the government's role as one rather of facilitating and encouraging private experimentation. The OWMR Advisory Board drew the following conclusions from the report:

> Guaranteed wage plans should not be the subject of legislative action but should be referred to free collective bargaining.
>
> Employers and employees should take "definite responsibility" for stabilizing operations in individual plants and industries in order to raise the level of general economic security.
>
> Existing statutes dealing with social insurance, minimum wages, fiscal and tax policies should be "reviewed and evaluated" to determine whether they help or hinder the establishment of private guarantee plans.
>
> The guaranteed wage should be considered a "significant, but not all-sufficient, tool" for maintaining full employment.
>
> A "continuing study" of guaranteed wage plans should be made, preferably by the President's Council of Economic Advisers, and government agencies should provide data to those interested in wage guarantees.[12]

Advocates, particularly the CIO, felt that the community tended to benefit from the guaranteed wage. Workers who felt secure in their jobs would make better customers for local merchants. They were more likely to make planned long-term expenditures on homes and durable goods if they were able to count on a steady future income. If the guaranteed wage reduced the total of unemployment in a community it would also tend to reduce relief expenditures by the community in periods of depression.

Still more far-reaching benefits were claimed for the guaranteed wage when the CIO asserted that universal adoption of the guaranteed wage would stabilize the whole economy and would go far toward providing full employment at all times. A CIO pamphlet claimed that:

If employers will agree to give labor regular work and pay, the whole community will benefit. When factories run full blast, farmers and storekeepers prosper. When plants and men are idle, farm prices fall and business loses. A floor under the income of wage-earners would mean a floor under the national income.[13]

Even though there were no major postwar developments in the area of guaranteed annual wages, a need was served by the Truman administration's detailed analysis of the problem. Since there was no sharp drop in employment after World War II, labor's demands for a guaranteed wage became less frequent by 1948.

But the American experience with unemployment following the 1929 depression was too recent and too vivid to make it necessary to have to convince organized labor that a policy implementing full employment would be beneficial. The background of the Employment Act of 1946 revealed several precedents for such action.

The immediate legislative precedent for the Employment Act of 1946 was contained in the statute setting up the Office of War Mobilization and Reconversion which was passed October 3, 1944. In addition to this function as coordinator of the nation's war mobilization program, the director was to formulate and recommend, in consultation and cooperation with state and local governments, industry, labor, agriculture and other groups, plans to meet the problems arising out of the transition from war to peace. The original proposal for this legislation went further toward a genuine full employment program than the final act, since the latter was limited to transitional problems. Failure to include more specific planning machinery in the War Mobilization and Reconversion Act led to further discussion during the debate on this legislation. James Patton, President of the National Farmers Union, submitted a proposal to the War Contracts Subcommittee of the Committee on Military Affairs to have the government guarantee a $40 billion level of capital investment every year, estimated as being necessary for a full-employment gross national product of $200 billion.[14] The War Contracts Subcommittee, after securing the viewpoints of interested government agencies and departments drew up a new bill, known as the "Full Employment Bill," in which the concept of a guaranteed fixed level of capital investment was rejected for a more comprehensive but a less specific approach to full employment. This bill was transmitted to the Military Affairs Committee on December 18, 1944, by Democratic Senators James Murray of Montana and Harry S Truman of Missouri in connection with the Subcommittee's report entitled "Legislation for Reconversion and Full Employment." On January 12, 1945, a revised bill, S. 380, was introduced in the Senate by Senator Murray and referred to the Banking and Currency Committee. An identical bill, H. R. 2202, was introduced in the House by Democrat Wright Patman of Texas on February 15, 1945, and was referred to the Committee on Expenditures in the Executive Departments.[15]

In the Senate, hearings were held during July and August, 1945, before a subcommittee of the Banking and Currency Committee, of which Senator Wagner of New York was chairman. Testimony at these hearings crystallized both the support and the opposition of full employment. Labor leaders argued for federal legislation to protect the interests of labor as a basic condition for a full employment economy. Philip Murray and other labor leaders placed great emphasis on proposals asking for higher minimum wages, fair employment practices, and the cooperative planning of government, business, and labor. On the full employment bill in general, friendly witnesses said that it would provide purchasing power and an expanded market which would aid the entire economy. They also argued that it would help prevent depressions and their accompanying human miseries.[16]

Opposition witnesses came from business spokesmen led by the National Association of Manufacturers and the U.S. Chamber of Commerce. These witnesses placed their emphasis upon a reduction of the government's activities in the economy, and argued that the purposes of the full employment bill could not be achieved in the free enterprise system; that it would result in regimentation, inflation, and continual deficit spending. Other persistent arguments advanced by the opposing witnesses were that depressions were inevitable and that fear of unemployment was a necessary incentive for good work.[17]

With a few minor changes, the subcommittee gave its approval to the original bill in its report to the full committee on September 15, 1945. The full committee likewise gave its approval to the bill, issuing its final report on September 22, 1945.[18] A dissenting report was also issued at this time and included Democratic Senators George Radcliffe and J. William Fulbright of Arkansas, and Republican Senators Robert Taft of Ohio, C. Douglass Buck of Delaware, and Bourke Hickenlooper of Iowa. Among those voting for the original bill were Democratic Senators Wagner, Glen Taylor of Idaho, Hugh Mitchell of Washington, Abe Murdock of Utah, and Republican Senator Charles Tobey of New Hampshire.[19]

In the course of the Senate's debate on the measure, which was held from September 25 to 28, 1945, three amendments proposed by Senators Radcliffe and Taft were accepted in modified form. One amendment provided that any outlays by the federal government needed to attain full employment must be consistent with the needs and obligations of the government, and that other essential considerations of national policy needed to be taken into account. A second amendment provided for a balanced budget over a reasonable number of years, "without interfering with the goal of full employment." The third, and last amendment of any importance, provided that employment should be considered as including self-employment in agriculture, commerce, industry, or the professions. On September 28, 1945, the amended bill was passed by a roll call vote of 71–10.[20]

In the House of Representatives hearings on the proposal were held by the Committee on Expenditures in the Executive Departments. The hearings lasted for six weeks, beginning on September 25, 1945.[21] The arguments used by witnesses on both sides of the question were similar to those delivered at the Senate hearings.

On October 25, 1945, Truman wrote to John McCormack, the House Majority Leader, urging him to secure the passage of the full employment legislation in the House. The letter said in part:

Dear John:

I am most anxious that the House Committee on Expenditures of Executive Departments report out the Full Employment legislation. Such legislation is of the utmost urgency and importance to the future of our nation. . . .

Full employment legislation has the firm and complete support of my administration. The Senate has already passed such legislation, and I am sure that the House will want to make its position clear to the American people at the first possible opportunity.

I do not refer to any specific bill. I refer to the general purposes and principles of full employment legislation.

If this legislation could be reported out of committee so that it could be passed by the Congress by Thanksgiving, it would give that day particular significance for millions of American families who remember only too well the dark days of the depression, and want reassurance that we shall never again have another 1932.

Very sincerely,
Harry S Truman[22]

Despite these efforts by Truman to secure prompt action, the House Committee's report was not issued until December 5, 1945, approximately a month after the hearings were ended. The House substitute bill differed from the Senate version in several important respects. The declaration of the right of every worker to employment opportunity and of the federal government's responsibility for full employment was eliminated. Instead, it was provided that the policy of the government was to be aimed at a high level of employment, production and purchasing power, at prevention of economic fluctuations by expanding and contracting public works and loans, and at the avoidance of competition with private business on the part of the government.

The House Committee's bill, while rejecting the proposal for a national budget, provided machinery to accomplish much of the same purpose. Provision was made for an annual economic report on general business conditions, tendencies toward inflation or deflation, and recommendations for further action. Under the House Committee bill, a three-man Council of Economic Advisers was to be established to submit reports and recommendations to the President. The bill also established a joint committee of Congress to act upon the President's report and recommendations.[23]

Two minority reports were issued, one stating that the measure was just another way to spend the taxpayer's money, and the other that the House measure gave inadequate recognition to the government's obligation. Debate in the House, was held on December 13 and 14, 1945, but various amendments were defeated and the substitute bill as reported by the majority was passed 255–126.[24] During the conference committee's consideration of the two bills, Truman made it clear on several occasions that he favored the Senate version and opposed the bill passed by the House.

During the debate in the House, Democrat Walter

Granger of Utah caustically referred to the bill as the "Alabama Hayride of 1946."[25] Party lines vanished during the debate, and many of the arguments were the same as those which had been used in the Senate. In favor of the strongest bill possible were Democrats Wright Patman of Texas and George Outland of California. Many members from both parties were satisfied with the committee's bill, among them Democrat William Whittington of Mississippi, and Republican Walter Judd of Minnesota. A small group, led by Republican Clare Hoffman of Michigan and Democrat John Gibson of Georgia, were opposed to any kind of full employment legislation.

Some changes were incorporated by the conference committee which narrowed the gap between the bills originally passed by the two bodies, but a number of basic differences from the Senate measure still remained. On February 5, 1946, the Conference Committee reported out a bill, entitled the "Employment Act of 1946." The Conference bill was passed in the House of Representatives on February 6, 1946, by a vote of 320–84, and in the Senate by a voice vote.[26]

Much of the activity under the Employment Act was directed toward making known employment conditions and needs by means of an Economic Report made by the President. Such a report was to be transmitted to Congress within sixty days after the beginning of each regular session, starting with the year 1947. It was required to contain information on:

1). The levels of employment, production, and purchasing power obtaining in the United States and such levels needed to carry out the policy declared in section 2;

2). Current and foreseeable trends in the levels of employment, production, and purchasing power;

3). A review of the economic program of the Federal Government and a review of economic conditions affecting employment in the United States or any considerable portion thereof during the preceding year and of their effect upon employment, production, and purchasing power; and

4). A program for carrying out the policy declared in section 2, together with such recommendations for legislation as [the President] may deem necessary or desirable.[27]

Supplementary reports were to be made to Congress by the President, including such recommendations as he deemed necessary or desirable to achieve the policy of affording employment opportunities. When transmitted to Congress, the Economic Report and supplementary reports were to be referred to the Joint Committee that would be created under the terms of the legislation.

Membership in the specially created Council of Economic Advisers was to consist of three persons appointed by the President, by and with the consent of the Senate. Each member was to receive a salary of $15,000 a year. The duties and functions of the Council were as follows:

1). To assist and advise the President in preparation of the Economic Report;

2). To gather timely and authoritative information concerning economic developments and economic trends, both current and prospective, to analyze and interpret such information in the light of the policy declared in section 2 for the purpose of determining whether such developments and trends are interfering, or are likely to interfere, with the achievement of such policy, and to compile and submit to the President studies relating to such developments and trends;

3). To appraise the various programs and activities of the Federal Government in the light of the policy declared in section 2 for the purpose of determining the extent to which such programs and activities are contributing, and the extent to which they are not contributing, to the achievement of such policy, and to make recommendations to the President with respect thereto;

4) . To develop and recommend to the President national economic policies to foster and promote free competitive enterprise, to avoid economic fluctuations or to diminish the effects thereof, and to maintain employment, production, and purchasing power;

5) . To make and furnish such studies, reports thereon, and recommendations with respect to matters of Federal economic policy and legislation as the President may request.[28]

In the exercise of its duties, the Council could establish advisory bodies and consult with such representatives of industry, agriculture, labor, consumers, state and local governments, and other groups as was deemed advisable. The Council had, to the fullest extent possible, to utilize the services, facilities, and information of other government agencies as well as of private research agencies, to avoid duplication of effort and expense.

The seven members each of the Senate and House of Representatives, who were to make up the Joint Committee on the Economic Report provided for by the Employment Act, were chosen by the President of the Senate and the Speaker of the House of Representatives, respectively. As nearly as was feasible, the party representation had to reflect the relative membership of the majority and minority parties in the two chambers of Congress. The functions of the Joint Committee were:

1) . To make a continuing study of matters relating to the Economic Report;

2) . To study means of coordinating programs in order to further the policy of this act; and

3) . As a guide to the several committees of the Congress dealing with legislation relating to the Economic Report, not later than May 1 of each year (beginning

with the year 1947) to file a report with the Senate and the House of Representatives containing its findings and recommendations made by the President in the Economic Report, and from time to time to make such other reports and recommendations to the Senate and House of Representatives as it deems advisable.[29]

Vacancies in the membership of the Joint Committee were not to affect the power of the remaining members to execute the functions of that body. Either the Joint Committee or any duly authorized subcommittee could hold hearings. To enable the Council of Economic Advisers to carry on its work, the Act authorized the appropriation of necessary sums; a limit of $345,000 per fiscal year was fixed for the salaries of the members and of officers and employees. For the operations of the Joint Committee on the Economic Report, the law authorized $50,000 for each fiscal year, or as much thereof as might be necessary.[30]

When he signed the bill on February 20, 1946, Truman said that it was not all he had hoped for, but he termed it a constructive beginning.[31] Recalling his ideas concerning full employment, he stated in his *Memoirs:*

> I knew that full production would be our greatest weapon against inflation. . . . That was my reason for requesting, in the twenty-one-point message to the Congress on September 6, 1945, full-employment legislation. My objective was to carry out, during the reconversion period, the economic bill of rights which had been formulated by President Roosevelt.
> By full employment, I meant the opportunity to get a good peacetime job for every worker who was ready, able, and willing to take one. Making jobs, or making people work, was in no sense a part of the full-employment program. I did feel, however, that it was the responsibility of the government to inspire private enterprise with confidence by giving assurances that all the facts about full employment and opportunity would be gathered periodically for the use of all . . .[32]

Despite its weaknesses and inadequacies, the Employment Act of 1946 was one of the most significant developments ever promulgated in American governmental policy concerning employment matters. One of its apparent weaknesses was to provide for the federal government's commitment to create job opportunities for all people who sought work, but without providing specific machinery such as a program of public works, needed in order to achieve this function. The steps needed to carry out the purposes of the Employment Act also required congressional authorization. With the authority of the law split between the executive and legislative branches of this government, the possibility of friction was increased.

The Employment Act, however, represented a tremendous change from the government's philosophy regarding labor problems that it had held only two decades previously. The Council of Economic Advisors in a sense replaced the National Resources Planning Board, which had been abolished in 1942 by a Congress that was suspicious of any board activities touching upon economic planning. Many members of Congress at that time doubted the propriety of any government agency that concerned itself with economic planning. The fact that the postwar Seventy-Ninth Congress established the Council of Economic Advisors in the Executive Office was an indication of a more general acceptance by the public of the role of government in economic affairs, and particularly those involving labor.

Truman thought of the full employment program for labor as an extension of the New Deal, and he also was convinced that he wanted to avoid the unemployment that followed World War I and therefore learn a lesson from history. It was clear, however, that the Truman administration undertook to have the government of the United States assume a vast responsibility with regard to the prevention and relief of unemployment. Truman also concluded that the Employment Act of 1946 gave "positive expression to a deep-seated desire of the American people for a sustained attack upon the perennial problem of mass unemployment."[33]

In a similar way, Truman also felt that the government was responsible for instituting a program for a fair as well as a full employment economy. During the postwar years, the question of racial discrimination in employment was one of the most difficult problems of labor relations. The movement to forbid discrimination in employment by federal statute developed out of the wartime experiences of the Fair Employment Practice Committee, from June, 1941, through June, 1946.

When Truman became President in 1945, his record in regard to the passage of a law that would create a permanent Fair Employment Practices Committee was superior to that of Franklin Roosevelt. Truman had long supported legislation to control discriminatory practices in employment. Although never considered as strong a liberal as Roosevelt, it was felt by one authority, Louis Kesselman, that Truman's record in this matter was better than Roosevelt's, "perhaps out of zeal to demonstrate his faithful adherence to liberal Democratic principles."[34] In the Senate, Truman had supported anti-poll tax bills and as Vice President favored a FEPC with strong powers of enforcement.

In his reconversion message to Congress on September 6, 1945, Truman had spoken of the "substantial progress" toward elimination of prejudice that had been made during the war and said "this American ideal" should be maintained as "an integral part of our economy."[35] He also advocated the establishment of a permanent FEPC. In his radio appeal for popular support for his legislative program on January 6, 1946, he criticized the "small handful of congressmen in the Rules Committee" who were blocking the FEPC bill in the House and said "I am sure that the overwhelming mass of our citizens favor this legislation and want their congressmen to vote for it."[36]

Truman thus made FEPC legislation one of the important points in his reconversion policies.

On June 5, 1945, Truman sent a letter to Democrat Adolph J. Sabath of Illinois, chairman of the House Rules Committee, in which he expressed a strong appeal for a FEPC. The letter said in part:

Dear Mr. Congressman:

I understand that the House Appropriations Committee has deleted from the War Agencies Appropriation Bill for the fiscal year beginning July 1, 1945, all appropriations for the Fair Employment Practice Committee.

This action will have the effect of abolishing the Committee and terminating its work without giving the Members of the House of Representatives an opportunity to vote on the question. . . . Discrimination in the matter of employment against properly qualified persons because of their race, creed, or color is not only un-American in nature, but will lead eventually to industrial strife and unrest. It has a tendency to create substandard conditions of living for a large part of our population. The principle and policy of fair employment practice should be established permanently as a part of our national law.[37]

Truman's letter to Sabath went a long way toward changing the public's attitudes toward the new President. An analysis of Truman's mail concerning the FEPC was drawn up by his staff and showed that the letter established him as a "liberal in the eyes of liberals."[38] Between June 1, and June 23, 1945, President Truman received about four thousand letters and telegrams concerning the FEPC. All but nineteen of the messages were in support of the FEPC and Truman's action concerning it.[39] Prior to Truman's letter to Congressman Sabath the messages asked Truman to act personally. Following Truman's letter all but a few messages congratulated the President on his action.[40]

Before June 5, there were frequent urgings for Truman to follow the lead set by President Roosevelt. A typical message of this type said, "We call upon you as President of the United States on the basis of your pledge to carry on the noble work of your predecessor, Franklin Delano Roosevelt to speak up boldly both for appropriations to continue FEPC and passage for permanent FEPC legislation." After the letter to Congressman Sabath, the congratulatory messages seldom referred to Roosevelt, but instead praised Truman for his clear statement. A typical message said: "Your courageous stand on the establishment of a permanent FEPC merits the gratitude of all Americans concerned with the basic principles of democracy."[41]

The mail also revealed that the FEPC had a great deal of group support in the postwar years. Labor organizations gave it the most support followed, in order, by community organizations, Negro organizations, churches, and women's groups. Of the messages received at the White House during this period nearly forty per cent were from labor organizations.

Although no permanent FEPC legislation had been enacted on a federal level by 1948, a number of states passed laws forbidding discrimination on the basis of race, color, or religion in public works, public employment, or in the performance of defense contracts. Among the states that passed laws that fell into any of the three categories were New York, New Jersey, California, Kansas, Nebraska, Oregon, Illinois, Pennsylvania, Minnesota, Connecticut, and Massachusetts. New York State pioneered these laws when it passed legislation that prohibited a labor organization from engaging in racial discrimination in membership or employment conditions, by union constitution, bylaws, ritual, or tacit agreement. Kansas, Nebraska, and Pennsylvania imposed similar bans on unions.[42]

President Truman's civil rights program, however, concerned much more than discrimination in employment. Truman viewed racial discrimination in much broader terms. On December 5, 1946, Truman issued Executive Order Number 9808 that created the President's Committee on Civil Rights.[43] The Committee was instructed to study the statutes and authority of the federal, state and local governments in their dealings with civil rights and to determine how their positions could be strengthened in that regard.

The Committee was an advisory board of fifteen eminent Americans including Charles E. Wilson, President of the General Electric Company, James Carey, Secretary-Treasurer of the CIO, the Right Reverend Henry Knox Sherill, Presiding Bishop of the Protestant Episcopal Church, and Boris Shishkin, an AFL economist. Wilson, who served as chairman, was a Republican, while most of the other members of the Committee were Democrats.[44] The Committee's report to the President was published in 1947 under the title, *To Secure These Rights*.[45]

In its report the Committee recommended that the President ask Congress to enact several new civil rights laws. The Committee also invited the states to enact similar laws. For example, it invited both to enact "fair employment practices laws" forbidding private employers from discriminating against persons seeking jobs because of their race, religion, or national origin.[46] The use of the power of government to protect through law civil liberty against invasion by private persons is controversial. The recommendations of the President's Committee on Civil Rights that such legislation be extended started a public debate that is still in progress. Opponents of civil rights legislation used a variety of arguments.

They argued that civil rights violations committed by private persons had their origin in prejudice and intolerance and consequently could not be prevented by law and government action. The conclusion was drawn that the only feasible way of opposing private interference with civil rights was through education and voluntary activity looking toward a lessening of prejudice and intolerance. The President's Committee anticipated this argument and attempted to answer it in these terms: The Committee agreed that education and other long-term methods had to play an important part in creating greater respect for civil rights on the part of all people, but it insisted that human conduct, as opposed to human nature, could be controlled by laws. The Committee said, "It may be impossible to overcome prejudice by law, but many of the evil discriminatory practices which are the visible manifestations of prejudice can be brought to an end through proper government controls."[47]

The Committee believed that a law forbidding racial and religious discrimination in employment practices might not immediately persuade employers and older employees to drop their prejudices against hiring or associating with workers of different races and religions. But it was convinced that such a law could prevent such persons from putting their prejudices into practice by denying employment to otherwise qualified workers.

Permanent FEPC legislation represented a major portion of unfinished business by the Seventy-Ninth and Eightieth Congresses. Although Truman had repeatedly urged passage of such legislation, he should not be blamed for its failure. Politically, he became more and more intent on holding the Democratic Party together, a task that had been difficult for Roosevelt. Louis Kesselman said that Truman was criticized increasingly by FEPC proponents for failing to clarify the role of the President's Committee in the reconversion period and for not continuing his early courageous leadership for permanent legislation on the subject. Kesselman also asserted that the lack of a working majority in Congress served to limit President Truman's influence over passage of the legislation as it had his predecessor's.[48] Although Truman's primary purpose in appointing the Committee on Civil Rights had been to recommend civil rights legislation, Truman was often criticized as using this Committee's report not only for a foundation for legislative recommendations, but also for the political implications that it held. One author maintained that Truman used his entire civil rights program, to a certain degree, to gain votes; although he conceded that Truman's use of civil rights in his campaign was good politics and did not necessarily detract from his sincerity.[49] There is a great deal of truth in this assertion, since Truman was in politics to win reelection in 1948, and he was willing to use whatever were his strongest weapons to assure victory.

Truman appeared convinced that one of the principal economic problems facing the United States was the achievement of maximum production and continued prosperity. He knew that discrimination depressed wages and income of minority groups, resulting in curtailed purchasing power and reduced markets. Reduced markets cut down production which in turn lowered employment levels. Rising fear, prejudice, and insecurity aggravated discrimination in employment during the postwar years and after. But it can at least be said that Harry Truman set in motion the machinery to attempt to solve this vast social and economic problem.

It was also the Truman Administration's general contention that minimum wage laws would reduce dissatisfaction in industry and thus reduce labor strife; however, no such legislation had been passed by the end of 1948. The Truman administration also argued that minimum wage legislation would act as an incentive to the low-wage employers to improve methods in their plants. It was felt that if these employers were confronted by the necessity of paying higher wages they would introduce technological improvements and change their plant organization in an attempt to make the workers worth the new wages they would receive. Truman's strongest arguments for minimum wage legislation, however, were that it would give workers a better standard of living.

There were also a number of attempts made during the postwar years to provide a labor education extension. Because the language of the various labor extension bills was considered to be vague in many places about the actual machinery to implement the service, no action was ever taken on any of the bills in the Seventy-Ninth or Eightieth Congresses.[50] No subsequent Congress ever passed any legislation that would have established a labor extension service, although there was scattered support for it throughout the 1950's.

There was irony in the fact that any attempts at labor extension were made at all in the postwar years. With all of the bitter controversy over the Taft-Hartley Act, Congress, which was labeled by historians as extremely anti-labor, was at the same time seriously considering a measure of potentially great importance to labor. The fact that the labor extension bills were overlooked in later historical investigations created an imbalance in the image of the postwar Congresses. It was true that these Congresses were very much concerned with bills that were quite restrictive in regard to labor practices. But it was also true that the labor extension bills were modest, quiet, and nonprovocative. It was not an impossibility that, if passed, their final consequences would have been as far-reaching as those which generated all of the headlines.

Labor education extension was probably one of the only subjects during the postwar period upon which all major labor organizations agreed among themselves. At their 1947 Conventions, the AFL, the CIO, and the Railway Brotherhoods all adopted resolutions in favor of the legislation. The Truman administration's support was evident as Secretary Schwellenbach stated in 1947:

> It is appropriate that the Department of Labor should be the Federal agency to develop the minimum standards to guide the administration of programs at the local level by the States. The Department, through the work of the Bureau of Labor Statistics, the Division of Labor Standards, the United States Employment Service, the Women's Bureau, the Wage and Hour Division, and other divisions and bureaus, can make readily available much of the information which is needed in the development of such worker's education programs. It is the obviously logical clearing house for labor education, and for the development and promotion of the basic principles and techniques of workers' education.[51]

In his Economic Report of January 14, 1948, Truman pointed out:

> As members of labor unions voting on strike action and other union issues, and as citizens reacting to economic policies and candidates for office, they need a higher degree of economic and civic education. The general requirements of intellectual competence are steadily moving upward. . . . The adjustment of the labor force to the changing character of our economy thus commences with the problem of education.[52]

Although Truman evidently did not take as active a part in the efforts to provide a labor education extension as did Schwellenbach, the above statement indicated Truman's recognition of the need for such an institution. The attempt by the Truman Administration for such a service stands out during the course of the emotion-packed and troubled labor relations of the postwar years because of its potential importance to the betterment of those relations. And the bipartisan support that it received runs contrary to some of the more anti-labor tags placed on the postwar Congresses.

Time and again in the postwar years, Truman repeated his requests with a call for a health and decency standard for America's working force. He felt that this would improve morale and create more efficient workers while sustaining mass purchasing power and promoting high levels of employment. In this respect Truman once again transcended the desires of any economic or political interest group and made his appeals on the basis of what he felt was good for the country as a whole.

Notes: Chapter 10

1. Samuel I. Rosenman (comp.), *The Public Papers and Addresses of Franklin D. Roosevelt*: 1944–1945 (New York: Harper & Brothers, 1950), p. 41.
2. Alvin H. Hansen, *After the War—Full Employment* (Washington: National Resources Planning Board, February, 1943), p. 4.
3. *Ibid.*, p. 5.
4. *Public Papers of the Presidents: 1946*, p. 125.
5. Stephen K. Bailey, *Congress Makes A Law* (New York: Columbia University Press, 1950), p. 228.
6. U. S. Congress, Senate, *Hearings*, Subcommittee of the Committee on Banking and Currency, 79th Cong., 1st Sess., p. 224.
7. *American Federationist*, September, 1945, p. 4.
8. Joseph L. Snider, *Analysis of the Guarantee of Work and Wages* (Boston: Subdivision of Research, Graduate School of Business Administration, Harvard University, 1947), Record Group 250, National Archives.
9. Murray W. Latimer, *Guaranteed Wages*, Report to the President by the Advisory Board of the Office of War Mobilization and Reconversion (Washington: U. S. Government Printing Office, 1947).
10. *Ibid.*
11. *Ibid.*

12. *Ibid.*
13. Philip Murray, "Guaranteed Wages the Year Round" (CIO Pamphlet, 1945).
14. Analysis of Reconversion and Economic Problems, Record Group 250, National Archives.
15. *New York Times*, January 13, 1945.
16. Bailey, *op. cit.*, pp. 104–110.
17. *Ibid.*, pp. 133–143.
18. *Ibid.*, pp. 116–117.
19. *Ibid.*, pp. 117–118.
20. *Congressional Record*, 79th Cong., 1st Sess., p. 9304.
21. Bailey, *op. cit.*, pp. 155–160.
22. Truman, *Memoirs*, Vol. I, p. 492.
23. Bailey, *op. cit.*, pp. 167–168.
24. *Ibid.*, pp. 220–221.
25. *Congressional Quarterly*, Vol. II, 1946, p. 70.
26. Bailey, *op. cit.*, p. 227.
27. "Employment Act of 1946," *Monthly Labor Review* (April, 1946), pp. 586–587.
28. *Ibid.*, p. 587.
29. *Ibid.*, pp. 587–588.
30. *Ibid.*, p. 588.
31. *Public Papers of the Presidents: 1946*, p. 126.
32. Truman, *Memoirs*, Vol. I, p. 491.
33. *Ibid.*, p. 494.
34. Louis Kesselman, *The Social Politics of FEPC* (Chapel Hill: University of North Carolina Press, 1948), p. 212.
35. *Public Papers of the Presidents: 1945*, p. 282.
36. *Public Papers of the Presidents: 1946*, p. 6.
37. Harry S. Truman to Adolph J. Sabath, June 5, 1945, Truman Papers, OF 40, HSTL.
38. Analysis of the President's Mail on FEPC, Truman Papers, OF 40, HSTL.
39. *Ibid.*
40. *Ibid.*
41. *Ibid.*
42. David Ziskind, "Countermarch in Labor Legislation," *Labor in Postwar America*, ed. Colston E. Warne (New York: Remsen Press, 1949), pp. 687–688.

43. Executive Order No. 9808, Truman Papers, OF 40, HSTL.
44. Reynold J. Davis, "A Study of Federal Civil Rights Programs During the Presidency of Harry S. Truman" (unpublished Master's thesis, University of Kansas, 1959), pp. 47–48.
45. *To Secure These Rights*, The Report of the President's Committee on Civil Rights (Washington: U. S. Government Printing Office, 1947).
46. *Ibid.*
47. *Ibid.*, p. 103.
48. Kesselman, *op. cit.*, p. 214.
49. Davis, *op. cit.*, pp. 126–129.
50. *Congressional Quarterly Almanac*, Vol. V, 1949, p. 457.
51. Papers of Lewis B. Schwellenbach, Statement on S. 1390, February 16, 1948, Before the Senate Committee on Labor and Public Welfare, Library of Congress.
52. Economic Report of the President, House Document 498, 80th Cong., 2d Sess., Record Group 174, National Archives.

11

Labor's Postwar Political Role

ON THE MORNING OF NOVEMBER 3, 1948, JUST HOURS AFTER being elected in his own right as President of the United States, Harry Truman told a friend, "Labor did it."[1] Those words were uttered with the full knowledge that the political influence of organized labor had indeed played a tremendous part in Truman's victory. Political action on the part of organized labor, however, was not at all a new endeavor. The history of the American labor movement contained many examples of independent political action by organized workers, particularly in times of declining industrial activity and widespread unemployment. At such times the ordinary trade union methods of winning increases in wages and improvements in working conditions were largely ineffective. Legislation seemed the best means of advancing the interest of the wage earners and the unions were apt to turn to concerted use of the ballot to compel attention to their demands by state and national legislatures.

With the organization of the AFL and intensive use of the strike, the boycott, and other economic weapons during the closing decades of the nineteenth century, less and less attention was given to grandiose projects for an independent labor party or a combination with farmers to control the national government. A nonpartisan political policy was

213

gradually developed by the AFL and thus afforded an outlet for the energies of politically minded union members while avoiding the danger of diverting the whole attention of the organized workers to politics.

The nonpartisan political policy resulted in endorsement during the ensuing years of more candidates of the Democratic party than of the Republican party. Republicans sometimes charged that organized labor had become an adjunct of the Democratic party, but President Samuel Gompers of the AFL consistently maintained that there had been no departure from policy of nonpartisanship. This policy was temporarily put aside, however, in the Presidential campaign of 1924 when the AFL pledged its support to the Progressive candidacies of Senators Robert La Follette and Burton Wheeler for President and Vice President. The AFL leaders afterwards asserted that there had been no departure from the nonpartisan political policy in 1924, but that the union had merely thrown its support to an independent ticket in one election as it was free to do.

Organized labor failed to play an important part in national politics during the 1920's and this was attributed by most political writers to the relatively small proportion of American workers who were members of trade unions and to the predominance of the craft-union form of organization in which the workers could expect to gain more through negotiation than through mass political activity.

A radical change was brought about by the rise of industrial unionism during the 1930's under the protection and encouragement of such New Deal measures as the National Industrial Recovery Act, the Guffey Coal Act, and the National Labor Relations Act. In order to channel the political power of a broader-based unionism, a new organization known as Labor's Non-Partisan League was set up in April, 1936, under George Berry, President of the Pressman's Union, with the support of John L. Lewis and Sidney Hillman.[2]

Although the immediate objective was the reelection of President Roosevelt, resolutions adopted at the first convention of the League, in August, 1936, said it was to be a permanent organization that would serve in future years as an instrument of independent political action by organized labor. The AFL refused to join the League because it felt that it was a political movement not in keeping with the AFL's nonpartisan political stand. The sweeping victory of President Roosevelt in the 1936 election, when he received over four million more votes than he had in 1932, was attributed by Labor's Non-Partisan League principally to the votes and support given him by the expanded industrial unions of the CIO.[3]

By 1940, however, the League had lost much of its effectiveness because of the hostility between the AFL and the CIO. At the 1937 convention of the AFL a resolution was adopted which said that the union would oppose every candidate "who would in any way favor, encourage, or support the CIO."[4] After the election of 1940, labor support for the New Deal was further divided by the withdrawal of the United Mine Workers from the CIO. John L. Lewis made good his promise to resign as President of the CIO if President Roosevelt were elected for a third term. Philip Murray, an ardent supporter of the New Deal, was chosen as his successor. By the end of the 1930's there was little doubt that organized labor had acquired a new sense of the importance of meaningful political action.

During the immediate postwar years the political interests of organized labor were given expression through various channels and with varying degrees of success. The two principal organizations involved in this political activity were the Political Action Committee of the CIO and Labor's League for Political Education, founded by the AFL in 1947.

The Political Action Committee of the CIO was established on July 7, 1943, in order to bring labor's political force to bear in the 1944 campaign.[5] The new committee was charged by the Executive Council of the CIO with the "task of conducting a program of political education in the deepest and most practical sense of that word—education in the full and enlightened exercise of the responsibilities of citizenship." Its activities were to be nonpartisan in the sense that the committee would not accord support wholly to any existing political party. It was to be partisan in the sense that the committee would "coordinate and assist in the political activities of organized labor."[6] Under the leadership of Sidney Hillman, President of the Amalgamated Clothing Workers, the CIO–PAC played an active role in the 1944 election campaign.

The CIO–PAC published figures after the election showing how it had helped to "win the election."[7] Hillman and the CIO–PAC were praised at the 1944 CIO Convention, and extensive plans were laid for another major effort in the 1946 elections.[8] The 1946 election went badly for the CIO–PAC, however, when most of its endorsed candidates were defeated soundly. The CIO–PAC efforts in the 1946 election were less forceful because of some of the anger that Truman had incurred in his strike policies. Much of its effectiveness was, however, neutralized by the charges of Communist influence in the CIO brought about by the increasing anti-Communist feeling after the war.

After the passing of the Taft-Hartley Act the AFL, which had been relatively passive, felt the need for making a change in its political methods. The 1947 AFL convention, therefore, ordered the establishment of a special political agency, and in December of that year Labor's League for Political Education was established.[9] The LLPE was financed by voluntary contributions and it was directed to acquaint the workers of the country with the economic and political views of the AFL, to prepare and disseminate information on the attitude of candidates for nomination or election to federal office, raise funds, and employ a staff for carrying out its duties. A conference of international presidents was called in December, 1947, to make final plans for launching the LLPE. In explaining the need for an intensified political program by the AFL, President William Green informed the conference that he had been surprised by the strength of anti-labor feeling in Congress and by the overriding of President Truman's veto of the Taft-Hartley Act.[10]

The postwar pattern of political action followed by the CIO was essentially the same as the AFL pattern. The CIO–PAC sought to exert influence at election times, following more the nonpartisan policy that had long been used by the AFL. It tried to influence the course of legislation by acting as a pressure group and it was interested in the administration and interpretation of whatever legislation was passed. Like the AFL, the CIO was active in municipal and state as well as national politics.

Financial support was also a significant part of organized labor's strength in political action. Congress, however, after 1943, began to limit union political expenditures. The Smith-Connally Act prohibited contributions by labor unions to national elections, but the law contained loopholes which were fully exploited by CIO–PAC in the 1944 election. The Smith-Connally Act referred to national "elections," but said nothing about nominations. The CIO–PAC was thus able to collect contributions and spent over $475,000 on a publicity campaign prior to the national convention which nominated Roosevelt and Truman.[11]

The Taft-Hartley Act of 1947 changed this temporary nature of the expired Smith-Connally Act's prohibitions by prohibiting political contributions by unions in elections, primaries, or conventions which involved federal offices. Some state legislatures enacted similar bans on union action in state elections, but neither federal nor state legislation covered independent political affiliates of unions such as the CIO–PAC or the AFL–LLPE.[12] There was, therefore, still room for large amounts of financial help for candidates during the elections of 1948.

In the postwar period the most important political activity of organized labor was reserved for the 1948 election where its participation reached a peak. By 1948, Truman felt that he owed much of his political success to organized labor. He had received the support of the railroad brotherhoods in his 1940 senatorial campaign; he felt that labor support was responsible for his nomination in 1944 as Vice President; and he thought that his reelection in 1948 would again prove that organized labor still supported him at the polls.

Prior to his election, however, Truman strove for labor's support from his first 1948 campaign efforts, and at no time did he ever take that support for granted. His whole campaign was geared to gathering labor's votes by his extensive use of the Taft-Hartley Act as a main issue. Truman also thought that politically labor would stay with the Democratic Party. During the course of the campaign he did everything in his power to see to it that labor stayed there, but he was very aware of the pro-Wallace feeling among labor, particularly in the CIO.

Even before his nomination in July, 1948, it was clear what Truman's plans were in regard to the role of the labor vote in the election. On June 3, 1948, Truman left Washington aboard an eighteen-car train for Berkeley, California, to deliver the annual commencement address at the University of California.[13] The trip was ostensibly one of a "nonpolitical" nature. It could hardly have turned out to be more political, however, as Truman spoke from the rear platform of the train on numerous occasions as he traveled Westward. At Crestline, Ohio, he told a crowd that "on this nonpartisan, bipartisan trip that we are taking here, I understand there are a whole lot of Democrats present, too."[14] After being presented a pair of spurs at Grand Island, Nebraska, he said "When I get them on, I can take Congress to town."[15] At Spokane, Washington, he said, "I understand that you are not very happy over the Labor Act of 1947. . . . Your only remedy is November, 1948."[16]

The trip ended on June 18, and so did the first phase of Truman's campaign. Truman later wrote that the purpose of the trip was to give the people a chance to "form their opinions of me and my program" and to "discuss the facts of the situation" in 1948.[17] The crowds had grown bigger as the trip progressed and Truman grew more confident in his delivery. Truman was never a spellbinding speaker, but the crowds warmed to his "off-the-cuff" approach, and the President was convinced that the "average, everyday American" would vote for his reelection if he could only give him "the full story."[18]

During the trip he was informed of the death of Secretary of Labor Schwellenbach on June 10. Truman was saddened by the death of his old friend and termed him "a great Senator, a great judge, and a great Secretary of Labor."[19] Schwellenbach's successor was Maurice Tobin, a former Governor of Massachusetts. Tobin's labor record was a good one and he was an excellent speaker. Tobin's appointment was delayed until August, after the Demovratic Convention had nominated Truman. Truman obviously wanted to use Tobin's noted speaking ability in his campaign, and his appointment no doubt helped the campaign for labor's votes. During the course of the campaign Tobin delivered more than a hundred speeches in twenty states and the Taft-Hartley Act was the theme of most of them.[20]

The Republicans were the first to hold a nominating convention in 1948, beginning it in Philadelphia on June 21. In that year, in the belief that it was the Republicans' turn to win a Presidential election, many prominent aspirants in the GOP sought the nomination. Senator Taft entered the race first, since he was in command of the

Republican Senate after the victory of 1946. Governor Thomas Dewey, titular leader of the party because of his nomination in 1944, moved softly prior to 1948, saying little about national issues. Harold Stassen revived the aspirations he had held ever since 1940 when he gained recognition for restoring the Republicans to power in Minnesota. He angered Senator Taft, however, by entering the Ohio primaries against the Senator, and annoyed the internationalist Republicans by debating with Governor Dewey in Oregon. Stassen was victorious in the Wisconsin and Nebraska primaries but lost the Oregon primary, which all but eliminated him for the nomination. Governor Earl Warren of California, like Dewey, took no stand on the leading controversial issues of the times and did no active campaigning. Taft's conservatism was Dewey's gain. Warren's geographic remoteness in California and his inactivity on the national level, Stassen's mistakes, and Dewey's control of the New York delegation all combined to produce the latter's nomination.[21]

President Truman's political fortunes had gone up and down after the 1946 elections. They went up after the veto of unpopular GOP bills; they went down when prices rose and during the preconvention attempts by fractional groups such as the Dixiecrats and the Americans for Democratic Action to replace him on the ticket. The desire of these groups to get rid of Truman was surpassed, however, by their inability to agree on anyone to take his place. As time went on, it became clear that Truman would be the Democratic candidate.

After a movement to nominate Dwight Eisenhower collapsed, and after the majority of the delegates had adopted a strong civil rights plank, the Democratic convention, also meeting in Philadelphia, nominated Truman for President and Senator Alben Barkley of Kentucky, with a reputation for leadership in action and moderation in attitude, for Vice President. The Southern Democratic revolt started early in 1948 after Truman's announcement of his civil rights program: his recommendations for a federal anti-lynch law, for the repeal of poll taxes, and for federal fair employment practices legislation.[22]

After the Democratic Convention, in which a strong civil rights plank was put into the party's platform, many Southern delegates rejected it and in less than a week established the States Rights Party, which nominated Governor J. Strom Thurmond of South Carolina for President and Governor Fielding Wright of Mississippi for Vice President.[23]

But Truman stood his ground on the civil rights issue. He had, since the early days of his Presidency, advocated a "workable fair employment practices program," [24] and he did not change that idea in 1948. He lost the votes of many Southerners by his stand, but he also won labor votes at the same time.

Despite many predictions and polls from all sides stating that Truman was a sure loser, a faint hope began to stir when Truman aroused the tired and disunited Democratic Convention with the declaration:

> I am therefore calling this Congress back into session July 26th. On the 26th of July, I am going to call Congress back and ask them to pass laws to halt rising prices, to meet the housing crisis—which they are saying they are for in their platform. . . . Now, what that worst 80th Congress does in this special session will be the test.[25]

Labor leaders had no qualms about the special session being "politics." On the contrary they welcomed the opportunity to put parties and candidates on record on the questions of inflation and housing. Union members were generally responsive to Truman's declaration to the reassembled Congress that, "Positive action by this government is long overdue. It must be taken now."[26] Labor leaders were also heartened by his willingness to carry the fight to the Republicans.

The open division in the Democratic Party caused the CIO–PAC to postpone its Presidential endorsement. With Dixiecrats and Wallace Progressives resorting to secession and party regulars plotting to sidetrack Truman for another candidate, there was considerable indecision in the ranks of the Democrats, even among those who had firmly opposed an alliance with the Progressive Party movement. Consequently, the CIO–PAC built its campaign around issues rather than personalities, and avoided either rejecting or defending Truman. Until well after the party conventions, the CIO–PAC was against the policies of the Republican Eightieth Congress rather than for any particular Presidential candidate. It was not until the end of August that the CIO Executive Board formally endorsed Truman for the Presidency.[27]

One of the most difficult problems which labor faced was that of overcoming the public fear of unions which had originally brought the Republicans into control of Congress in 1946. With that purpose in mind the CIO–PAC made inflation rather than repeal of the Taft-Hartley Act the principal issue of the campaign. In terms of political exploitation the choice could scarcely have been better, since nearly every citizen had in his own daily experience convincing proof that the rising cost of living had not been checked by the policy of decontrolling prices. That fact alone gave weight to the CIO–PAC's contention that the policies of the Republican Congress held no solution for postwar economic problems.

There was one embarrassing aspect of this line of attack, however, in the fact that a Democratic-controlled Congress had been responsible for the original decision to abandon price controls. The CIO–PAC made a special effort, therefore, to demonstrate that the leadership of the organized campaign against the OPA had come from groups holding a strategic position in the Republican Party. It capitalized upon the NAM's admission that it had spent $3,000,000 to kill OPA, and publicized damaging quotes from the NAM's nationwide campaign against controls.[28] As proof that the NAM view was the Republican view, the CIO–PAC cited the Eightieth Congress's refusal to adopt adequate anti-inflation measures even after six months of competition had led to a twenty per cent increase in consumer prices.[29]

The CIO–PAC contended that savings had cushioned the widening gap between effective consumer demand and production. They insisted that if the trend were permitted to continue until savings were completely exhausted, depression would result. In line with its belief that placing greater purchasing power in the hands of the consumer was the key to inflation control, the CIO specifically advocated the enactment of an excess profits tax, price control of basic commodities, that the federal government should be given the authority to allocate and ration commodities in short supply, and the control of bank and consumer credit.[30] Once the CIO had carefully defined its position on inflation, the CIO–PAC repeated and elaborated its parent organization's basic arguments. It also consistently related other issues to public concern over the rising cost of living. In demanding a seventy-five cent hourly minimum wage and broader coverage for the wage-hour law, one of its most effective points of attack was the incredulousness of expecting a forty-cent hourly minimum to act as a safeguard against substandard living conditions.[31]

The CIO–PAC also demanded a fifty per cent increase in old-age benefits, and campaigned for an expansion of social security coverage, a program of sickness and disability insurance, and a nationwide system of unemployment insurance.[32] The questions of rent control and tax policy also lent themselves to an exploitation of the issue of inflation. The CIO–PAC hammered at the Eightieth Congress's favoritism to the higher income groups in tax matters, and at its failure to adjust wage minimums or social security benefits. Transcending all other criticisms, however, was the assertion that the Republicans were responsible for continued inflation and, therefore, that the privations of the aged, the widow, and the orphan rested upon their heads. Many of these arguments were at best good political fodder, but many voters accepted their premise.

Although the CIO used inflation as its chief issue, it was the Taft-Hartley Act that was responsible for the tremendous effort exerted by the AFL in the 1948 election. The AFL launched a program in the summer of 1947 that was dedicated to the repeal of the law and to the defeat of every Congressman who had voted for it. The Executive Council of the AFL decided to circumvent Section 304 of the Taft-Hartley Act which banned direct union contributions to federal political campaigns. It advised the 1947 AFL Convention to create a new political body to be supported by one-dollar contributions, given voluntarily by AFL members.[33]

The convention resolution which established the LLPE stated that the organization was being created "in order to serve most effectively the interest of the workers of the nation," and "to further the economic and political policies of the American Federation of Labor."[34] The resolution went on to elaborate:

1). It shall be the duty of "Labor's Educational and Political League" to prepare and disseminate information by such media of communication as the League may decide for the purpose of acquainting the workers of the nation with the economic and political policies of the American Federation of Labor.
2). The League shall prepare and disseminate information concerning the attitude of candidates for nomination and/or election to federal offices, with par-

ticular reference to their attitude toward the American Federation of Labor.[35]

This policy represented no real change from the political techniques previously employed by the AFL. The new body was finally named Labor's League for Political Education and was composed of four operating departments. The Department of Finance was given the job of collecting one dollar from each AFL member. The Department of Public Relations prepared leaflets, pamphlets, press releases, articles, and cartoons. The Department of Political Direction prepared, maintained, and distributed the records of all public office holders and prospective candidates for federal office.[36]

The Department of Organization was given the task of coordinating the local and state bodies, and of helping to persuade other groups to cooperate with the AFL in its political program. The emphasis was placed on the close congressional races, where it was felt anti-labor congressmen could be defeated, and men more favorable to labor could be elected.[37]

The states in which the AFL concentrated its efforts for the Senate contests were West Virginia, Illinois, Minnesota, Idaho, Iowa, and Tennessee, while the major elections to the House centered primarily on the larger industrial centers. The AFL's stress was placed on getting out a large labor vote, and appeals were made to get every union member to register, especially since there could be no legal limitation on such appeals. Mass meetings, rallies, and newspaper and radio appeals were employed more widely than ever before, while the printing of the candidates' records, comparisons of the various party platforms, and electioneering were resorted to on a large scale. The AFL also hired a commercial public relations firm to publicize its cause in a more professional manner, utilizing all media of influencing public opinion. The use of radio was relied on heavily.[38]

One of the AFL's greatest contributions to Truman's campaign came in September, 1948. Identical invitations were issued to Dewey and Truman to write Labor Day messages on subjects of interest to labor for the AFL's widely circulated monthly magazine *American Federationist*.[39] Dewey put himself in the position of defending the Eightieth Congress and the Taft-Hartley Act. Truman, however, hammered at the law, and taunted that "The Republican platform is afraid to mention the Taft-Hartley Act."[40] Truman also listed some of the omissions of the Eightieth Congress's legislative record, such as public housing, an increased minimum wage, and improved old-age assistance and survivors benefits.[41]

Dewey's arguments were less specific and in many instances vague. He never mentioned the Taft-Hartley Act by name, but rather pledged himself to maintain the freedom of the American labor movement, declaring that the first act of the Hitler dictatorship had been to destroy the German unions. He stated that "we must zealously guard against any attempts at union busting and against efforts to make the American labor movement a political company union."[42]

Dewey's tone was "lofty," while Truman employed sharply worded barbs thrown at the Republicans, and specifically discussed those "bread and butter" issues of interest to working men. The AFL no doubt knew that Truman would use this approach, and his forceful denunciation of the Taft-Hartley Act was in keeping with its own political goals.

The support for Truman by organized labor was far from unanimous. A. F. Whitney endorsed him, but Alvanley Johnston and most others refused to come out for the President. Dan Tobin of the AFL Teamsters said that he wanted "nothing to do with him."[43]. John L. Lewis attacked Truman in what Alfred Steinberg called his "fault-less Shakespearean language."[44] At the UMW convention in October in Cincinnati, Lewis declared "If there is any man in this convention or any man in this organization that wants to trade me off for a Truman, let him trade and be damned to him." The UMW convention adopted a political report that characterized Truman as being "unfriendly" to the union. The report gave indirect support to Dewey by stating that he had never "uttered any statements that reflect upon the integrity or the objectives of the United Mine Workers or its officers or members." The report also emphasized the right of every UMW member to vote in accordance with his own convictions, but avoided putting the union definitely on record for Dewey.[45]

The pollsters almost unanimously predicted Truman's defeat. The Gallup, Crossley, and Roper polls all indicated a Dewey victory because of the votes that would be drawn away from the Democrats by the Progressives and the Dixiecrats. Wallace ran on a platform advocating "peace and prosperity." He made a strong bid for labor votes by advocating the restoration of price controls, repeal of the Taft-Hartley Act, and raising the minimum wage to a dollar per hour. Wallace blamed postwar troubles on the "Truman-Taft" group and was critical of Truman's "big-business appointments" and dismissal of prominent New Dealers during his administration. The nationwide pollsters thus were certain of Truman's defeat, and by a substantial margin. For days and even weeks before the election, columnists Drew Pearson, Joseph and Stewart Alsop, Arthur Krock, and Walter Lippmann predicted Dewey's election and discussed what he would do when he became President of the United States.[46] Harry Truman, however, had different ideas as to whether the electorate was ready to afford Dewey a victory that was "a sure thing."

Truman did not officially open his campaign until September, 1948, but it was obvious that he had "unofficially" opened it in his State of the Union message on January 7, 1948. In that speech he referred to the Taft-Hartley Act by saying, "I made my attitude clear on this act in my veto message to the Congress last June. Nothing has occurred since to change my opinion of this law."[47] His "nonpolitical" tour in June was another step in his campaign, as was his calling Congress back for a special session after his nomination. He had carefully calculated his campaign moves with an eye toward the labor vote. It was therefore no accident that his first official campaign speech was given before a huge crowd on Labor Day in Detroit's Cadillac Square.

In that speech Truman set the tone of his entire campaign. He warned, "that Eightieth Republican Congress failed to crack down on prices but it cracked down on labor all right!"[48] He asked the crowd if they wanted the Taft-Hartley Act which would "enslave" the workingman or if they wanted to "go forward with an administration whose interest is the welfare of the common man?" Truman concluded that "we are going to win this crusade for the right!"[49]

Truman's aggressive stumping on his famous "whistle-stop" campaign was to carry him nearly 32,000 miles and include approximately 350 speeches, most of which pertained to "That do-nothing Eightieth Congress." One newspaper sneeringly reported that "Evidently he has yet to learn that an intelligent public long ago wearied of this type of campaigning."[50] Much that Truman said was strictly campaign bombast, and was not always very original. Former Republican President Herbert Hoover was once again set up as a straw man for attack. Truman reminded a New York City crowd:

Over in Central Park men and women were living in little groups of shacks made of cardboard and old boxes.

They were known as "Hoovervilles." Out here on Eighth Avenue veterans were selling apples. Ragged Individualism, I suppose that's what you would call it.[51]

In Raleigh, North Carolina, he described a "Hoover Cart" . . . the remains of the old tin lizzie being pulled by a mule because you can't afford to buy a new car or gas for the old one."[52] When Truman attempted to draw the broad social issues of the campaign his vocabulary was reminiscent of election campaigns of fifty years before. He told an Iowa audience:

> The Republican strategy is to divide the farmer and the industrial workers—to get them to squabbling with each other—so that big business can grasp the balance of power and take the country over, lock, stock and barrel.[53]

He also included the melodramatic warning:

> These Republican gluttons of privilege are cold men. They are cunning men. And it is their constant aim to put the Government of the United States under the control of men like themselves. They want a return to the Wall Street economic dictatorship.[54]

More than 12 million people turned out to hear Truman speak during the campaign. Curiosity and the prospect of political sensationalism may have accounted for the presence of many, but the speeches probably had more substance than the political name-calling which made the headlines. Before the end of the campaign the listeners had become quite responsive. Most observers, however, failed to realize the changing temper of the crowds and to understand the significance of their numbers. Nearly all of the polls were still predicting that Truman would be soundly defeated.

Truman was most effective in discussing specific policies affecting the interests of the various economic classes. Long before they had reached a decision for whom to vote, many of those listening in the whistlestops of the farm states must have felt an uneasy concern as he reminded them that:

In 1948, the Republican's Eightieth Congress refused to grant funds for the Commodity Credit Corporation to provide storage space for grains. This means that farmers will have to sell their grain at dump prices or let it rot in improper storage.[55]

Capitalizing upon the farm element's concern over the future price supports, Truman declared, "Parity must be our continuing goal."[56] The President warned, however, that the Republicans would not continue farm aid, and quoted the prediction of Republican Senator Arthur Capper of Kansas, Chairman of the Senate Committee of Agriculture, ". . . that there would be a drive in the next Congress to reduce the support price levels in 1949."[57] Truman quoted the blunt statement of Republican Representative Leon Gavin of Pennsylvania, "I'm telling you right now that sooner or later you'll have to discontinue the price support program, and you may as well start reconciling yourself to that fact. The sooner you stop it the better off the country will be."[58] Truman's attack along this line had a telling effect on election day.

In industrial centers Truman followed the lead of the CIO–PAC and LLPE and concentrated upon the questions of inflation, and the labor policies of the Eightieth Congress. He declared in his Detroit speech, "Make no mistake, you are face to face with a struggle to preserve the very foundations of your rights and your standards of living."[59] Frequently he cited the statement of Republican Senator Kenneth Wherry of Nebraska to the NAM who said, "I do not need to remind the membership of this association that it was the Republican leadership in the Senate and the House that was responsible for ending OPA."[60] Truman offered this statement as proof that "the forces of big business, operating through the Republican Party, tore down the protection against high prices which had been built up for our people."[61]

With equal effectiveness he played upon labor's fear that a Republican victory would lead to renewed attacks upon the rights of unions. In Akron, Ohio, Truman quoted the statements from Representative Fred Hartley's book *Our New National Labor Policy*. Hartley had written, "I am well aware . . . of the political difficulties of eliminating the New Deal social legislation. It cannot be repealed at a single stroke."[62] Truman also delighted in noting Hartley's statement that:

> No sooner had the Taft-Hartley Law been enacted over the Truman veto than the Republican leaders of both House and Senate . . . decided that no more legislation to which organized labor could object would be passed until after the presidential election of 1948.[63]

Truman's appeal to class fears was not his only effective campaign technique. He was apparently correct in his analysis of the character of the public's aspirations. He believed that a majority of the voters were motivated more by the hope of a better and more secure life, than by the fear of too much governmental intervention. For that reason he took an unequivocal stand in favor of broader social benefits. At Indianapolis he stated:

> I am proud of our record on Social Security. But it is not enough. Millions of workers are not yet covered by its benefits, and those benefits are not nearly high enough to meet today's excessive prices.[64]

In another speech at Buffalo, New York, he maintained:

A great, rich country like ours can afford decent housing for its citizens. We must do three things: We must build more homes, we must build homes that people—particularly young people—can afford, and we must clear out and rebuild the slums.[65]

And he also asserted at Indianapolis:

The best health facilities and the finest doctors in the world are not much help to the people who cannot afford to use them. I proposed a national system of health insurance in 1946 and I have urged it repeatedly since that time. There is no other way to assure that the average American family has a decent chance for adequate medical attention.[66]

Such declarations, as it turned out, included nearly everything for everyone, and had great appeal for voters.

Truman wound up his campaign in St. Louis with another hard-hitting speech. He again pounded at the Taft-Hartley Act by saying that "It was passed with the idea, so the Republican leaders in the Congress said, of putting labor in its place. They wanted to take the bargaining power away from labor. . . ."[67] After this address Truman retired to his home in Independence to await the verdict of the voters as to whether his energetic efforts had been enough to return him to the White House.

Voters were unable to learn the results of the election until the following morning. Truman was elected with 303 electoral votes. Dewey received 189 electoral votes and Thurmond 39, while Wallace failed to gain a single electoral vote despite the fact that his popular vote was nearly as large as Thurmond's. Truman carried all Western states except Oregon, all Southern states except Alabama, Louisiana, Mississippi, and South Carolina. In the Midwest, he took Minnesota, Wisconsin, Iowa, Illinois, and Ohio. He also won in Kentucky, Missouri, and West Virginia.[68] As the Republicans had anticipated, Truman lost several Southern states to the States Rights' candidates. The votes cast for the Progressive Party, led by Wallace, cost Truman New York and Maryland. Truman lost heavily in the Northeast, but he did manage to salvage Rhode Island and Massachusetts. What the Republicans had not counted on was that Truman would carry much of the Midwest and California. Truman became one of the few Presidents to win without New York.

It was a tremendous personal triumph for Truman. He had won on his own merits; he had beaten Wallace and the Dixiecrats; and he had smashed several prominent local Democratic bosses, notably Boss Ed Crump of Tennessee, who had formally endorsed Thurmond and opposed the pro-Truman candidate for United States Senator, Estes Kefauver. The 1948 election also was notable for the large number of non-voters and also for those who made up their minds late in the campaign. This helped to impair the accuracy of the public opinion polls. For those who did vote, one study of voting behavior found that Negroes voted almost two to one for Truman, as did the Catholics. Truman received a majority of the votes cast by those under thirty-five years of age and those who had less than a college education. There was a high percentage of non-voters among farmers, but those who voted went about two to one for Truman. He also carried practically all of the nation's biggest cities, and Democrats won both houses of Congress by comfortable margins.[69]

There was some truth to the quip that "Dewey snatched defeat out of the jaws of victory."[70] The result of the election was very close and Dewey could have won if he had carried California, Illinois, and Ohio. If he had won in these three states he would have had 267 electoral votes, and if he had carried any two of them, it would have thrown the election into the House of Representatives. Dewey would have won if there had been a shift of 29,000 votes out of more than 10,000,000 votes cast in these three states.[71]

These states had large agricultural populations which were extremely important in Truman's victory, but they were also states with large blocs of labor votes. It seems doubtful that Truman could have won without the large numbers of labor votes in the industrial areas. Truman himself conceded that Ohio and California were the "key states in the election."[72] He had confounded the pollsters with his victory, and organized labor was not shy about claiming credit for their part in it. The *CIO News* said, "Frankly, we don't intend to be a bit modest about the part organized labor played in the Democratic victory."[73]

Harry Truman had calculated correctly that labor would stay with the Democratic Party. One poll showed that of those workers who voted only eleven per cent of those with union membership voted for Dewey, while only seventeen per cent of the nonunion workers voted for him. Truman at the same time received fifty-six per cent of the union members vote and thirty-seven per cent of the nonunion vote.[74] These figures would seem to indicate that labor had indeed "done it" for Truman, or at the very least, had played a significant part in reelecting him as President of the United States.

Notes, Chapter 11

1. *New York Times*, November 4, 1948.
2. Joseph G. Rayback, *A History of American Labor* (New York: The Macmillan Company, 1959), p. 357.
3. Philip Taft, *The A. F. of L. from the Death of Gompers to the Merger* (New York: Harper & Brothers, Publishers, 1959,) p. 305.
4. *Report of the Proceedings of the Fifty-Seventh Annual Convention of the American Federation of Labor, 1937,* p. 115.

5. Joseph Gaer, *The First Round* (New York: Duell, Sloan, and Pearce, 1944), pp. 176–180.
6. *Ibid.*
7. *CIO News*, November 13, 1944.
8. *CIO News*, November 27, 1944.
9. *Report of the Proceedings of the Sixty-Sixth Annual Convention of the American Federation of Labor, 1947*, p. 607.
10. Philip Taft, *Organized Labor in America* (New York: Harper & Row, 1964), p. 613.
11. Lloyd G. Reynolds, *Labor Economics and Labor Relations* (New York: Prentice-Hall, Inc., 1954), pp. 388–389.
12. *Ibid.*, p. 389.
13. R. Alton Lee, "Harry S. Truman and the Taft-Hartley Act" (unpublished Ph.D. dissertation, University of Oklahoma, 1962), p. 146.
14. *Public Papers of the Presidents: Harry S. Truman, 1948*, Washington: U. S. Government Printing Office, 1964), p. 284.
15. *Ibid.*, p. 297.
16. *Ibid.*, p. 307.
17. Truman, *Memoirs*, Vol. II, pp. 178–179.
18. *Ibid.*
19. *Public Papers of the Presidents: 1948*, p. 313.
20. Lee, *op. cit.*, p. 160.
21. Robert Blanchard, Richard Meyer, and Blaine Morley, *Presidential Elections, 1948-1960,* Research Monograph No. 4, Institute of Government, University of Utah, 1961, pp. 8–9.
22. *Ibid.*, p. 9.
23. *Ibid.*
24. Truman, *Memoirs*, Vol. II, p. 182.
25. *Public Papers of the Presidents: 1948*, pp. 409–410.
26. *Ibid.*, p. 418.
27. Taft, *Organized Labor in America, op. cit.*, p. 613.
28. "Brother, What a Congress," *Economic Outlook* (August, 1948), p. 2.
29. *Ibid.*
30. *Here's How They Stack Up*, cio–pac pamphlet (1948), Record Group 174, National Archives.
31. "Raise Wage-Hour Act to 75¢," *Economic Outlook* (April, 1948), p. 3.

32. "Brother, What a Congress," *op. cit.*, p. 4.
33. Morton Leeds, "The AFL in the 1948 Elections," *Social Research*, XVII (1950), p. 208.
34. *Report of the Proceedings of the Sixty-Sixth Convention of the American Federation of Labor, 1947*, p. 407.
35. *Ibid.*
36. Leeds, *op. cit.*, p. 209.
37. *Ibid.*, p. 210.
38. *Ibid.*, p. 211.
39. *American Federationist*, September, 1948.
40. *Ibid.*, p. 30.
41. *Ibid.*
42. *Ibid.*
43. Alfred Steinberg, *The Man From Missouri* (New York: G. P. Putnam's Sons, 1962), p. 309.
44. *Ibid.*
45. *New York Times*, October 9, 1948.
46. Blanchard, Meyer, and Morley, *op. cit.*, pp. 10–12.
47. *Public Papers of the Presidents: 1948*, p. 6.
48. *Ibid.*, p. 477.
49. *Ibid.*, p. 479.
50. *New York Sun*, October 8, 1948, Record Group 174, National Archives.
51. *Public Papers of the Presidents: 1948*, pp. 909–910.
52. *Ibid.*, pp. 823–824.
53. *Ibid.*, p. 505.
54. *Ibid.*, pp. 505–506.
55. *Ibid.*, p. 795.
56. *Ibid.*, p. 764.
57. *Ibid.*, p. 762.
58. *Ibid.*, p. 606.
59. *Ibid.*, p. 478.
60. *Ibid.*, p. 655.
61. *Ibid.*
62. *Ibid.*, p. 746.
63. *Ibid.*, p. 747.
64. *Ibid.*, p. 803.
65. *Ibid.*, p. 722.
66. *Ibid.*, p. 805.

67. *Ibid.*, p. 936.
68. *New York Times*, November 3, 1948.
69. Blanchard, Meyer, and Morely, *op. cit.*, pp. 10–11.
70. Jules Abels, *Out of the Jaws of Victory* (New York: Henry Holt and Company, 1959).
71. *Ibid.*, p. 290.
72. Truman, *Memoirs*, Vol. II, p. 221.
73. Quoted in Abels, *op. cit.*, p. 272.
74. Angus Campbell and Robert L. Kahn, *The People Elect a President* (Ann Arbor: University of Michigan Press, 1952), p. 28.

12

Conclusions

IT IS AN UNDENIABLE FACT THAT HARRY TRUMAN THOUGHT of his entire domestic policy as an extension of Franklin Roosevelt's New Deal. Truman, therefore, approached the problems of labor relations with a sense of continuing the policies of his predecessor. During his first term in office, Truman made his efforts concerning labor's problems an integral part of his proposals for Congressional action in the fields of economic and social welfare. From his September 6, 1945, "reconversion" speech to his most ardent political appeals during the 1948 campaign, Harry Truman made labor questions an important segment of what was to be known after 1948 as the "Fair Deal."

There are three general conclusions that can be drawn from the Truman administration's efforts to solve the problems of labor relations from 1945 to 1948. First, the complexity of the problems was enormous, and this complexity made implicit the difficulty of solving them. Secondly, the 1945–1948 period was not so anti-union as it appeared on the surface. And thirdly, it was Truman's intention to make certain that none of these problems disturbed his objective of maintaining national stability.

In order to be able to understand any of Truman's policies dealing with labor relations, an effort must be made to understand certain parts of Truman's personality.

In doing so, one of the first things to consider is that Truman's most dominant quality was an elemental sense of responsibility. This is the quality that made men trust him and turn to him in his early days in the Senate, and is the quality that people instinctively recognized when he was in the White House.

It is important, however, to bear in mind that in mental habit Truman was first, last, and always a politician. Much of the confusion that arose in the historical investigation of the postwar years revolved around this point. Truman's partisan political attitudes and his elemental sense of responsibility seemed to many observers to be contradictory. This was not the case.

Because of this responsibility Truman felt little pain in making the decisions to stand up to labor leaders when their actions threatened the national welfare. In the 1946 railway strike crisis, Truman humbled A. F. Whitney and Alvanley Johnston with probably as little pain as would have been suffered by any man ever in the White House. Truman saw two men whom he felt could strangle the transportation of the United States, with consequences that could have reached from a standstill of industry to stoppage of food supplies to individual homes. To Truman, the actions of these two men were unendurably irresponsible. He was therefore less bothered than more studious men would have been by the implications of his drastic remedy. Truman saw in simple and stark terms an outrage upon the people of the United States, and the most dominant quality of his personality reacted simply and starkly. In this instance, whatever partisan political ideas entered his mind were subordinated to the response of his character.

There was also a permeation of traditionalism and patriotism in Truman's actions toward labor relations, especially in strikes that threatened the national welfare. Truman thought that in a democratic society the public interest in labor relations in general had to be displayed through its elected governmental officials. In its simplest form, Truman's idea of his administration's role in the public's interest in labor relations was to find ways to harmonize the aspirations of employers and employees in order to promote and maintain general economic progress for the benefit of all, and at the same time provide security for those who worked. Truman also knew that production of needed commodities and services was essential to the maintenance of a modern industrial society in the United States. The average man's expectations of improving his economic status depended for their fulfillment largely upon the United States's capacity as a nation to achieve maximum levels of production.

It was for these reasons that Truman persistently presented as the goals of his labor policies the development of greater equality of economic opportunity for all citizens and the refusal to permit individual citizens to fall below a certain minimum level of existence. He was convinced that these goals could be met in part through programs designed to improve the standard of living for workers. Truman's basic idea in the postwar period was to promote the public interest in the improvement of living standards by proposing measures that called for the establishment of such things as full employment and minimum wages for workers.

During the first term of Truman's administration there were three main alternative ways open for the governmental adjustment of labor–management difficulties. The first was to maintain a strict hands-off attitude in accordance with laissez-faire economic thought. The second alternative was for the government to encourage collective bargaining and to use its facilities to promote voluntary settlement of differences between industry and labor. A third alternative was in the direction of compulsory arbitration, in which the government could force both labor and management to abide by its decisions concerning their relative rights and privileges.

Truman's labor policy was based primarily on varying though vigorous conceptions of the second of these three alternatives. The first alternative was rejected by Truman because of the recognized need to give the American worker an opportunity to protect his interests by organizing and joining a union of his own choosing. The third alternative was rejected because of the fear of concentrating excessive power in the hands of the government.

The President's Labor–Management Conference in 1945 was one of the first steps taken by the Truman administration in an effort to get both management and labor to agree upon some form of mutually acceptable program to minimize the use of strikes and to gain support for the government's stabilization program. The conference was credited with a few accomplishments including the fact that it marked point in history in which American industry formally accepted the principle of collective bargaining. The inability of the conference, however, to handle the labor–management disputes over the Wagner Act must be counted as its greatest failure. Experience had shown that the law needed improvements, and if the interested parties could have agreed upon some milder changes in organizational rules, some of the more restrictive parts of the Taft-Hartley Act could have been avoided, to the best interests of both labor and management.

When Truman's conference was not able to solve some of the long-range problems of labor relations, the postwar atmosphere was further ripened for the later enactment of the Taft-Hartley Act. After the conference it became apparent that a broad extension of government regulation over labor relations was inevitable. Truman's later political pronouncements in 1948 concerning the Taft-Hartley Act were overemphasized by historical investigators as portraying Truman's true feelings toward government participation in labor relations. Truman's "pro-labor" image was enhanced by this overemphasis, but his actions throughout his first term present a much different picture.

President Truman must therefore be given some responsibility for the eventual enactment of the Taft-Hartley Act. Truman would hardly be flattered by that appraisal, but nevertheless he did directly contribute to the climate of opinion which made the law possible. His repeated insistence upon regulatory measures to insure responsible action on the part of both management and labor was an important part of his proposed legislative program during his first term. His early proposals in 1945 to create fact-finding machinery for the adjustment of labor disputes with provision for "cooling-off" periods were an example of his insistence. In 1946 Truman added to this by his near acceptance of the Case bill, his proposal for a Temporary Disputes Settlement bill, his acceptance of the Hobbs Anti-Racketeering Act, and his firm handling of the coal, railroad, and other strikes which threatened the national safety.

The Taft-Hartley Act eventually became the established federal policy on settlement of labor disputes. Despite Truman's political protestations against the law, much of his first-term labor policy ran parallel to the functions of the Taft-Hartley Act. Truman always maintained that the law went too far, but it nevertheless contained much of what he had called for since assuming the Presidency. The function, formerly divided among several federal offices, of aiding in the resolution of labor disputes by means of impartial persuasion, was vested in an independent agency, the Federal Mediation and Conciliation Service. Under the act either party to a labor dispute affecting interstate commerce had to give the other party a sixty-day notice of intention to terminate or modify a labor contract; and within thirty days after expiration of the contract, the

FMCS had to be notified. During the "cooling-off" period of sixty days, employees could not strike. Strikes which affected an entire industry and imperiled the national health or safety could be prohibited for a maximum of eighty days. Most of these provisions had been previously suggested by Truman in similar forms in his efforts to achieve stability in postwar labor relations. He also made use of these provisions of the law during his second term in office.

But the role of the Taft-Hartley controversy in the postwar labor scene has been overemphasized to the extent that the importance of other facets of Truman's labor policies have been downplayed and in some instances completely overlooked by historians. A wider look at these policies presents a more balanced picture.

The Truman administration spearheaded the most significant modern development in employment matters with the passage of the Employment Act of 1946. The Employment Act represented an acceptance by the federal government of a new responsibility for promoting and maintaining national economic stability. Although the record of the Council of Economic Advisors since 1946 has been disappointing to many observers, the Act nevertheless placed a public obligation on the federal government to use all of its resources to prevent or overcome depressions and unemployment. President Truman and his successors have frequently acted on this responsibility. The great support that Truman and his administration gave this legislation represented a giant step forward in the history of American labor relations.

Truman's program for providing fair employment practices was another important part of his labor policy. Although no federal legislation providing for a permanent FEPC was passed, his repeated efforts at trying to get such legislation set a standard for later Presidents. Much of the later success of civil rights legislation can be traced back to Truman's appeals. The 1947 report of the President's Committee on Civil Rights underscored many of the economic reasons Truman had for advocating fair employment practices. Truman was aware of the fact that economic discrimination hampered full use of the nation's resources and achievement of economic progress and industrial stability.

From his wartime investigations, Truman also was convinced that the shortages of labor supply that occurred might not have been so serious if minorities frequently had not been denied opportunities for training and experience. He felt that this discrimination imposed a direct cost upon the American economy which he was determined to stop. These economic arguments for civil rights legislation were many times de-emphasized by historians in comparison with the social and political aspects of the quest for making civil rights more secure after World War II.

A neglected aspect of the postwar labor relations scene was the quest for extending a federally sponsored labor education service to American workers. The troubled postwar period paradoxically was the time when the strongest efforts at providing such a service were put forth. The failure of legislative efforts to establish a permanent labor education extension was probably the reason that historians overlooked its significance. But the bipartisan efforts in Congress and the attempts of many members of the Truman administration to establish it represent a forward-looking policy. Labor education extension proposals represented an important part of the Truman Administration's concern for the "human side" of reconversion for labor after World War II. If the Administration failed, it did help municipalities, states, labor organizations, and educational groups to fortify labor education.

Despite these and other positive aspects of Truman's labor policies, serenity was not one of the chief characteristics of labor relations during his first term in office. It is apparent, however, that the postwar years contained much more than a constant political struggle between management and labor over the Taft-Hartley legislation. Definite steps were taken to insure that the rights of both labor and management were protected. Truman attempted to steer a course aimed at preserving the dignity of the American working man, but at the same time, he adequately demonstrated his conviction that organized labor had to act responsibly in its economic actions while considering the nation's welfare.

Bibliography

NOTE: *A major portion of the unpublished material for this study is contained in the Presidential papers located at the Harry S Truman Library in Independence, Missouri. Materials pertaining to the role of John R. Steelman as a labor advisor during the Truman years are not available to the researcher. Steelman's oral history memoirs at both Columbia University and the Truman Library are closed until 1985, making it very difficult to adequately assess his participation in decisions involving labor. The Papers of Lewis B. Schwellenbach at The Library of Congress are very thin and contain material that is quite limited in value.*

The National Archives in Washington, D.C., also has provided valuable primary material, particularly the General Records of the Department of Labor, Record Group 174. The Records of the Office of War Mobilization and Reconversion, Record Group 250 are useful. Letters, reports, and other documents contained in these files help to furnish an insight into many aspects of the policies of the Truman administration with regard to postwar labor problems.

ABELS, JULES. *Out of the Jaws of Victory.* New York: Henry Holt and Company, 1959.

ALINSKY, SAUL. *John L. Lewis: An Unauthorized Biography.* New York: G. P. Putnam's Sons, 1949.

BAILEY, STEPHEN K. *Congress Makes a Law: The Story Behind The Employment Act of 1946.* New York: Columbia University Press, 1950.

BAILEY, STEPHEN K. and HOWARD, SAMUEL D. *Congress at Work.* New York: Henry Holt and Company, 1952.

BARBASH, JACK. *Unions and Telephones: The Story of the Communications Workers of America.* New York: Harper & Brothers, 1952.

BERELSON, BERNARD. *Voting: A Study of Opinion Formation in a Presidential Campaign.* Chicago: University of Chicago Press, 1954.

BERNSTEIN, BARTON J., and MATUSOW, ALLEN J. eds. *The Truman Administration: A Documentary History.* New York: Harper & Row, 1966.

BLANCHARD, ROBERT; MEYER, RICHARD; and MORELY, BLAINE. *Presidential Elections, 1948–1960.* Research Monograph No. 4, Institute of Government, University of Utah, 1961.

BROWN, EMILY CLARK. *National Labor Policy: Taft-Hartley After Three Years and the Next Steps.* Washington, D.C.: Public Affairs Institute, 1950.

CALKINS, FAY. *CIO and the Democratic Party.* Chicago: University of Chicago Press, 1952.

CAMPBELL, ANGUS, and KAHN, ROBERT L. *The People Elect a President.* Ann Arbor: University of Michigan Press, 1952.

CANTERBERY, E. RAY. *The President's Council of Economic Advisors: A Study of its Function's and Its Influence on the Chief Executive's Decisions.* New York: Exposition Press, 1961.

CANTRIL, HADLEY (ed.), prepared by Mildred Strunk. *Public Opinion, 1935–1946.* Princeton, New Jersey: Princeton University Press, 1951.

CARNES, CECIL. *John L. Lewis: Leader of Labor.* New York: Robert Speller Publishing Corporation, 1936.

CHAMBERLAIN, EDWARD H.; BRADLEY, PHILIP D.; REILLY, GERALD D.; POUND, ROSCOE. *Labor Unions and Public Policy.* Washington, D.C. American Enterprise Association, 1958.

CHAMBERLAIN, NEIL W. *Social Responsibility and Strikes.* New York: Harper and Brothers, 1953.

CHAMBERS, WALTER. *Labor Unions and the Public.* New York: Coward-McCann, Inc., 1936.

CLARK, JOHN MAURICE. *Demobilization of Wartime Economic Controls.* 1st ed. New York and London: McGraw-Hill Book Company, Inc., 1944.

COHEN, SANFORD. *Labor in the United States.* Columbus, Ohio: Charles E. Merrill Books, Inc., 1960.

COLE, GORDON H.; STEIN, LEON; and SOBOL, NORMAN L. *Labor's Story as Reported by the American Labor Press.* Glen Cove, N.Y.: Community Publishers, 1961.

CORWIN, EDWIN S. and KOENIG, LOUIS W. *The Presidency Today.* New York: New York University Press, 1956.

DANIELS, JONATHAN. *The Man of Independence.* New York: J. B. Lippincott Company, 1950.

DANKERT, CLYDE E. *An Introduction to Labor.* New York: Prentice-Hall, Inc., 1954.

DERBER, MILTON and YOUNG, EDWIN (eds.) . *Labor and the New Deal.* Madison: University of Wisconsin Press, 1957.

DRURY, ALLEN. *A Senate Journal 1943–1945.* New York: McGraw-Hill Book Company, Inc., 1963.

DULLES, FOSTER RHEA. *Labor in America: A History.* New York: Thomas Y. Crowell Company, 1955.

DUNN, STEPHEN FRANCIS. *Management Rights in Labor Relations.* Grand Rapids: Woodbeck Publishing Co., 1946.

ERNST, MORRIS L. *The People Know Best: The Ballots vs. The Polls.* Washington, D.C.; Public Affairs Press, 1949.

FAINSOD, MERLE; GORDON, LINCOLN; and PALAMOUNTAIN, JOSEPH C., JR. *Government and the American Economy.* 3rd ed. New York: Norton, 1959.

FAULKNER, HAROLD UNDERWOOD. *American Economic History.* 8th ed. New York: Harper & Brothers, 1960.

FINE, SIDNEY. *Laissez-Faire and the General Welfare State.* Ann Arbor: University of Michigan Press, 1956.

GAER, JOSEPH. *The First Round.* New York: Duell, Sloan, and Pearce, 1944.

GALENSON, WALTER. *The CIO Challenge to the AFL: A History of the American Labor Movement, 1935–1941.* Cambridge: Harvard University Press, 1960.

GARFINKEL, HERBERT. *When Negroes March: The March on Washington Movement in the Organizational Politics for FEPC.* Glencoe, Illinois: Free Press, 1959.

GOLDMAN, ERIC F. *The Crucial Decade—and After: America 1945–1960.* New York: Random House, 1961.

GRAVES, W. BROOKE. *Fair Employment Practice Legislation in the United States, Federal-State-Municipal.* Library of Congress Legislative Reference Service, Public Affairs Bulletin No. 93. Washington: April, 1951.

GREGORY, CHARLES OSCAR. *Labor and the Law.* 2nd ed., revised. New York: W. W. Norton, 1958.

HANSEN, ALVIN H. *Economic Policy and Full Employment.* New York: Whittlesey House, 1947.

HARDMAN, J. B. S. and NEWFELD, MAURICE F. (eds.). *The House of Labor: Internal Operations of American Unions.* New York: Prentice-Hall, Inc., 1951.

HARTLEY, FRED ALLAN. *Our New National Labor Policy: The Taft-Hartley Act and the Next Steps.* New York: Funk & Wagnalls Co., 1948.

JAFFE, ABRAM J. and STEWART, CHARLES D. *Manpower Resources and Utilization: Principles of Working Force Analysis.* New York: Wiley, 1951.

JOSEPHSON, MATHEW. *Sidney Hillman: Statesman of American Labor.* Garden City, New York: Doubleday & Company, Inc., 1952.

KAPLAN, A. D. H. *The Guarantee of Annual Wages.* Washington, D.C.: The Brookings Institution, 1947.

KARSH, BERNARD. *Diary of a Strike.* Urbana: University of Illinois Press, 1958.

KELLY, THOMAS. *A History of Adult Education in Great Britain.* Liverpool: Liverpool University Press, 1962.

KESSELMAN, LOUIS COLERIDGE. *The Social Politics of FEPC: A Study in Reform Pressure Movements.* Chapel Hill: University of North Carolina Press, 1948.

KOENIG, LOUIS W. *The Chief Executive.* New York: Harcourt, Brace & World, Inc., 1964.

250   THE TRUMAN ADMINISTRATION

KOENIG, LOUIS W. (ed). *The Truman Administration: Its Principles and Practice*. Washington Square, New York: New York University Press, 1956.

LAZARUS, HERMAN and GOLDBERG, JOSEPH P. *The Role of Collective Bargaining in a Democracy*. Washington, D.C.: Public Affairs Institute, 1949.

LEE, R. ALTON. *Truman and Taft-Hartley: A Question of Mandate*. Lexington: University of Kentucky Press, 1966.

LEEK, JOHN H. *Government and Labor in the United States*. New York: Rinehart & Company, Inc., 1952.

LIEBERMAN, ELIAS. *Unions Before the Bar: Historic Trials Showing the Evolution of Labor Rights in the United States*. Revised ed. New York: Oxford Book Co., 1960.

LEISERSON, WILLIAM M. *American Trade Union Democracy*. With a Foreword by Sumner H. Slichter, New York: Columbia University Press, 1959.

LENS, SIDNEY. *Left, Right & Center: Conflicting Forces in American Labor*. Hinsdale, Illinois: Henry Regnery Company, 1949.

MCNAUGHTON, WAYNE L. *The Development of Labor Relations Law*. Washington, D.C.: American Council on Public Affairs, 1944.

MCNAUGHTON, WAYNE L., and LAZAR, JOSEPH. *Industrial Relations and the Government*. New York: McGraw-Hill Book Company, Inc., 1954.

METZ, HAROLD W. *Labor Policy of the Federal Government*. Washington, D.C.: Brookings Institution, 1945.

MIDDLETON, PHILIP HARVEY. *Railways and Organized Labor*. With Introduction by Harry A. Wheller. Chicago: Railway Business Association, 1941.

MILLER, GLEN W. *American Labor and the Government*. New York: Prentice-Hall, Inc., 1948.

MILLIS, HARRY ALVIN and BROWN, EMILY CLARK. *From the Wagner Act to Taft-Hartley: A Study of National Labor Policy and Labor Relations*. Chicago: University of Chicago Press, 1950.

NEUSTADT, RICHARD E. *Presidential Power, The Politics of Leadership*. New York: Wiley, 1960.

NORTHRUP, HERBERT R. *Labor Adjustment Machinery.* New York: American Enterprise Association, Inc., 1946.

NORTHRUP, HERBERT R. *Organized Labor and the Negro.* Foreword by Sumner H. Slichter. New York and London: Harper & Brothers, 1944.

NOURSE, EDWIN G. *Economics in the Public Service: Administrative Aspects of the Employment Act.* New York: Harcourt, Brace and Company, 1953.

PECK, GUSTAV. *Industrial Relations Policy.* Library of Congress Legislative Reference Service, Public Affairs Bulletin No. 48. Washington: January, 1947.

PETERSON, FLORENCE. *Survey of Labor Economics.* Revised ed. New York: Harper & Brothers, 1951.

PHILLIPS, CABELL. *The Truman Presidency: The History of a Triumphant Succession.* New York: The Macmillan Company, 1966.

RAYBACK, JOSEPH G. *A History of American Labor.* New York: The Macmillan Company, 1959.

REDDING, JACK. *Inside the Democratic Party.* New York: Bobbs-Merrill Company, Inc., 1958.

REYNOLDS, LLOYD G. *Labor Economics and Labor Relations.* New York: Prentice-Hall, Inc., 1954.

RICH, BENNETT MILTON. *The Presidents and Civil Disorder.* Washington, D.C.: The Brookings Institution, 1941.

RIDDLE, DONALD H. *The Truman Committee: A Study in Congressional Responsibility.* New Brunswick, New Jersey: Rutgers University Press, 1964.

ROE, WELLINGTON. *Juggernaut: American Labor in Action.* 1st ed. Philadelphia: J. B. Lippincott Co., 1948.

ROSEBOOM, EUGENE H. *A History of Presidential Elections.* New York: The Macmillan Company, 1957.

ROSENMAN, SAMUEL I. (comp.). *The Public Papers and Addresses of Franklin D. Roosevelt: 1944–1945.* New York: Harper & Brothers, 1950.

ROSSITER, CLINTON L. *The American Presidency.* New York: Harcourt, Brace and Company, 1956.

RUCHAMES, LOUIS. *Race, Jobs and Politics: The Story of FEPC.* New York: Columbia University Press, 1953.

SEIDMAN, JOEL. *American Labor from Defense to Reconversion.* Chicago: University of Chicago Press, 1953.

SHISTER, JOSEPH (ed). *Readings in Labor Economics & Industrial Relations.* Chicago: J. B. Lippincott Company, 1951.

SOMERS, HERMAN MILES. *Presidential Agency, the Office of War Mobilization and Reconversion.* Cambridge: Harvard University Press, 1950.

STARR, MARK. *Labour Politics in U.S.A.* Foreword by Margaret Cole. London: Fabian Publications, 1949.

STEINBERG, ALFRED. *The Man From Missouri: The Life and Times of Harry S. Truman.* New York: G. P. Putnam's Sons, 1962.

SUFRIN, SIDNEY and SEDGEWICK, R. C. *Labor Economics and Problems at Mid-Century.* New York: Alfred A. Knopf, 1956.

TAFT, PHILIP. *Organized Labor in American History.* New York: Harper & Row, 1964.

TAFT, PHILIP. *The A.F. of L. From the Death of Gompers to the Merger.* New York: Harper & Brothers, 1959.

TAYLOR, GEORGE W. *Government Regulation of Industrial Relations.* New York: Prentice-Hall, Inc., 1948.

TRUMAN, HARRY S. *Memoirs.* 2 vols. Garden City, New York: Doubleday and Co., 1955, 1956.

VELIE, LESTER. *Labor U.S.A.* New York: Harper & Brothers, 1958.

WARNE, COLSTON E. (ed.). *Labor in Postwar America.* Brooklyn, N.Y.: Remsen Press, 1949.

Who's Who in Labor: The Authorized Biographies of the Men and Women Who Lead Labor in the United States and Canada and of those Who Deal With Labor. New York: The Dryden Press, 1946.

WITNEY, FRED. *Government and Collective Bargaining.* Chicago: J. B. Lippincott Company, 1951.

YOUNG, ROLAND. *Congressional Politics in the Second World War.* New York: Columbia University Press, 1956.

Government Publications

LATIMER, MURRAY W. *Guaranteed Wages*. Report to the President by the Advisory Board of the Office of War Mobilization and Reconversion. Washington: U.S. Government Printing Office, 1947.

Public Papers of the Presidents of the United States: Harry S. Truman, 1945. Washington: U.S. Government Printing Office, 1961.

Public Papers of the Presidents of the United States: Harry S. Truman, 1946. Washington: U.S. Government Printing Office, 1962.

Public Papers of the Presidents of the United States: Harry S. Truman, 1947. Washington: U.S. Government Printing Office, 1963.

Public Papers of the Presidents of the United States: Harry S. Truman, 1948. Washington: U.S. Government Printing Office, 1964.

SUFFERN, ARTHUR E. *Labor-Management Disputes, Subsequent to August 17, 1945, Involving Possession of Properties by the Federal Government*. Washington: U.S. National Wage Stabilization Board, 1946.

To Secure These Rights. The Report of the President's Committee on Civil Rights. Washington: U.S. Government Printing Office, 1947.

U.S. Congress, House, Committee on Labor. *Investigation of the Causes of Labor Disputes*. Hearings, June 7–June 25, 1945. 79th Cong., 2d Sess., 1945.

U.S. Congress, Senate, Special Committee Investigating the National Defense Program. *Additional Report*. 78th Cong., 1st Sess., 1943.

U.S. Congress, Senate Committee on Education and Labor. *Fair Employment Practice Act, Hearings on S. 101 and S. 459*. 79th Cong., 1st Sess., 1945.

U.S. Congress, Senate, Subcommittee of the Committee on *Banking and Currency*. Hearings. 79th Cong., 1st Sess., 1945.

U.S. Congress, Senate, Committee on Education and Labor. *Hearings on a Bill to Provide for the Appointment of Fact-Finding Boards*. 79th Cong., 2nd Sess., 1946.

U.S. Congress, Senate. Senate Report No. 48. *Exempting Employers from Liability for Portal-to-Portal Wages in Certain Cases.* 80th Cong., 1st Sess., 1947.

U.S. Congress, Senate, Committee on Education and Labor. *Labor Relations Program.* Hearings. 80th Cong., 1st sess., 1947.

U.S. *Congressional Record.* Vols. LXXXI–XCVI.

U.S. Department of Labor. *The National Wage Stabilization Board, January 1, 1946–February 24, 1947.* Washington: U.S. Government Printing Office, 1947.

U.S. Department of Labor, Division of Labor Standards. *The President's National Labor-Management Conference, November 5–30,* 1945, Bulletin No. 77, 1946.

U.S. Department of Labor, Division of Labor Standards. *Resumé of the Proceedings of the Twelfth National Conference on Labor Legislation, December 5 and 6, 1945.* Bulletin No. 76, 1946.

U.S. *Federal Register,* 1941.

Reports

MIRE, JOSEPH. *Labor-Education.* A Study Report on Needs, Programs, and Approaches. Conducted on Behalf of the Inter-University Labor Education Committee, 1956.

Proceedings of the Fifty-Seventh Annual Convention of the American Federation of Labor, 1937.

Proceedings of the Sixty-Fourth Convention of the American Federation of Labor, 1945.

Proceedings of the Sixty-Fifth Convention of the American Federation of Labor, 1946.

Proceedings of the Sixty-Sixth Convention of the American Federation of Labor, 1947.

Proceedings of the Sixty-Seventh Convention of the American Federation of Labor, 1948.

Proceedings of the Eighth Constitutional Convention of the Congress of Industrial Organizations, 1946.

Proceedings of the Ninth Constitutional Convention of the Congress of Industrial Organizations, 1947.

Proceedings of the Tenth Constitutional Convention of the Congress of Industrial Organizations, 1948.

Articles and Periodicals

American Federationist. 1944–1950.

BERNSTEIN, BARTON J. "The Truman Administration and its Reconversion Wage Policy," *Labor History,* VI (Fall, 1965), 214–231.

BERNSTEIN, BARTON J. "The Truman Administration and the Steel Strike of 1946," *The Journal of American History,* LXII (March, 1966), 791–803.

Business Week. 1945–1948.

CHAMBERLAIN, NEIL. "Nature and Scope of Collective Bargaining," *Quarterly Journal of Economics,* LVIII (May, 1944), 359–387.

CHAMBERLAIN, NEIL W. "Obligations Upon the Union Under the National Labor Relations Act," *American Economic Review,* XXXVII (March, 1947), 170–177.

C.I.O. News. 1944–1948.

Congressional Digest. 1945–1948.

Congressional Quarterly, Vol. I, Washington: Congressional Quarterly, Inc., 1945.

Congressional Quarterly, Vol. II, Washington: Congressional Quarterly, Inc., 1946.

Congressional Quarterly, Vol. III, Washington: Congressional Quarterly, Inc., 1947.

Congressional Quarterly Almanac, Vol. IV, Washington: Congressional Quarterly News Features, 1948.

Congressional Quarterly Almanac, Vol. V., Washington: Congressional Quarterly News Features, 1949.

Economic Outlook. 1948.

Editorial Research Reports. 1944–1953.

FITCH, JOHN A. "The New Congress and the Unions," *Survey Graphic,* XXXVI (April, 1947), 231–235, 262–264.

Fortune. 1946–1948.

GREEN, WILLIAM. "Labor Relations Bills: View of American Federation of Labor," *Vital Speeches,* XIII (March 1, 1947) , 294–300.

HERRICK, E. M. "National Labor Relations Act," *Annals of the American Academy of Political and Social Science,* CCXLVIII (November, 1946) , 82–90.

KROLL, JACK, "Why Labor is in Politics," *New York Times Magazine,* October 27, 1946, 15.

Labor and Nation. 1945–1952.

Labor Information Bulletin. 1947–1948.

Labor Law Journal. 1945–1948.

Labor Relations Reporter. 1943–1948.

Labor's Daily. 1957.

LEEDS, MORTON. "The A.F.L. in the 1948 Elections," *Social Research,* XVII (June, 1950) , 207–218.

LEISERSON, WILLIAM M. "Public Policy in Labor Relations," *American Economic Review,* XXXVI (May, 1946) , 336–346.

Life. 1944–1948.

MASLOW, WILL, "FEPC—A Case History in Parliamentary Maneuver," *University of Chicago Law Review,* XIII (June, 1946) , 407–444.

MEANY, GEORGE. "Taft-Hartley Law, A Slave Labor Measure," *Vital Speeches,* XIV (December 1, 1947) , 119–123.

Monthly Labor Review. 1943–1950.

"Mr. Truman Turns to Fascist Remedies," *Christian Century,* LXIII (June 5, 1946) , 707.

MURRAY, ROBERT K. "Government and Labor During World War II," *Current History,* (September, 1959) , 146–152.

New Republic. 1945–1948.

NEUSTADT, RICHARD. "Congress and the Fair Deal: A Legislative Balance Sheet," *Public Policy,* V (1954) , 351–381.

Newsweek. 1945–1948.

New York Times. 1935–1950.

NORTHRUP, HERBERT R. "Literature of the Labor Crisis," *Political Science Quarterly,* LXI (September, 1946) , 420–433.

"Organized Labor and the Public Interest; Symposium," *American Economic Review,* XXXV (May, 1945), 193–228.

PARKINSON, ROYAL. "Fair Employment Practices Legislation," *Harvard Business Review,* XXVI (January, 1948), 115–128.

"Political Aims of Organized Labor; Official Proposals of A.F. of L. and C.I.O.," *Annals of the American Academy of Political and Social Science,* CCLIX (September, 1948), 144–152.

POMPER, GERALD. "Labor Legislation: The Revision of Taft-Hartley in 1953–1954," *Labor History,* VI, No. 2 (Spring, 1965), 143–158.

Railway Age. 1945–1948.

RAY, JETER S. "The Portal-to-Portal Act of 1947," *Tennessee Law Review,* XX (February, 1948), 151–168.

REISEL, VICTOR. "Labor is Big Business," *American Mercury,* LXI (December, 1945), 728–734.

ROSSITER, CLINTON. "The President and Labor Disputes," *Journal of Politics,* XI (1949), 193–220.

Saturday Evening Post. 1943–1948.

SLICHTER, SUMNER H. "Labor Crisis," *Atlantic,* CLXXIII (February, 1944), 37–41.

SLICHTER, SUMNER H. "Needed: A Basic Labor Policy," *New York Times Magazine,* June 9, 1946, 10.

SLICHTER, SUMNER H. "Strikes and the Public Interest," *Yale Review* XXXV, Vol. 2 (December, 1945), 207–221.

SLICHTER, SUMNER H. "Taft-Hartley Act," *Quarterly Journal of Economics,* LXIII (February, 1949), 1–31.

TAFT, PHILIP. "Jurisdictional Disputes," *Annals of the American Academy of Political and Social Science,* CXLVIII (November, 1946), 37–43.

TANNENBAUM, FRANK. "Social Function of Trade Unionism," *Political Science Quarterly,* LXII (June, 1947), 161–194.

TELLER, LUDWIG, "Government Seizure in Labor Disputes," *Harvard Law Review,* IX (September, 1947), 1017–1059.

The Nation. 1945–1948.

"The Smith-Connally Act," *Lawyers Guild Review,* III (July–August, 1943), 46–51.

"The Smith-Connally Act," *Temple University Law Quarterly,* XVIII (April, 1944), 275–281.

Time. 1945–1948.

United Mineworkers Journal. 1946–1948.

U.S. News & World Report. 1946–1948.

WARNE, COLSTON E. "Why Strikes?" *Forum,* CVII (February, 1947), 105–110.

WARREN, EDGAR L. "Conciliation Services in Labor Relations," *Annals of the American Academy of Political and Social Science,* CCXLVIII (November, 1946), 120–129.

WARREN, EDGAR L. "The Conciliation Service: V-J Day to Taft-Hartley," *Industrial Labor Relations Review,* I (April, 1948), 351–362.

WITTE, EDWIN E. "Appraisal of the Taft-Hartley Act," *American Economic Review,* XXXVIII (May, 1948), 368–382.

Manuscript Sources

Papers of John D. Clark, (Council of Economic Advisors, 1946–1948), Harry S. Truman Library, Independence, Missouri.

Papers of Warner Gardner, (Assistant Secretary of the Interior, 1946–1947), Harry S. Truman Library, Independence, Missouri.

Papers of John W. Gibson, (Assistant Secretary of Labor, 1946–1948), Harry S. Truman Library, Independence, Missouri.

Papers of Paul M. Herzog, (Chairman, National Labor Relations Board, 1945–1948), Harry S. Truman Library, Independence, Missouri.

General Records of the Department of Labor, Records of Successive Secretaries of Labor and Their Assistants, 1933–1953, Record Group 174, National Archives, Washington, D.C.

Letter from Hilda W. Smith to the author, August 14, 1965.

Records of the Office of War Mobilization and Reconversion, Record Group 250, National Archives, Washington, D.C.

Papers of Samuel I. Rosenman, (Special Counsel to the President, 1945–1948), Harry S. Truman Library, Independence, Missouri.

Papers of Lewis B. Schwellenbach, (Secretary of Labor, 1945–1948), Library of Congress, Washington, D.C.

Papers of Harry S. Truman, Harry S. Truman Library, Independence, Missouri.

Papers of James E. Webb, (Director, Bureau of the Budget, 1945–1948), Harry S. Truman Library, Independence, Missouri.

Unpublished Material

DAVIS, REYNOLD J. "A Study of Federal Civil Rights Programs During the Presidency of Harry S. Truman." Unpublished Master's thesis, Department of History, University of Kansas, 1959.

HARTMANN, SUSAN M. "President Truman and the Eightieth Congress," Unpublished Ph.D. dissertation, Department of History, University of Missouri, 1966.

JONES, DAVID L. "Senator Harry S. Truman: The First Term." Unpublished Master's thesis, Department of History, University of Kansas, 1963.

LEE, R. ALTON. "Harry S. Truman and the Taft-Hartley Act." Unpublished Ph.D. dissertation, Department of History, University of Oklahoma, 1962.

SCHMIDTLEIN, EUGENE FRANCIS. "Truman the Senator." Unpublished Ph.D. dissertation, Department of History, University of Missouri, 1962.

Index

261

HD   McClure
8072.   The Truman administration
M184   and the problems of post-war
        labor, 1945-1948.